The Great Shutout Pitchers

The Great Shutout Pitchers

*Twenty Profiles
of a Vanishing Breed*

Joe MacKay

McFarland & Company, Inc., Publishers
Jefferson, North Carolina, and London

LIBRARY OF CONGRESS CATALOGUING-IN-PUBLICATION DATA

MacKay, Joe, 1936–
 The great shutout pitchers : twenty profiles of a vanishing breed / Joe MacKay.
   p.   cm.
 Includes index.

   ISBN 0-7864-1676-9 (softcover : 50# alkaline paper) ∞

   1. Pitchers (Baseball)—United States—Biography. 2. Shutouts (Sports) I. Title.
 GV865.A1M22   2004
 796.357'092'2—dc22   2003017942

British Library cataloguing data are available

©2004 Joe MacKay. All rights reserved

No part of this book may be reproduced or transmitted in any form or by any means, electronic or mechanical, including photocopying or recording, or by any information storage and retrieval system, without permission in writing from the publisher.

On the cover: Walter Johnson *(Early-era Baseball Photos)*

Manufactured in the United States of America

McFarland & Company, Inc., Publishers
 Box 611, Jefferson, North Carolina 28640
   www.mcfarlandpub.com

To my good and true friend Larry Pileggi, whose help carried me through. He painstakingly edited and typed without complaint. Without his efforts, this book would never have been possible.

I cannot forget my beautiful wife, Rosemarie, whose patience and encouragement will always be cherished. She gave up her quality time with me so I could complete my endeavor.

Acknowledgments

No project can be completed by just one man. If it's making a movie, painting a portrait, or composing a piece of music, the artist must have help. This can be in the form of inspiration, encouragement or writing. A book is no different.

I mentioned in my dedication that my good friend Larry Pileggi was a vital assistant. I would like to include in my thanks the Mastics-Moriches-Shirley Community Library in Shirley, New York. Thanks to the people there. Under supervisor J. Robert Verbesey (who is now retired) and his successor, William Cicola, I enjoyed the greatest help in gathering material. Mr. Verbesey personally encouraged me to continue towards the completion of my work. He and his staff of librarians showed great concern in aiding me with the research for this book. I'm compelled to list each and every one of them to show my gratitude for their devoted service: Dana Hickling, Dawn Triche, Denise Boinay, Kathleen Carter and Deborah Ward. Their professionalism and conscientiousness was beyond the call of duty. They and the library administration have made it the finest library I have ever been in. I don't think there is a finer facility in New York State.

Contents

Acknowledgments	vii
Introduction	1
Walter Johnson, "The Big Train" *The Greatest of Them All*	5
Grover Cleveland Alexander *A Winner Wherever He Went*	17
Christy Mathewson *A True Baseball Idol*	27
Cy Young *So Great They Named an Award After Him*	39
Eddie Plank *The First Great Left-Hander*	51
Warren Spahn *The Greatest Left-Hander Ever*	62
Tom Seaver *The Franchise*	74
Nolan Ryan *Mr. No-Hitter*	86
Bert Blyleven *A Class Act*	98
Don Sutton *A Quiet and Consistent Performer*	110
Ed Walsh *King of the Spitballers*	123
Bob Gibson *The Intimidator*	135
Steve Carlton *Mr. Lefty*	147

Mordecai "Three Finger" Brown
The Mainstay of the Cubs — 158

Jim Palmer *From Oblivion to Greatness* — 170

Gaylord Perry *The Master of Deception* — 177

Juan Marichal *The Dominican Dandy* — 187

Rube Waddell *The Man-Child of Major League Baseball* — 196

Vic Willis *Ultimate Recognition at Long Last* — 208

Jim Galvin *The "Little Engine That Could"* — 216

Index — 227

Introduction

During the long history of baseball, 20 pitchers have achieved 50 or more complete-game shutouts. Eighteen of these men did it under the present rule that requires the distance between the pitching rubber and home plate be 60'6". However, Cy Young pitched three years under the rule that had the distance at 50'. Nine of his 77 shutouts were at this distance. Another pitcher, James "Pud" Galvin, pitched 11 of his "whitewashes" at the original distance of 45' and the rest of them at 50', after the rule dictating the gap between pitcher and batter was changed in 1881. Galvin retired from the game in 1892, one year before the present rule came into effect. Galvin never threw a pitch in a major league game with the distance at 60'6". All of these men, with the exception of Bert Blyleven, have been enshrined in the Baseball Hall of Fame at Cooperstown, New York. (It's my personal belief that Blyleven should be given that honor he so richly deserves.) This achievement of excellence in that area of pitching could be one of the reasons that they earned the highest reward: immortality in their sport.

In all probability this list has seen its last new member. This is partly due to the specialization of relief pitching seen in the "pitching revolution" that began in the 1970s and continues to the present day. Since the use of the relief pitcher has emerged as an integral part of managerial strategy, the complete-game statistic has almost faded into oblivion. The almost sacred "pitch count" dictates when to remove a pitcher, even if the hurler doesn't feel fatigued or isn't showing any signs of weakening.

And, of course, this could very well happen right in the middle of a shutout! *If a pitcher reaches a certain pitch count or certain inning, in comes the reliever.* The starter gets credit for the win but not a shutout.

I remember a game back in 1980 when Luis Tiant was pitching a shutout for the New York Yankees. He was in the eighth inning when he got into a jam. He had a comfortable lead with two outs and two runners on base. Manager Dick Howser decided that Tiant had been in long enough and that it was time for a change. Tiant stormed off the mound because, like so many able professionals of his trade, he wanted to complete what he started.

His removal from the game deprived him of a complete-game shutout. If given the opportunity, he might have gained his 50th career shutout. Perhaps this feat, if accomplished, would have been what he needed to enrich his credentials for entering the Baseball Hall of Fame. He finished his career with 49 shutouts.

The present-day pitchers who are the closest to the 50 milestone are Roger Clemens, who has 46, and Randy Johnson and Greg Maddux, who both have 34. Clemens has been stuck at 46 for several years because his current team, the New York Yankees, wouldn't let him overexert himself as he aged past 40. Clemens' 45th complete-game shutout occurred during the 2000 American League Championship Series against the Seattle Mariners, when he shut them out 5–0 on one hit. His 46th came on July 30, 2003, against the Anaheim Angels. Clemens shut down the world champions, 8–0.

Johnson is approaching his 40th birthday and to reach the 50-shutout milestone seems to be a far-fetched dream. There are just so many pitches in an arm, even a great arm. Maddux also seems to be slowing down. The way the Atlanta Braves protect their prized investment, he hardly reaches the seventh inning anymore.

Another reason the 50 career shutout goal will probably not be reached again is because of shorter playing careers. Due to the large salary increases of the '80s and '90s and the astronomical sums that players now make, many opt for earlier retirement. Because of their newly found security, players are becoming involved in successful business ventures. It is rare, indeed, to see a ball player go past the 40-year-old age mark like Nolan Ryan and Bert Blyleven. It could very well be that 35 is the magic number that will be the common retirement age, especially for pitchers. Financial security would be more attractive than the rigors of training and keeping in shape. This, coupled with the prolonged absences from family during

Introduction 3

extended road trips, make a player's exit from the game more inevitable.

While compiling the data for this book, I originally decided to eliminate Pud Galvin from it because he never pitched at the 60'6" distance. Later I decided that he should be included, mainly because he was the first to achieve the mark and because he belonged regardless of the rules at the time. He shouldn't be excluded just because he was a part of a different era.

I dreaded the difficult research due to the poor record-keeping of Galvin's time and lack of material at hand, but I succeeded in finding all of his games. This entailed a trip to the Baseball Hall of Fame library. Once I started researching Galvin, I found him to be an interesting individual—he was arrested while taking a train so he could play for the Buffalo team.

I did, however, find an error in his total shutouts. He was given credit for 57 shutouts, but he should have 58. This is explained in the chapter devoted to him.

I am quite convinced this list will never be expanded. The 20 named here will be the only ones. Due to the nature of today's game, *these men are truly a vanishing breed.*

Walter Johnson, "The Big Train"
The Greatest of Them All

If one can compare Walter Johnson to someone outside of baseball, he would be the quiet, unassuming marshal championing the cause of justice in the old, wild West. Like Gary Cooper's portrayal of Will Kane in *High Noon* or even Alan Ladd's characterization of Shane in the movie of that title, Johnson would fit the image perfectly. Playing all of his career with the lowly Washington Senators, he stoically performed his duty with dedication that made him tower over his contemporaries on the mound.

He made his debut versus the Detroit Tigers at the tender age of 19, but he lost 3–2. This was the Tiger team anchored by Ty Cobb and Sam Crawford (both of Hall of Famers) that would capture the American League pennant for the next three years (1907–1909). His strong achievement was the advent of greatness waiting to be fulfilled. Although his first three years were on the rocky side mainly due to the lackadaisical performances behind him, the Senators finished eighth, seventh, and eighth, respectively. Walter could not be blamed; his winning percentage and E.R.A. were superior to that of his team. In 1907, he fashioned a 1.86 E.R.A. with two shutouts, his first being a 1–0 seven-hitter against Boston and Cy Morgan. There would be many more to come, as he would spin 109 more shutouts! In his next start, he wrapped up his second whitewash, besting the New York Highlanders 2–0. This wasn't bad for a 19-year-old pitching for a tail-ender.

In 1908, he improved his record to an even .500, helping to raise Washington to seventh place, which was a lofty position for them. This was the season, though he didn't start until June because of illness, when he got rolling. He became the brightest star in a dull constellation. In his 14 victories there were six shutouts and three of them came in a four-day period against the lowly Highlanders. On September 4, 1908, he hooked up with "Happy Jack" Chesbro and defeated the all-time single-season winner of modern baseball 3–0. In that game he gave up six hits and walked one. On September 5, 1908, he took the mound against Rube Manning and won 6–0, giving up four hits and walking none. The next day was Sunday and no baseball was played on Sunday in New York during those years. With a day of rest, he came back and started the first game of the Labor Day doubleheader. He proceeded to blank the Highlanders again, this time 4–0. Here, he gave up only two hits and again walked no one; the loser of this game was Chesbro for the second time. In fewer than four days, he tossed three complete-game shutouts, giving up 12 hits and walking one in 27 innings, while beating the two best pitchers (one of them a Hall of Famer) the Highlanders had. As each game day progressed, he got better and stronger as his declining hit total attests to. To rub salt into the New Yorkers' wounds, Walter shut out the Highlanders for a fourth time on October 7, 1908.

In 1909, he struggled valiantly, compensating for his team's ineptness. They were a pitiful bunch. He posted a 13–25 record and four of his victories were shutouts, three of them by the identical score of 1–0. His fourth shutout was a luxurious 2–0 win against the Tigers. He was able to blank Detroit twice that year on their way to a third straight pennant. In his other two, he defeated two future Hall of Famers, Cleveland's Addie Joss and Philadelphia A's "Chief" Bender. In many of his games he did not have the security of more than a one-run lead. Out of his total shutouts, 37 would be by the score of 1–0.

The 1910 season became Walter's first winning year as he posted 25 wins for the seventh-place Senators. He was the mainstay of the staff and the league's rising star. The old adage of Washington being first in war, first in peace, and last in the American League would never apply again as long as Johnson was pitching for them. The darkness of the cellar would be abandoned due to Walter's matchless right arm. He notched a 25–17 record that embraced eight shutouts. One was an opening-day 3–0 one-hitter against the Athletics left-handed ace Eddie Plank. Frank "Home Run" Baker spoiled his masterpiece. This game also marked the first appearance of a president at the opening ceremonies, which started a long-standing tradition by having him toss out the first ball to inaugurate the baseball season. The Philadelphia team was the first of the fabled Connie Mack dynasties, which would win four pennants in the next five years along with three World Series championships.

His shutout of the St. Louis Browns on September 25 flirted with near perfection but was spoiled by Frank Truesdale's leadoff single. Walter was spectacular as he led the league in games pitched, games started and complete games. His 1.35 E.R.A. was only good for third place behind Ed Walsh and Jack Coombs. His winning percentage was 158 points higher than his team's! He also led the league in strikeouts, posting 313 of them to become the second man during the modern baseball era to break that number. He was now on his way to stardom.

In 1911, he again hit the 25-win plateau with Washington who still finished in seventh place. His E.R.A. was a shining 1.89, but still he could only place second behind Vean Gregg. Six shutouts helped lower his E.R.A. below 2.00 for the second time. His shutout of the St. Louis Browns by a 7–0 score on August 17, 1911, was the 25th of his career. His shutout on October 3, 1911, was a six-inning one-hitter that was stopped by darkness. His mound opponent, Eddie Plank, hit the single. Again his winning percentage was well over 100 points higher than his team's!

If one could search the annals of baseball history and look to see where two pitchers stood as titans on the mound for the whole season, it would be the 1912 season that showcased the performances of Joe Wood and Walter Johnson. This was the first and only time in American League history two pitchers broke the 30-win barrier. Wood fashioned a 34–5 record as he led the Boston Red Sox to the pennant and world championship, and Johnson logged a 32–12 record, moving Washington into the first division for the very first time in the franchise's history. They finished a distant second behind the Red Sox. Another extraordinary accomplishment happened during the season when both men rattled off 16-game winning streaks, which is still the league record. This was tied by "Lefty" Grove and "Schoolboy" Rowe. Walter had the distinction of setting the record first, but the streak was stopped by a relief loss against the St. Louis Browns on a scorer's quirk. Because of the significance of the feat, league president Ban Johnson ruled in favor of the scorer's decision.

Wood, on the other hand, duplicated Johnson's performance a short while later as he approached the record. An inevitable matchup with Walter was irrepressible. After 13 straight wins, Wood's next assignment was against Washington at Boston. Wood and Johnson matched zeroes until the sixth inning when Boston broke the scoring drought and pushed a run across. This was enough for Wood and he held Washington at bay for the rest of the game. Washington made a last gasp effort in the ninth, but Wood prevailed for his 14th-straight victory. He was able to add two more wins to match Walter's 16 in a row. Wood also manufactured ten shutouts compared to Johnson's seven, but one of Johnson's was a one-hitter on August 16, 1912. It was spoiled by Rath's scratch hit.

Due to Wood's extraordinary performance, Johnson has to play second fiddle when the season is analyzed by historians, although he led the league with 303 strikeouts, becoming only the second man in modern history to reach the 300 mark twice. The year of glory really belonged to Wood. Walter Johnson's imprint of greatness was his stellar performance during 1913. As great as 1912 was, 1913 was even more magnificent as Walter surpassed many of his 1912 statistical achievements. Sporting a 36–7 record, which meant a .837 winning percentage, his achievements kept Washington in the pennant race with Philadelphia. They finished only 6½ games out, which was amazing for a team who only two years earlier was mired in seventh place. He was the franchise, and his supernatural performances made the entire league hold him in awe. He completed only 30 of 36 starts, which was low for him in both categories, but this could be attributed to his being a reliever in 11 games of which he won 7. He set a league record E.R.A. low of 1.14 until Hubert "Dutch" Leonard broke it the following year with a 1.00. Included in Walter's 36 wins were 11 shutouts, 5 by the score of 1–0. His shutout of Boston on July 3, in 1913, went 15 innings, and he defeated their ace Ray Collins. One must not forget that they were the world champions of the previous year who boasted Tris Speaker and Harry Hooper (both Hall of Famers) in their lineup. Walter was truly the team savior as a starter and reliever. Not only was he the toast of the D.C. fans but of the league. His pleasant demeanor made him heir apparent to Christy Mathewson in image as well as talent, but Walter played for weaker teams while "Matty" pitched for contenders and champions.

The start of 1914 began with grand expectations as Walter shut out Boston in Fenway Park 3–0. His Atlas-like achievements were becoming axiomatic. Opponents knew that they would have to match Washington's best with one of their own. Although he did not duplicate 30 wins as he did in the previous two years, he still led the league with 28 victories. He also led the league in shutouts with nine, making that the third time he became the league leader in that category with nine. One significant note was on July 13, 1914, when he shut out the Tigers, led by Ty Cobb, 5–0 allowing only three hits while striking out ten. This was the 50th of his career and he wasn't even at the halfway point of his career total. By year's end, he would only be four behind Ed Walsh and six behind league record setter Eddie Plank (at this time Plank would have 59 and finish with a total of 69, 63 in the American League and 6 in the Federal League).

At the start of 1915, Walter again opened the season with a shutout over the New York Yankees and Jack Warhop (who will always be noted as the man who gave up Babe Ruth's first home run). Ironically, he only struck out one as he yielded two hits. He was again going to lead the league in wins with 27 (7 of those were shutouts). On September 8, 1915, he again bested New York; this time by a score of 1–0 defeating Bob Sharkey. This shutout moved him ahead of Walsh, and only Plank stood in his way of the inevitable record pace.

From 1915 through 1917, Walter would have a rival in grabbing the headlines and superlatives. He was the elite of the American League, but Grover Cleveland Alexander would become the major's premier hurler during those three years. Alex would capture 30 or more wins for those years, and his shutout totals would dwarf even the great Johnson.

In 1916, Washington slid back into the second division finishing seventh. Because of the closeness of the pennant race, they logged a won-loss record of 76–77, which left them only 14½ games behind the champion Red Sox. Walter won 25 games, leading the league in that department, which accounted for almost one third of the team's wins, but he could only manufacture three shutouts. This was his lowest total since his rookie year. His first shutout was against the defending world champion Red Sox, but his third was his most significant. On September 5, 1916, he defeated the New York Yankees 2–0 ceding only one hit. This shutout tied him with Eddie Plank for the league record of 63.

In 1917, his victory total fell below 25 for the first time since 1909, but he twirled eight shutouts, one behind league-leader Stan

Coveleski. His first shutout on opening day against Philadelphia set the league record with only Christy Mathewson and Cy Young ahead of him. By year's end, he would be within striking distance of the two former stalwarts. Two of these shutouts were against the Chicago White Sox who would go on to be crowned world champions that year. One of them was a one-hitter defeating Urban Faber. Walter was denied a no-hitter by Ray Schalk. In this game Johnson again showed his ability as a bat man by going three for three with two doubles. It must be noted that when he shut out the St. Louis Browns, he bested Eddie Plank, which was Plank's last game. Also, on September 5, 1916, he fashioned another one-hitter versus the Yankees. "Rube" Oldring's single in the fifth inning with no one out spoiled Johnson's attempt at a no-hitter. Walter also hit a homer to aid his own cause.

Just as he started the season with a shutout, he ended it with one against the Red Sox, beating their heralded left-hander, George "Babe" Ruth.

Because of World War I and the efforts that were needed for war production, baseball had to abbreviate the season. On September 2, the curtailment took place, which did exclude the World Series from any cancellations. Regardless of this, Walter had another outstanding year. He pitched Washington to within four games of the pennant, which was the closest they ever came. His eight shutouts tied him with Carl Mays for the league lead. The game of May 15, 1918, versus Chicago went 15 innings as he prevailed against Claude Williams. On June 9, 1918, he shut out Detroit with one hit and tied him with Cy Young's total. This shutout was marred by Vitt's only hit for the Tigers. His eighth of the year tied him with Matty for the Major League record.

The year 1919 saw another short season but not as drastic as 1918. Walter won 20 again for the tenth consecutive year. He spun seven shutouts, five by the score of 1–0. His first whitewash was a 1–0 victory over Philadelphia, which gave him the Major League record. On May 11, 1919, he hooked up in a duel with the Yankee Jack Quinn, which ended in a 0–0 tie after 12 innings. Darkness ended the game.

As the advent of the Roaring Twenties emerged on the American scene, the "Black Sox" scandal would erupt and shake the foundations of baseball. The throwing of the 1919 World Series by the Chicago White Sox would leave a sour aftertaste in mouths of fans that would be relieved by a miraculous evolution named Babe Ruth. He would be the fresh mint that would alleviate the foul odor remaining from 1919.

His heroic deeds committed through his patented use of the home run revolutionized the game forever. In a single season he would lay on the back burner the scandalous memories and announce the demise of the "dead ball" era.

He would be aided by Judge Kenesaw "Mountain" Landis whose rule as the first commissioner would cast a menacing shadow over those who harbored thoughts of any illegalities towards the game. The season of 1920 would be bittersweet for Johnson. At 32 he still was a formidable foe at the onset of the season, but as it progressed he would be jinxed by injury. This losing season would be his first since 1909. The brighter side of the season in which he only won eight games saw him attain two milestones. The first was his 300th victory on May 14, 1920. Because of extensive research on Walter's 1912 season, they have given him credit for another victory. His win on May 14, 1920, is regarded as his 300th win.

One authoritative source, *Total Baseball*, has recognized the stat as being correct, while Macmillan's *Baseball Encyclopedia* and Neft and Cohen have not substantiated it. Still, the year did promote Walter's 300th victory. In his last shutout, he finally pitched his only no-hitter to defeat Boston 1–0. Only an error by second baseman "Bucky" Harris prevented him from having a perfect game. Also, he achieved this no-hitter by stifling Boston 1–0 with ten strikeouts. A short while later, the "Big Train" was derailed for the remainder of the season by a sore arm.

Everyone must have doubted whether Walter could rebound from his injury of 1920. He was now in his mid–30s, which now planted the proverbial seeds of doubt in the minds of his fans and supporters. Had the many campaigns taken their toll on the immortal warrior? He dispelled any doubts by having a winning season with 17 victories, which included one shutout. His E.R.A. was uncharacteristically high at 3.51, and two of the members of the pitching staff topped his victory total. Regardless, he was instrumental in moving the Senators back into the first division.

The following year his record stood at 15–16, but he did lead the team in E.R.A. (2.99), which was aided by four shutouts. His efforts could not stop the slide of his team into sixth place.

In 1923 he again led his team with 17 victories, but he had a 3.54 E.R.A. This could have been due to the emergence of the home run as well as some diminishing velocity on his once-masterful fastball. His efforts did propel Washington into the first division—three percentage points ahead of St. Louis.

If any pitcher had a rejuvenating year, it would have to be Walter Johnson in 1924. He was the catalyst in bringing Washington its first pennant, stopping the Yankees from a record four in a row. If awards were in vogue at that time, Walter would have won all of the pitching categories. He led the league in wins, percentage, strikeouts, shutouts and E.R.A.! He annexed the triple crown of pitching for the second time (his career year of 1913 being the other).

In hurling his six shutouts, he notched the 100th of his career. This was a shining 4–0 one-hitter on May 23, 1924, versus Chicago. Harry Hooper spoiled Walter's opportunity for a spectacular milestone win. On August 25, 1924, he pitched his team to a 2–0 victory over St. Louis without allowing a hit. Because of rain, the game was shortened to seven innings preventing Walter from achieving his second no-hitter.

In the World Series, the Senators combated the Giants who were making a record fourth consecutive appearance. Johnson was given the honor of opening the Series, a privilege he so richly deserved. If it wasn't for him, Washington would not have made it. He was the sentimental favorite of the nation to defeat the McGraw-led Giants. Fans were pulling for him to wear the mantle of champion. After so many years of playing with a non-contender, he had the chance to succeed in the twilight of a great career. As if frustration was to follow him in his moment of glory, he lost a heartbreaking 4–3 decision in 12 innings. He was hit hard, and gave up 14 hits but showed a tenacity in going the route.

He started the fifth game going the distance and was charged with his second loss of the Series. It seemed that the quest for the championship would never really materialize. Washington forced the Giants to a seventh and deciding game, which afforded Johnson the opportunity for a reprieve for his elusive dream. He made his first relief appearance of the season in the ninth. He held the Giants for the next three innings. In the bottom of the 12th, Washington fulfilled its Cinderella role by pulling the game out of New York's grasp. Eric McNeely's hopper to third bounced over Fred Lindstrom's head bringing in the decisive and winning run. Johnson gained the victory. He was now at the moment of his glorious achievement, which was long in coming.

In 1925 Washington again captured the pennant with no strong opposition from anyone, including the dominant Yankees. The Yankees fell early in the season when Babe Ruth was incapacitated with abdominal complications. This aided the Senators in their goal for consecutive pennants. Walter was again instrumental in achieving that with another 20-win season. He had help from Stan Covelski who also contributed 20 victories.

In the Series, Johnson was spectacular in his first two starts. He defeated the Pirates 4–1 in the opening game at Pittsburgh and followed that up with a 4–0 whitewash in the fourth game, yielding only six hits and giving the Senators a comfortable 3–1 game lead. The Pirates fought back and then tied the Series and had to face Walter in the deciding seventh game. Staked to a 6–3 lead during a rain-soaked afternoon, Johnson couldn't secure it. He faltered badly giving up five runs in the seventh and eighth innings. He was hammered hard and gave up 15 hits while going the route. It was a disappointing finish with the elements and the Pirate bats playing major roles.

The following year Washington faded to fourth as some of their veterans started to show their age (Walter among them). He was now 38, and the inevitable end of the road was drawing closer each passing day. He posted a 15–16 record and led the team with his 15 wins.

In his final year, a broken leg exacerbated his decision to hang up his glove. On May 30, 1927, he pitched his final shutout to beat Boston 3–0. After 21 challenging seasons, the "Big Train" had entered the terminal with 110 shutouts in his career and 37 of those by the score of 1–0! Over 25.4% of his victories were shutouts. He was truly the greatest and if he had the luxury of pitching with a contender most of his career, his final statistics would have been even more brilliant.

Walter Johnson's Shutouts

Date	Team	Score	Hits	S.O.	Walks	Loser
9/7/07 (A)	Bos.	1–0	7	7	1	Morgan
9/12/07 (A)	N.Y.	2–0	6	4	1	Newton
8/14/08 (H)	Chi.	1–0	2	10	1	White
8/28/08 (H)	Cleve.	8–0	9	5	2	Liebhardt
9/4/08 (A)	N.Y.	3–0	6	4	1	Chesbro
9/5/08 (A)	N.Y.	6–0	4	3	0	Manning
9/7/08 (A)	N.Y.	4–0	2	5	0	Chesbro
10/7/08 (H)	N.Y.	1–0	5	8	0	Warhop
6/11/09 (H)	Det.	1–0	4	7	1	Killian
8/4/08 (H)	Cleve.	1–0	4	8	2	Joss
8/17/09 (H)	Phi.	1–0	4	5	6	Bender

The Great Shutout Pitchers

Date	Team	Score	Hits	S.O.	Walks	Loser
9/21/09 (H)	Det.	2–0	6	5	2	Killian
4/14/10 (H)	Phi.	3–0	1	9	3	Plank
5/14/10 (H)	Cleve.	1–0	5	8	0	Joss
5/19/10 (H)	St. Louis	5–0	7	8	3	Graham
8/11/10 (A)	Cleve.	6–0	2	7	1	Fanwell
8/19/10 (H)	Cleve.	10–0	6	3	0	Koestner
8/13/10 (H)	St. Louis	8–0	5	14	4	Bailey
9/25/10 (A)	St. Louis	3–0	1	11	0	Molloy
10/3/10 (A)	N.Y.	4–0	5	4	2	Vaughn
5/2/11 (A)	Bos.	3–0	7	3	0	Collins
6/14/11 (H)	St. Louis	13–0	9	4	1	Nelson
7/17/11 (A)	Chi.	3–0	5	6	1	Lang
8/4/11 (H)	Chi.	1–0	5	4	3	White
8/17/11 (H)	Stl.	5–0	4	7	4	Nelson
10/3/11 (H)	Phi.	2–0	1	4	0	Plank (6 inn.)
4/15/12 (A)	N.Y.	1–0	4	6	4	Quinn
4/19/12 (H)	Phi.	6–0	3	8	2	Brown
4/29/12 (H)	N.Y.	2–0	5	5	1	Vaughn
5/11/12 (H)	Cle.	8–0	2	11	0	Mitchell
5/30/12 (A)	Bos.	5–0	5	13	4	O'Brien
8/2/12 (A)	Det.	4–0	7	8	1	Willett
8/16/12 (H)	Chi.	4–0	2	7	0	Benz
4/19/13 (A)	N.Y.	3–0	6	8	0	Keating
4/23/13 (H)	Bos.	6–0	2	7	2	Collins
4/30/13 (A)	Phi.	2–0	4	10	1	Plank
5/10/13 (A)	Chi.	1–0	2	4	1	Benz
6/6/13 (H)	Stl.	1–0	5	8	1	Leverenz
6/10/13 (H)	Det.	3–0	2	7	1	Clauss
6/21/13 (H)	N.Y.	6–0	2	7	4	Keating
6/27/13 (H)	Phi.	2–0	3	6	1	Brown
7/3/13 (A)	Bos.	1–0	15	4	1	Collins (15 inn.)
9/15/13 (H)	N.Y.	1–0	3	8	1	Ford
9/29/13 (H)	Phi.	1–0	5	9	0	Wyckoff
4/14/14 (A)	Bos.	3–0	5	8	0	Collins
5/5/14 (H)	N.Y.	6–0	4	6	1	McHale
5/20/14 (H)	Cle.	5–0	5	2	2	Gregg
5/29/14 (A)	Bos.	1–0	2	3	1	A. Johnson
7/6/14 (H)	Bos	1–0	3	6	1	A. Johnson
7/13/14 (H)	Det.	3–0	3	10	2	Main
7/21/14 (H)	Chi.	4–0	7	4	0	Benz
8/1/14 (A)	Det.	3–0	7	5	6	Williams
9/18/14 (A)	Stl.	1–0	5	6	2	Hoch
4/14/15 (H)	N.Y.	7–0	2	1	3	Warhop
4/28/15 (H)	Phi.	1–0	7	4	1	Wyckoff
6/23/15 (H)	Bos.	5–0	7	7	2	Mays
6/28/15 (H)	Phi.	2–0	6	7	0	Crowell
9/3/15 (H)	N.Y.	2–0	4	7	0	Pieh

Date	Team	Score	Hits	S.O.	Walks	Loser
6/28/15 (H)	Phi.	2–0	6	7	0	Crowell
9/3/15 (H)	N.Y.	2–0	4	7	0	Pieh
9/8/15 (A)	N.Y.	1–0	6	10	2	Sharkey
9/28/15 (H)	Det.	3–0	3	10	2	Oldham
4/29/16 (H)	Bos.	4–0	4	6	0	Foster
8/28/16 (H)	Cle.	2–0	3	3	2	Boehling
9/5/16 (H)	N.Y.	2–0	1	8	1	Cullop
4/11/17 (A)	Phi.	3–0	3	11	3	R. Johnson
6/7/17 (H)	Chi.	1–0	3	6	1	Russell
6/19/17 (H)	Det.	3–0	5	6	2	James
8/6/17 (H)	Stl.	1–0	5	3	1	Plank
8/10/17 (H)	Chi.	4–0	1	1	3	Faber
9/7/17 (H)	N.Y.	6–0	3	4	1	Love
9/15/17 (H)	Phi.	4–0	6	7	1	Schauer
10/3/17 (H)	Bos.	6–0	7	7	2	Ruth
5/1/18 (A)	Bos.	5–0	4	3	3	Mays
5/11/18 (H)	Cle.	1–0	5	5	4	Bagby
5/15/18 (H)	Chi.	1–0	10	9	1	Williams (15 inn.)
5/26/18 (H)	Det.	4–0	4	3	2	Kallin
6/9/18 (A)	Det.	2–0	1	7	3	Boland
6/27/18 (H)	Phi.	8–0	6	5	0	Adams
7/25/18 (A)	Stl.	1–0	4	3	2	Sotheron
8/10/18 (A)	Phi.	1–0	7	10	0	Watson
4/23/19 (H)	Phi.	1–0	9	6	3	Perry
5/11/19 (A)	N.Y.	0–0	2	9	1	Quinn (12 inn.)
6/13/19 (H)	Cle.	1–0	4	2	3	Morton
6/29/19 (H)	Phi.	1–0	6	4	1	Naylon
7/3/19 (H)	N.Y.	1–0	7	4	2	Shore
7/15/19 (A)	Cle.	3–0	8	4	1	Bagby
7/24/19 (H)	Phi.	1–0	6	8	1	Kinney
4/25/20 (H)	Bos.	2–0	7	5	2	Bush
5/29/20 (A)	Phi.	5–0	4	6	0	Moore
6/27/20 (H)	Phi.	7–0	3	2	0	Moore
7/1/20 (A)	Bos.	1–0	0	10	0	Harper
9/14/21 (H)	Stl.	1–0	4	5	0	Davis
6/18/22 (A)	Chi.	10–0	4	1	4	Faber
6/23/22 (H)	Phi.	3–0	5	5	1	Heimach
6/28/22 (H)	N.Y.	1–0	7	9	0	Hoyt
8/24/22 (H)	Chi.	1–0	5	5	0	Blankenship
5/2/23 (H)	N.Y.	3–0	3	4	4	Sharkey
7/30/23 (H)	Det.	1–0	6	6	3	Dauss
9/26/23 (H)	Chi.	1–0	6	5	0	Thurston
4/15/24 (H)	Phi.	4–0	4	8	2	B. Harris
5/23/24 (H)	Chi.	4–0	1	14	1	Leverette
6/6/24 (A)	Det.	2–0	4	7	4	Whitehill
6/26/24 (H)	Phi.	5–0	8	3	1	Baumgartner
8/12/24 (H)	Cle.	4–0	5	8	0	Smith

Date	Team	Score	Hits	S.O.	Walks	Loser
8/25/24 (H)	Stl.	2–0	0	2	2	Davis (7 inn.)
5/11/25 (A)	Chi.	9–0	5	4	2	Blankenship
6/16/25 (H)	Stl.	3–0	9	7	2	Giard
6/30/25 (H)	Phi.	7–0	2	7	0	Harriss
4/13/26 (H)	Phi.	1–0	6	12	3	Rommel (15 inn.)
7/3/26 (A)	Stl.	9–0	6	4	1	Gaston
5/30/27 (H)	Bos.	3–0	3	1	0	Welzer

Walter Johnson

Year	Home	Away	Total
07	2	0	2
08	3	3	6
09	4	0	4
10	5	3	8
11	4	2	6
12	4	3	7
13	7	4	11
14	5	4	9
15	5	1	7
16	3	0	3
17	6	2	8
18	4	4	8
19	5	2	7
20	2	2	4
21	1	0	1
22	3	1	4
23	3	0	3
24	5	1	6
25	2	1	3
26	1	1	2
27	1	0	1
	76	34	110

Johnson's Shutouts by Team

Bos.	Chi.	Cle.	Det.	N.Y.	Phi.	Stl.	Total
15	14	12	12	21	23	13	110

Johnson's Shutouts by Team Finish

1	2	3	4	5	6	7	8	Total
15	13	8	10	19	9	10	26	110

Grover Cleveland Alexander
A Winner Wherever He Went

Baseball historians can look back at 1911 and realize that it would be the only year the four winningest pitchers of all time would be contemporaries. It would be Cy Young's last year while Walter Johnson would emerge as the greatest of all pitchers. Christy Mathewson, who still had some glorious years left, would still be the bell cow of the Giants, leading them to three consecutive pennants. This would be the year that Grover Cleveland Alexander would erupt on the scene setting a record for victories (28) by a rookie. When historians select the all-time team; these four are the first selectees of the starting rotation. It can't be a coincidence that of the first nine players selected to baseball's Hall of Fame, they were the only pitchers who were immortalized.

Alexander stormed onto the scene with the Philadelphia Phillies leading the league in wins, shutouts, complete games, and innings pitched. Of his seven shutouts, the first coming against Brooklyn 5–0, he meagerly doled out three hits. He had only three when September came, but he seemed to find added momentum when he hooked up in a classic pitching duel with Cy Young, defeating the all-time victory leader 1–0. Alexander gave up only one hit to "Doc" Miller. This was also the first National League loss by Young since 1900 when he defected to the then new American League. It was a classic showcase of the new guard versus the old guard. Alexander threw three more consecutive shutouts during September.

The year 1912 was a season of struggle for Alexander and the Phillies. Alex doubled as a starter and reliever winning 19 and losing 17. The Phils fell to the second division finishing under .500. "Alex" again led the league in strikeouts and innings pitched. His E.R.A. was substantially below the team's even though he pitched three shutouts.

In 1913 the Phillies rose to second place (their highest finish since 1901). Alexander broke the 20-win club for the second time, but his status as the team ace was interrupted for the year when teammate Tom Seaton led the league in wins with 27. This was Seaton's career year, but Grover was a contributing factor with nine shutouts, one of which was an extra-inning tie. The one on April 25, 1913, versus the Giants went nine innings, but New York employed two pitchers against him. On September 5, 1913, he matched zeroes with the Braves' "Lefty" Tyler in a game that went ten innings. When he defeated the Cubs on September 22, he earned the distinction of shutting out every club in the league at least once. He would do that three times during his career!

September also showed that he seemed to gain strength as the year progressed when the rigors of a long campaign takes its toll on most pitchers.

The following year saw Alexander become the ace of the staff again, but the Phils tumbled into sixth place. This could be attributed to the defection of Tom Seaton to the newly derived Federal League. Alex contributed 27 wins and again led the league in wins, strikeouts, complete games, and innings pitched. He pitched six shutouts after June which was a further indication of his resilience. On September 19, 1914, St. Louis became his 25th career shutout victim.

Starting with 1915, Alexander would have the three most outstanding years of his brilliant career. During these years the label "Alexander the Great" would become synonymous with his pitching feats. He would duplicate Christy Mathewson's three consecutive years of 30-plus wins. "Matty" had a 94–33 record. During his three years Alex matched this victory total but lost two more games. It was in the shutout category that Alexander was overwhelming in comparison to Mathewson. For the three years Grover blanked the opposition 36 times while "Big Six" achieved only 16. These three years for Alexander were extraordinary because of where he pitched.

The Phils home park, Baker's Bowl, was claustrophobic. It had the smallest dimensions of any park in the majors. Yet, Alexander performed with aplomb, as he led the Phillies to their first pennant ever. In his 31 victories, there were 12 shutouts with 4 of them being one-hitters. On June 5, 1915, he pitched a 3–0 one-hitter versus St. Louis with Art Butler getting a hit in the ninth inning with two outs. In this game, Alex retired the first 15 men he faced. On June 26, 1915, he defeated Brooklyn 4–0 on one hit. In the eighth inning, Zack Wheat singled for Brooklyn's only hit. In this game, Alex threw only 76 pitches as he disposed of the Dodgers in rapid fashion. On July 5, 1915, he beat the Giants 2–0, again yielding only one hit. Fred Merkel led off the second inning with a double but was unable to dent the plate. Grover had the privilege of clinching the pennant on September 29, 1915, with a 5–0 shutout. This also was a one-hitter with the culprit, Sherwood McGee, leading off the fourth inning with a single, depriving Grover of another potential no-hitter. These four games would be the last time he would ever come close to pitching a no-hitter. Grover's year was so outstanding that he led the league in seven major pitching categories, including the triple crown of pitching (wins, strikeouts, and E.R.A.).

He was given the honor of opening the World Series versus the Red Sox which showed the opposing league his brilliance as he stifled Boston 3–1. In game three, he yielded a run in the last of the ninth which gave the Red Sox the Series lead that they never relinquished. Alex was the only Phillies pitcher to win a World Series game until Bob Walk defeated the Kansas City Royals in the opening game of the 1980 World Series.

As great as he was in 1915, he was even greater in 1916. He led the league in eight pitching categories, including his second triple crown of pitching! The Phillies failed to repeat as champions but no one could fault Alexander and his effort. He kept them in the pennant race until the fading days of the campaign. His 33 victories would be the third highest total for the league in this century in which there were 16 shutouts. This is a record that one can assume will never be broken, especially with today's present-day usage of relievers. He again shut out every team at least once with the Cincinnati Reds feeling the sting five times. On August 18, 1916, he reached the 50-shutout mark beating Cincinnati 3–0.

The 1917 season saw the Giants gain dominance over the league after a three-year hiatus as also-rans. Alex repeated as a 30-game winner to keep Philly as the bridesmaid for the second consecutive year. It was now obvious that as Alexander goes so go the Phillies. His right arm was a tower of strength that held the team up as respectable and made them a shade above the others. He annexed his third straight triple crown, another achievement that cements his uniqueness throughout the annals of the game.

During the off-season, the Phils dropped a bombshell on the baseball world. Alexander had asked for $12,000 a year for three years and was rewarded with being sold to Chicago Cubs along with his battery mate Bill Killefer for Cub catcher Dil Hoffer and pitcher Mike Pendergast plus $50,000 in cash. Phils president, Baker, felt that Alexander was too expensive to keep and that he wouldn't be able to afford the price of his services. Cub president Charlie Weeghman was elated to attain baseball's greatest pitcher. He now had built the Cubs into a fierce and legitimate contender with the addition of Alex. This gave him a starting rotation which included Jim "Hippo" Vaughn, Claude Hendrix, and "Lefty" Tyler.

In 1918, Alex, after completing a 2–1 record, was drafted into the army. But regardless of his absence, the Cubs still romped to the pennant in the abbreviated season due to World War I.

In 1919, he was released from the army and reported to the Cubs well after the season started. But he did not seem to lose any luster from his lack of competition. He posted a 16–11, won-loss record with a 1.72 E.R.A. which led the league. This was definitely helped by nine shutouts which also was the top mark in that category. He again shut out every team at least once, which was the third time he accomplished the feat. On June 12, 1919, he shut out his old team 3–0 doling out seven hits and walking only one.

In 1920, the Cubs floundered and finally finished in a tie for fifth with a record below .500. Alex was the only shining light in what was to become a dismal year for Chicagoans who would be stricken with the disgrace of the infamous Black Sox scandal. Grover logged a 27–14 record. He won his fourth triple crown of pitching. He threw seven shutouts with four of them coming against the World Champion Cincinnati Reds who were bitten four times by the shut out bug. Excluding the 1918 season because of his military call up, he shut out the Reds every year. Also, during that year he tossed his 75th-career shutout beating the pennant-bound Dodgers. This gem was a 1–0 six-hitter against their ace, Burleigh Grimes.

As the decade of the 20s emerged, the offensive impact of the home run became vital to the game. Due to the transference of Babe Ruth from a pitcher to a hitter. He totally revolutionized the game, and by doing so, he helped to erase the stigma of the Black Sox scandal. The dead-ball era was clearly over and so were E.R.A.s below 2.00 except for Dolph Luque of Cincinnati who had a 1.93 E.R.A. in 1923. Twice the league leaders would post E.R.A.s of 3.00 and over.

The shutout totals would also dwindle with six being the high for the league leader during the decade. It was a certainty that the old game of pitching and defense was being sacrificed with the more attractive offensive deeds. The increase of attendance was indicative of fan support for the new game.

In 1921, Grover pitched three shutouts. Unbelievably, it led the league with six other pitchers tying him for the top spot! At 34, he was still the ace of the Cubs staff, and his 3.39 E.R.A. led the team. At this time he was starting to feel the effects of epilepsy, and he was trying to wash away his frustrations with epilepsy by indulging in alcohol. His old catcher, Bill Killefer, became the manager of the Cubs and would tolerate his behavior due to past loyalties. He won 16 games in 1922 giving the Cubs a winning season after two sub .500 finishes in the second division. His shutout on September 14, 1921, defeated his old team (Philadelphia) 10–0 to give him the National League record as he passed Mathewson by one (his 80th).

In 1923 he sported a 22–12 record to boost the Cubs back into the first division. He fashioned three shutouts, two of them against the Reds, defeating two of their three 20-game winners.

In 1924, he was felled by the injury jinx for the first time in his career. His record of 12–5 with a .706 winning percentage was stopped by a broken wrist. He seemed to have control of himself and his personal problems with the guidance of Killefer.

In 1925, the Cubs disastrously fell into the cellar. Alex at the age of 38 was the only winning pitcher with a 15–11 record. The Cubs released Killefer and replaced him with "Rabbit" Maranville who subsequently was dumped for George Gibson.

Joe McCarthy took over the helm for the Cubs in 1926 and this would have a bearing on Grover for the rest of his career. McCarthy decided to drop Alexander from the team because he had a 3–3 record. "Marsh" Joe could not give in to Alex's continual bouts and binges. He could not justify having a 39-year-old setting a poor example for the younger players. Besides, McCarthy had revived the Cubs and they were in a pennant fight with the other three Western Division clubs.

Baseball is filled with ironic twists throughout its history. When

"Old Pete" was given his walking papers, all felt that it was the proverbial end of the line. The Cardinals were fighting for their first pennant. They were the only National League team to never fly a flag and that city was agog over the possibility of having a winner. Even the Browns in the American League failed in their quest to capture a championship for St. Louis.

Cardinal manager Rogers Hornsby was criticized for picking up Alex for the pennant drive. Alexander did not disappoint his new manager even though he did get suspended once for his drinking. He won nine games, two of them shutouts, and also contributed two saves which showed that he was responsible for helping St. Louis to gain its first pennant. On September 2, 1926, he shut out with sweet revenge the Cubs 2–0. This was payback time as he showed McCarthy that he wasn't over the hill.

The 1926 World Series was a classic versus the Yankees who flaunted the greatest one-two punch in baseball history called Ruth and Gehrig. The Yankees were overwhelming as they took a one-game lead. In the second game, Alex stymied the Yankees 6–2 tying the Series. The New Yorkers took the fourth and fifth games, giving them a one-game lead as the Series traveled back to New York.

When all odds were against St. Louis, Alex rejuvenated them by defeating the Yankees 10–2. The Series was all even as game seven dawned on the horizon. It was said that Hornsby gave Alex the day off so he could unwind celebrating a victory with "John Barleycorn." It was stipulated that "Alex" would show up for the next game if needed. In the seventh inning of the seventh game, the Cards were ahead 3–2 when the Yankees rallied with the bases loaded. The starter, Jesse Haines, developed a blister on his finger and Hornsby had to make a pitching change. Mulling in his mind, he decided on Alexander, who only the day before, pitched a complete-game victory and was still under the effects of his night out. He came in to face the ominous Tony Lazzeri. With one strike on him, Lazzeri sizzled a ball down the left field line that just hooked foul at the last moment. The next pitch he swung and missed which quelled the uprising.

Alex held the Yankees at bay and the Series ended when Ruth, on with a walk, was thrown out trying to steal second base. The Cards had won the Series and Alex was the hero. Hornsby's faith in him paid off with a championship for St. Louis!

In 1927, Alex showed that his performance in the Series was no fluke as he captured 21 victories with a new manager, Bob O'Farrell.

O'Farrell had replaced Hornsby when club president Sam Braedeon decided he couldn't relent to the constant demands that Rogers wanted in the form of salary and decision-making power. During the off-season, Hornsby was traded to the Giants for Frankie Frisch.

With Alex's efforts, St. Louis made another strong showing falling 1½ games short of repeating as champions. Alexander was now 40 and still contributing. His 20-win season made him one of a few pitchers who could boast about having a 20-game-win season for three different teams. He was able to secure two shutouts in his victory total.

In 1928, the Cardinals won their second pennant with the aid of Grover's 16 wins—not bad for a 41-year-old reject. He manufactured his last career shutout beating Pittsburgh and Burleigh Grimes 5-0. That made 90 shutouts for his career! In the Series, he showed little against the Yankees as they drubbed him 9-3.

In 1929, he saw his final days with the Cardinals. He was suspended because of his drinking which was now becoming a detriment to the team. Released at the end of the season, he hooked up with the Phillies who gave him a chance in 1930. Sporting a 0-3 record and being 43 years old, he was given his release.

There is no doubt that when historians look back upon the career of Grover Cleveland Alexander, a great deal of his incredible achievements will never be duplicated. Those 16 shutouts in one season and the National League career total of 90 seem to be beyond the grasp of present-day pitchers. Regardless of his frequent bouts with alcoholism, he was a winner wherever he went.

Grover Cleveland Alexander

Date	Team	Score	Hits	S.O.	Walks	Loser
5/8/11 (H)	Brk.	5-0	3	9	3	Bell
6/26/11 (H)	Bos.	5-0	5	5	5	Ferguson
8/22/11 (H)	Pitt.	3-0	8	6	3	Ferry
9/7/11 (A)	Bos.	1-0	1	7	0	C. Young
9/13/11 (H)	Brk.	2-0	4	8	2	Barger
9/17/11 (A)	Cin.	6-0	5	6	2	Boyd
9/21/11 (A)	Chi.	4-0	4	2	2	Ruelbach
7/16/12 (A)	Cin.	5-0	4	4	3	Suggs
9/20/12 (H)	Stl.	5-0	5	4	2	Burke
9/26/12 (A)	Brk.	7-0	2	7	3	Curtis
4/25/13 (A)	N.Y.	0-0	9	6	1	Demaree Crandall
5/1/13 (H)	N.Y.	1-0	6	2	1	Tesreau
5/24/13 (A)	Brk.	3-0	9	4	0	Ragan

Date	Team	Score	Hits	S.O.	Walks	Loser
6/4/13 (A)	Pitt.	4–0	6	3	2	Camnitz
8/5/13 (A)	Stl.	1–0	4	7	1	Salee
8/14/13 (H)	Cin.	1–0	5	5	1	Ames
9/5/13 (A)	Bos.	0–0	7	4	1	Rudolph
9/13/13 (A)	Stl.	2–0	4	2	0	Perritt
9/22/13 (A)	Chi.	2–0	4	3	2	Humphries
7/1/14 (A)	Bos.	5–0	5	4	1	Rudolph
7/25/14 (H)	Stl.	3–0	10	5	2	Perdue
8/3/14 (H)	Chi.	5–0	6	2	1	Stack
8/7/14 (H)	Cin.	2–0	6	7	0	Ames
9/12/14 (H)	N.Y.	1–0	4	8	1	Marquard
9/19/14 (H)	Stl.	7–0	2	11	0	Perdue
4/14/15 (A)	Bos.	3–0	6	5	2	Rudolph
5/25/15 (H)	Chi.	3–0	2	9	3	Humphries
6/5/15 (A)	Stl.	3–0	1	8	1	Meadows
6/26/15 (H)	Brk.	4–0	1	6	0	Coombs
7/5/15 (H)	N.Y.	2–0	1	6	0	Perritt
7/13/15 (H)	Stl.	8–0	6	3	1	Griner
7/21/15 (H)	Chi.	1–0	2	4	1	Adams
7/24/15 (H)	Cin.	4–0	8	4	0	McKerney
8/25/15 (H)	Cin.	8–0	4	5	3	Schneider
9/2/15 (A)	N.Y.	2–0	7	7	1	Mathewson
9/9/15 (H)	N.Y.	3–0	3	4	2	Benton
9/29/15 (A)	Bos.	5–0	1	4	1	Rudolph
4/8/16 (H)	Bos.	4–0	5	2	3	Rudolph
5/3/16 (A)	Bos.	3–0	6	2	0	Barnes
5/13/16 (A)	Cin.	5–0	3	4	0	Dale
5/18/16 (A)	Pitt.	3–0	4	3	1	Kantlehner
5/26/16 (H)	Brk.	1–0	8	9	0	Smith
6/3/16 (H)	Stl.	2–0	9	5	0	Meadows
7/7/16 (A)	Stl.	1–0	6	2	1	Meadows
7/15/16 (A)	Pitt.	4–0	4	5	0	Jacobs
7/20/16 (A)	Cin.	6–0	2	3	0	Toney
8/2/16 (H)	Chi.	1–0	7	7	3	Pendergast (12 inn.)
8/9/16 (H)	Cin.	1–0	3	7	0	Schultz
8/14/16 (H)	N.Y.	8–0	4	7	0	Benton
8/18/16 (A)	Cin.	3–0	7	2	0	Schneider
9/1/16 (H)	Brk.	3–0	8	4	0	Coombs
9/23/16 (H)	Cin.	4–0	8	4	1	Toney
10/2/16 (H)	Bos.	2–0	3	7	0	Ragan
5/10/17 (H)	Stl.	1–0	4	7	1	Meadows
6/6/17 (A)	Chi.	4–0	5	7	0	Seaton
7/13/17 (H)	Chi.	7–0	7	5	1	Douglas
7/16/17 (H)	Cin.	1–0	6	1	1	Ragan
7/31/17 (A)	Stl.	6–0	4	1	1	Meadows
8/22/17 (H)	Chi.	5–0	7	3	0	Pendergast
9/3/17 (A)	Brk.	5–0	4	5	1	McQuard

Grover Cleveland Alexander

Date	Team	Score	Hits	S.O.	Walks	Loser
9/13/17 (H)	Brk.	1–0	7	8	1	Pfeffer (11 inn.)
6/2/19 (H)	Pitt.	7–0	9	1	0	Mayer
6/12/19 (H)	Phi.	3–0	7	8	1	Jacobs
7/23/19 (A)	Brk.	3–0	5	6	0	Mamaux
7/27/19 (A)	Stl.	4–0	5	5	1	Tuero
8/10/19 (H)	N.Y.	2–0	4	7	3	Benton
8/14/19 (A)	Brk.	2–0	4	5	0	Smith
8/31/19 (II)	Stl.	1–0	3	2	0	Woodward
9/21/19 (H)	Bos.	3–0	6	4	0	Causey
9/28/19 (A)	Cin.	2–0	6	5	1	Eller
5/3/20 (A)	Cin.	5–0	7	0	3	Fisher
5/24/20 (H)	Phi.	6–0	5	9	0	Rixey
7/1/20 (A)	Cin.	1–0	7	5	1	Luque
8/14/20 (H)	Cin.	5–0	5	5	1	Reuther
8/28/20 (H)	Brk.	1–0	6	1	1	Grimes
9/5/20 (H)	Pitt.	2–0	3	8	0	Ponder
9/25/20 (A)	Cin.	2–0	6	1	2	Fisher
7/20/21 (A)	Phi.	10–0	6	3	1	G. Smith
9/2/21 (A)	Cin.	7–0	5	2	0	Rixey
9/14/21 (H)	Phi.	10–0	8	1	0	Hubbell
7/21/22 (H)	Brk.	1–0	4	0	2	Reuther
5/25/23 (H)	Cin.	4–0	2	1	0	Donoghue
6/24/23 (H)	Cin.	2–0	3	6	1	Luque
7/11/23 (A)	Brk.	2–0	6	3	1	Reuther
9/16/25 (H)	Bos.	3–0	7	1	0	Genewich
8/7/26 (A)	Brk.	3–0	4	1	0	Grimes
9/2/26 (A)	Chi.	2–0	3	0	2	Root
6/5/27 (H)	Brk.	8–0	8	1	0	Petty
7/11/27 (A)	Phi.	7–0	4	0	0	Preutt
4/12/28 (H)	Pitt.	5–0	7	3	1	Grimes

Year	Home	Away	Total
11	4	3	7
12	1	2	3
13	2	7	9
14	5	1	6
16	8	4	12
16	9	7	16
17	5	3	8
19	5	4	9
20	4	3	7
21	1	2	3
22	1	0	1
23	2	1	3
25	1	0	1
26	0	2	2

Year	Home	Away	Total
27	1	1	2
28	1	0	1
	50	40	90

Alexander's Shutouts by Team

Bos.	Brk.	Chi.	Cin.	N.Y.	Phi.	Pit.	Stl.	Total
11	16	10	20	8	5	7	13	90

Alexander's Shutouts by Team Finish

1	2	3	4	5	6	7	8	Total
7	7	14	11	7	13	15	16	90

Christy Mathewson
A True Baseball Idol

Before I start to discuss Christy Mathewson and his outstanding career, it must be noted that the era he pitched in is one when baseball statistics were poorly kept. This was due to the fact that most followers of the game at that time did not revere them as today's fans do. Record keeping was not as fully accurate and the wire services of the day that transmitted data from each city did it without state-of-the-art technology. Christy Mathewson's shutout total varies with each of the following four major resource books: *Total Baseball*, Macmillan's *The Baseball Encyclopedia*, Neft and Cohen's *The Baseball Encyclopedia*, and *The Sporting News Baseball Complete Record Book*. All four of these reference books should be a part of every purist's reference library. *Total Baseball* lists Matty's shutouts at 79; Macmillan gives him 80; Neft and Cohen credit him with 77; and *The Sporting News* show his totals at 83. Ronald A. May, in his book *Christy Mathewson: A Game by Game Profile of a Legendary Pitcher*, has researched every game that Mathewson has appeared in in his major league career and accurately recorded his game performances. He has Matty's total shutouts at 79, the exact number that *Total Baseball* records.

May, because of his intense research, must be credited with being the expert on "Matty." The difference between Macmillan and *Total Baseball* is due to a game that Mathewson pitched in 1908. On

September 1, 1908, Christy pitched an 8–0 victory over the Boston Doves. He only went eight innings because manager John McGraw wanted to rest his ace due to the team being in a fiercely fought pennant race with the Pittsburgh Pirates and the Chicago Cubs. This game gave him a victory but not a complete-game shutout. Macmillan has never corrected its total. Neft and Cohen's total of 77 is due to shortening his total by one in 1906 and 1910.

The Sporting News, on the other hand, credits him with 83, but his totals in their publication *Daguerreotypes* shows 84. I added the total in that book and it only added up to 83! What I believe is that they have given him credit for four shutout victories that he did not complete. *The Sporting News* has done that with others that have pitched during that period and further chapters will substantiate or discredit their totals. The total of 79 is the one that this writer will honor as the correct count.

Regardless of the discrepancies, Matty was the American idol during his era. He was the type of man that you wanted your son to grow up to be or your daughter to marry. His clean-cut appearance could have reflected that of a country parson or the family doctor with a warm bedside manner. He was the ideal Hollywood hero in a profession that was overwhelmed with rowdies and two-fisted drinkers. The personification of a ballplayer during these years was not one that was held in high esteem. Matty was the one flower blossoming in the garden of weeds. Not only did his physical appearance command attention, but being a product of Bucknell University added to his presence.

Mathewson, in making his debut in 1900, showed little that would portray his future greatness as he was promoted to the New York Giants from Norfolk of the Virginia League with a 20–2 record. He was only a youth of barely 20 years coming to the big city. To make matters even more strenuous for him was that the Giants were usually residents of the lower part of the standings of the National League. They did not project the image their moniker indicated.

The following year Matty would show considerable potential as he notched 20 victories against 17 losses for a team that escaped the cellar by one game. Five of his victories were shutouts, and his first on May 6th was a 4–0 five-hitter against the Phillies. The Phils were a contending team led by the bats of Ed Delahanty and Elmer Flick (both of whom would become batting champions in the newly formed American League). In pitching that game, he showed impeccable control (which would be a legendary trademark of his) by walking none. He was pitted against "Red" Donohue who was Philadelphia's ace. He tossed three more victories that month giving him a total of four. His fifth and last one of the year was on July 15 when he spun his first no-hitter against the St. Louis Cardinals, who led the league in home runs and boasted the league's leading hitter in Jesse Burkett. He walked four which was the highest number of walks that he ever issued in a shutout game. He was only one month shy of his 21st birthday when he posted this gem, which was the second no-hitter of the new century.

The Giants continued their rag-tag play even worse the following year which led them to become basement dwellers. One major event in the latter part of the year resulted when John McGraw deserted the American League due to his continuous feuds with Ban Johnson, the founder of the league, and took over the helm of the Giants. This was not only a fortuitous ray of blessing for New York baseball but for Christy personally. McGraw took the young phenom, who was struggling because of the ineptness of his team, and guided him with the tenderness that emerged from the crusted exterior of the "Little Napoleon." Matty finished the year at 14–17 with eight shutouts, leading the league in that department. His winning percentage was almost 100 points higher than the team's, and his E.R.A. over 70 points lower! The best was yet to come not only due to his age and ability but the ever-dominating presence of "Muggsy" McGraw. A new era for New York City baseball would explode on the scene not like a nova, but one of rapturous splendor that would last for decades.

The influence of McGraw took place immediately during the last half of 1902 when there was talk that Matty was being considered for first base. McGraw squelched that after appraising Christy's ability as a pitcher. One thing can always be said about "Mac" regardless of his abrasive personality was that he knew talent and he made sure pitching was always Matty's forte.

In 1903 dividends were shown instantly and abundantly with McGraw's leadership as the Giants finished second only 6½ games out of the lead. This was remarkable since the Pirates, who had now won three consecutive pennants, won the previous year by 27½ games! McGraw in 1902 induced Joe McGinnity over from the American League and the "Iron Man" teamed up with Mathewson as co-30-game winners! No team in modern baseball can make that claim except the 1904 Giants when the same two pitchers again duplicated the feat!

Matty in 1903 pitched only three shutouts but one was a one-hitter defeating Cincinnati and their ace, Frank "Noodles" Hahn, who is credited with the first no-hitter in modern-day baseball. Joe Kelley smacked a triple in the first with two outs that deprived him of his second no-hitter. Kelley was left stranded at third base.

With Matty and McGinnity again winning over 30 games each with a combined total of 68 victories, a modern baseball record by two pitchers on the same team in a single season, the Giants cakewalked to their fist pennant under McGraw. Their performances enabled the Giants to establish a record 106 wins. Mathewson had to play "second banana" to McGinnity who dominated many of the pitching categories. With the Highlanders in a dog fight for the American League pennant, it created the possible scenario of an all New York World Series. McGraw, who still had a vendetta against the American League and its founder Ban Johnson, strongly pronounced that his team would not engage in any post-season series with the upstart American League. This he stated more emphatically with the possibility that the New York entry could cop the American League flag. He also wanted nothing to do with post-season because of the chance that the new league could duplicate the upset they performed in the first series in the previous year. The possibility of the Giants' two aces facing a showdown with Boston's ace, Cy Young, or the Highlanders' ace, Jack Chesbro, would not be realized. The next World Series cancellation would occur 90 years later when the infamous strike of 1994 canceled the playoff and Series.

In 1904 Matty fashioned another one-hitter, this time against the Chicago Cubs, beating their ace Jake Weimer 5–0. Johnny Kling broke up his potential no-hitter with a single in the fourth inning.

The following year the Giants waltzed to their second consecutive pennant winning one less game from the following year. Matty posted his third-straight, 30-plus season as he notched 32 victories for the year. He had what almost any pitcher would call a career year, but Christy's best was still further down the road. He was the dominant pitcher of the year, and he proved it by annexing the triple crown of pitching (victories, strikeouts, and E.R.A.). During the year, he spun his second career no-hitter on June 13 versus the Cubs (1–0) and the man who would be his arch rival, Mordecai "Three Finger" Brown. They would lock up constantly in pitching duels, many of them legendary, and split 26 decisions throughout their careers.

Matty achieved another milestone when he tossed his 25th career shutout, also manufactured against the Cubs (1–0). This time he was opposed by Ed Ruelbach, who in 1908 gained fame by pitching two shutouts in a doubleheader.

Mathewson's accomplishments during 1905 also spilled over into the World Series, one in which every game was a shutout. Pitching was so dominant in this World Series with Matty achieving the greatest individual performance by a pitcher. Not to downgrade Don Larsen's masterpiece in 1956, but his was only a one-game showpiece, whereas Christy performed in three games.

Another team that could boast about pitching was the Philadelphia A's, a team rich in pitching that touted three future Hall of Famers in "Rube" Waddell, Eddie Plank, and "Chief" Bender. They were also supported by Andy Coakley who contributed 19 victories. The A's would enter the Series without their eccentric left-hander, Rube Waddell, who injured his pitching shoulder with unnecessary horseplay with teammate Coakley. Despite this, the A's still showed a formidable rotation.

The first game pitted Plank against Matty, which became the first World Series game that presented two future Hall of Famers pitching against one another. Matty prevailed with a brilliant four-hitter winning 3–0. Three days later he bested Coakley 9–0 giving up four hits again. Two days later, he shut out Philadelphia for the third time (giving up five hits), which clinched the Series by defeating Bender. Matty pitched three complete-game shutouts in five days! Only once since did anyone come close to matching 0.00 E.R.A. for 27 innings and that was Waite Hoyt who was victimized by two unearned runs in the 1921 World Series. In 1905 Matty's name would become legendary. He was not only the toast of baseball, but he was cheered nationally.

He started 1906 late due to illness but cracked the 20-game win column with 22 victories. His E.R.A. was an uncharacteristically high 2.97 despite logging six shutouts. Realistically, it must be stated that if he started the season promptly, the Giants would never have caught the Chicago Cubs who coasted to the pennant by 20 games. This was the record-setting 116-victory year that had not been duplicated until the Seattle Mariners matched the total in a 162 game schedule.

Matty was back to his old self with 24 wins in 1907 which included eight shutouts that tied him for the league lead with Orvil Overall of Chicago. He was able to shut out every team that year at least once, whitewashing the Pirates twice in the process. His blanking of Cincinnati was a struggle when he allowed 11 hits, but his pitching in the clutch prevented the Reds from denting the plate. As well as he did, he could not prevent the Giants from falling into fourth place, 25½ games behind the rampaging Cubs who breezed to their second-straight pennant by 17 games. The Giants were showing age at several positions which led McGraw to make some major revisions for the next season.

The year 1908 would go down as one of the most dramatic pennant races in the annals of the game with lasting implications. A three-way dogfight among the Giants, Cubs, and Pirates left the winner gasping for breath at the end. It was a bittersweet year for Matty. He had his career year, but it left him empty at the end. He was like the child enjoying the carousel but not able to obtain the brass ring for the extra ride. He did everything that an athlete had to do to put his team on the pinnacle of victory and it reflected in his all-dominating pitching stats. Winning the pitching triple crown was just an example of that. He carved out 11 shutouts which included his 50th career milestone. It was an abbreviated six-inning game but still a complete-game victory. Also, on April 27 he spun his third one-hitter against the Boston Doves with Claude Richey getting a single in the second inning.

His 37 victories were one short of reaching the pennant. This was the year of the famous Merkel boner where a youthful Giant failed to touch second base in a game they had apparently won versus the Cubs. This created chaos because of the fans, anticipating the Giants victory, stormed the field in jubilation. The game was declared a tie and was to be replayed as the last game of the season. Matty was assigned to pitch the clincher, but he fell short losing 4–2. It was an ironic finish to one of the most glorious seasons that a pitcher would witness. Also, his last shutout of the year on September 18 tied him for the National League record with "Pud" Galvin. Galvin, who never pitched at the 60'6" distance, recorded all of his shutouts at 45' and 50'. Matty had shut out Pittsburgh 7–0, giving up five hits.

It would be unrealistic for anyone to think Mathewson could duplicate or come close to matching his 1908 performance, but he did put up impressive numbers in 1909. His 25–6 record gave him a percentage that superseded his team's winning percentage by over 200 points. He led the league in E.R.A. with a 1.14 which was aided by eight shutouts. His superlative effort could not keep his team from falling into third place 18½ games behind the champion Pirates.

Also, he set the National League record for shutouts at 54. He pitched his first of the year on May 17th blanking Cincinnati 6–0 on six hits.

The year 1910 gave him another remarkable season. He won 27 games and led the league in that department. He only pitched two shutouts, one being his fourth career one-hitter again versus the Dodgers. This gem was spoiled by Pryer McElveen who got an infield hit in the eighth inning. The following day the *New York Times* credited Matty with a no-hitter! The *Brooklyn Eagle* of the same day credited Matty with a one-hitter! This was left up to the judgment of the individual scorers. A brief synopsis of the play reveals that Giant third baseman Art Devlin cut in front of shortstop Artie Fletcher in fielding the slow roller. His off-balance throw pulled Fred Merkel off the bag. In all probability, if Fletcher fielded the ball he would have had a better shot of getting the out and preserving the no-hitter. Oddly, in this game the only other Brooklyn base runners were on by errors. Regardless of his low number of shutouts, he still managed to notch an E.R.A. of 1.90.

The next three years the Giants presented a consecutive string of pennants to match the Pirates of 1901–1903 and the Cubs of 1906–1908. They would experience more frustration when it would come to the World Series. They were the only National League team to lose three in a row. This might have been due to the presence of Connie Mack's first dynasty in Philadelphia winning world championships in 1910, 1911, and 1913 plus another pennant in 1914. The Boston Red Sox interrupted Mack's string of successes in 1912 when they fielded one of the strongest Boston teams in history. This conglomeration of talent was anchored by Joe Wood whose 34 victories propelled the Red Sox to a large lead they never relinquished. Despite this, the Giants were still a highly respectable entry displayed by their dominance of the National League.

During the string of pennants, Matty was aided by George "Rube" Marquard in anchoring the Giants' pitching staff. All three years they would be the dominant righty-lefty tandem of the league as they posted 23 or more victories each of the three years. Twice during this stretch of pennants, Matty would lead the league in E.R.A.

In 1911, Matty spun five shutouts with a league-leading E.R.A. of 1.99. In the Series against the Philadelphia A's, he not only saw his string of shutout innings come to a halt at 28-plus, but he bitterly tasted defeat in Series play. In the first game, the A's crossed the plate in the second inning, but the Giants rallied to give him the win. Matty's shutout string lasted until 1918 when a lefty named George "Babe" Ruth topped his record. Ruth's record would be shattered by another left-hander by the name of "Whitey" Ford. Regardless, Matty still has the record for a right-hander and the record for consecutive scoreless innings by a National League pitcher.

Game three gave Matty his first loss in the Series. He had stymied the A's until the ninth inning when Frank "Home Run" Baker sent one of Matty's pitches into the crowd to score. In the top of the 11th, the A's put across two runs to defeat the Giant legend 3–2. He was also charged with the loss in the fourth game as Philadelphia rallied for four runs in the middle of the game defeating him 4–2.

In 1912, the Giants posted 103 victories and romped to the pennant by 10 games. Matty had to settle as second best on the staff to Marquard who rattled off 19 consecutive victories which enabled him to lead the league with 26. Matty contributed 23 wins and finished with an E.R.A. of 2.12, second to teammate Jeff Tesreau (1.96). Oddly, Christy did not pitch a single shutout during the regular season. The Series against the Boston Red Sox, who powered their way with 105 wins, became the showcase of two titans battling to a death finish. The American League champions were led by Joe Wood who dominated the pitching stats in the Junior circuit. Wood, who finished with a 34–5 record, faced the two Giant aces only once in the finale as a relief pitcher. It seemed that the managers didn't want to match up their aces in head-to-head competition.

Boston jumped out to a 3–1 lead with the second game started by Matty a tie. The Giants battled back to even the Series giving Wood a sound thrashing in the seventh game. It looked like momentum had swung to the Giants in the finale. They battled Boston evenly through the eighth when Wood came into relieve. They cuffed Wood for a run in the top of the tenth and it looked secure with Matty breezing. In the bottom of the tenth, as if Pandora's infamous box was opened, the Giants became unraveled. Fred Snodgrass, a sure-handed center fielder, dropped an easy fly ball which was later known as the $30,000 muff. With one out, a single left men at first and third. Tris Speaker then lifted a foul pop between the catcher and first baseman, Fred Merkel, who let it fall untouched. Merkel again would be blamed for this (remember the 1908 game when he failed to touch second base, costing the Giants the pennant). Given a reprieve, Speaker singled, tying the game and sending the winning run to third base. Next, sacrifice fly made the Red Sox the world champions.

In 1913, the Giants again outdistanced their foes for the pennant. This time the margin was 12½ games over the Phillies. Pitching was still the dominant aspect of a well-rounded team. Matty took his rightful place as the bell cow of the staff posting 25 wins. He also led the league in E.R.A. with an impressive 2.06 which was aided by four shutouts. His shutout on August 26 besting Cincinnati 1–0 was his 14th 1–0 complete-game victory. This record at the time has now been surpassed by Walter Johnson, Grover Alexander, and Bert Blyleven.

In the World Series the Giants again would assume the role of bridesmaid for the third consecutive time, a record that still prevails today. The only bright spot for the Giants was Matty who fashioned his fourth World Series shutout. This was accomplished in game two when he hooked up against Eddie Plank. They dueled into the tenth when the Giants broke through for three runs and made it hold up with Mathewson's stellar performance. This shutout, his fourth, gave him the record for World Series shutouts topping Three Finger Brown who had three.

The Giants pennant train in 1914 was derailed by the "Miracle" Braves who after July 4th burst forth and rollicked to the pennant by 10½ games over the Giants. No one could fault Matty because he supplied 24 victories, five being shutouts. His E.R.A. was uncharacteristically high (3.00), but he still was a formidable opponent even though he was getting on in years. Of his shutouts, the one on July 4 versus Philadelphia was the 75th of his career defeating the Phils 3–0. On August 26 he pitched his 76th career shutout which gave him a tie for the major league record with Cy Young. Then on September 11, he blanked Brooklyn 3–0 giving him the major league record at 77.

The Giants in 1915 fell from grace by tumbling into the cellar. This was the first time under McGraw's tutelage that the team wouldn't occupy a position in the first division. It seemed that Mathewson wearing out, who slowed to an 8–14 record, was the omen of decadence for the whole team. Christy did post one shutout in his win total. His E.R.A. of 3.58 was higher than the team's total which was an indication that "Big Six" was coming to the end of the line.

The 1916 season was his last. Later in the year, he was traded to Cincinnati and took over the reins as manager of the Reds. His last shutout was versus Boston defeating them on May 29 by 3–0. His glory days as a player were now over and he seemed bent on being a manager.

During World War I, he joined the American Expedition Force where he contracted lung disease from inhaling poison gas. This would eventually deteriorate his health. In 1925 during the opening game of the World Series, he passed away and sorrow filled everyone who had seen him during his majestic career. He was truly an idol to all Americans.

Christy Mathewson

Date	Team	Score	Hits	S.O.	Walks	Loser
5/6/01 (H)	Phi.	4–0	5	7	2	Donahue
5/11/01 (A)	Brk.	7–0	2	4	1	Kennedy
5/15/01 (H)	Chi.	4–0	9	2	2	Taylor
5/24/01 (H)	Cin.	1–0	3	4	1	Phillips
7/15/01 (A)	Stl.	5–0	0	4	4	Sudhoff
4/17/02 (H)	Phi.	7–0	4	6	4	Felix
5/1/02 (H)	Phi.	3–0	2	9	3	Vorhees
7/8/02 (A)	Chi.	1–0	6	5	1	Rhodes
7/24/02 (A)	Brk.	2–0	5	11	1	Newton
7/28/02 (H)	Brk.	2–0	2	5	3	Evans (5 inns)
8/18/02 (A)	Chi.	5–0	4	1	0	Taylor
8/26/02 (A)	Cin.	6–0	8	6	3	Thielman
9/10/02 (H)	Chi.	6–0	7	7	0	Rhodes
5/20/03 (H)	Pit.	2–0	6	5	1	Leever
5/29/03 (H)	Bos.	3–0	5	5	3	Pittinger
6/13/03 (A)	Cin.	4–0	1	5	2	Hahn
6/10/04 (H)	Chi.	5–0	1	5	4	Weimer
6/30/04 (H)	Bos.	3–0	8	3	2	Pittinger
8/20/04 (A)	Pit.	5–0	3	2	1	Leever (6 inns)
8/24/04 (A)	Chi.	3–0	3	3	1	Briggs
5/11/05 (H)	Stl.	4–0	5	3	4	Taylor
5/23/05 (H)	Cin.	7–0	3	8	1	Overall
6/13/05 (A)	Chi.	1–0	0	2	0	Brown
7/29/05 (A)	Cin.	3–0	6	6	1	Overall
8/10/05 (A)	Chi.	1–0	3	6	1	Ruelbach
8/17/05 (H)	Chi.	3–0	3	6	0	Wicker
8/24/05 (H)	Cin.	8–0	2	2	1	Chech
9/7/05 (H)	Bos.	3–0	3	9	2	Willis
6/23/06 (H)	Phi.	5–0	6	3	2	Richie
7/5/06 (H)	Bos.	1–0	5	6	2	Pfeffer
7/14/06 (A)	Stl.	4–0	6	4	2	Brown
7/25/06 (A)	Pit.	3–0	8	6	2	Phillippe
9/3/06 (H)	Bos.	4–0	3	2	2	Pfeffer
9/11/06 (A)	Bos.	3–0	6	9	3	Young
4/22/07 (A)	Bos.	1–0	8	7	1	Flaherty
5/3/07 (H)	Brk.	1–0	2	8	1	Stricklett

Christy Mathewson 37

Date	Team	Score	Hits	S.O.	Walks	Loser
5/8/07 (H)	Pit.	4–0	4	6	1	Leifield
7/13/07 (H)	Cin.	4–0	11	7	1	Hitt
7/20/07 (H)	Chi.	1–0	3	7	0	Lundgren
8/27/07 (H)	Stl.	1–0	3	5	1	Karger
9/6/07 (H)	Phi.	2–0	3	2	2	Moren (7 inns)
9/24/07 (A)	Pit.	2–0	8	4	1	Leifield
4/18/08 (A)	Brk.	4–0	6	12	1	Pastorius
4/27/08 (A)	Bos.	2–0	1	4	0	Young
5/29/08 (A)	Brk.	1–0	4	8	1	Rucker
6/3/08 (A)	Bos.	3–0	3	11	1	Young
6/20/08 (H)	Chi.	4–0	3	6	1	Fraser
7/13/08 (A)	Pit.	7–0	3	2	0	Leifield
7/29/08 (H)	Stl.	1–0	3	3	0	Sallee
8/17/08 (A)	Stl.	3–0	4	4	0	Sallee (6 inns)
8/20/08 (A)	Cin.	2–0	8	4	2	Coakley
9/8/08 (H)	Brk.	1–0	5	7	1	Rucker
9/18/08 (H)	Pit.	7–0	5	3	0	Maddox
5/17/09 (H)	Cin.	6–0	6	5	0	Rowan
5/28/09 (H)	Phi.	3–0	2	4	0	Coveleski
6/12/09 (A)	Cin.	2–0	4	7	1	Ewing
6/30/09 (A)	Brk.	3–0	4	9	0	Wilhelm
8/12/09 (A)	Chi.	3–0	4	5	0	Pfiester
8/21 09 (H)	Cin.	1–0	5	9	0	Rowan
8/30/09 (H)	Chi.	5–0	5	2	0	Ruelbach
9/11/09 (H)	Brk.	4–0	3	6	1	Knetzer
5/2/10 (A)	Brk.	6–0	1	8	0	Scanlon
9/7/10 (H)	Bos.	2–0	7	5	3	Frock
5/27/11 (H)	Phi.	2–0	8	6	0	Moore
6/21/11 (A)	Bos.	4–0	7	3	1	Weaver
6/28/11 (H)	Bos.	3–0	9	3	0	Mattern
8/11/11 (H)	Phi.	6–0	11	9	1	Burns
10/4/11 (A)	Brk.	2–0	7	5	0	Rucker
4/29/13 (A)	Brk.	6–0	8	1	0	Rucker
7/18/13 (H)	Stl.	5–0	5	5	1	Perritt
7/28/13 (A)	Stl.	4–0	4	5	2	Harmon
8/26/13 (H)	Cin.	1–0	8	2	0	Johnson
5/9/14 (H)	Bos.	2–0	10	1	0	Tyler
6/17/14 (H)	Pit.	5–0	5	4	0	McQuillan
7/4/14 (H)	Phi.	3–0	8	1	2	Mayer
8/26/14 (A)	Stl.	4–0	2	0	0	Sallee
9/11/14 (H)	Brk.	3–0	7	1	0	Schmutz
7/16/15 (H)	Chi.	2–0	5	4	0	Zable
5/29/16 (A)	Bos.	3–0	4	2	0	Rudolph

Year	Home	Away	Total
01	3	2	5

Year	Home	Away	Total
02	4	4	8
03	2	1	3
04	2	2	4
05	5	3	8
06	3	3	6
07	6	2	8
08	4	7	11
09	5	3	8
10	1	1	2
11	3	2	5
13	2	2	4
14	4	1	5
15	1	0	1
16	0	1	1
	45	34	79

Mathewson's Shutouts by Team

Bos.	Brk.	Chi.	Cin.	N.Y.	Phi.	Pit.	Stl.	Total
12	13	14	12	0	9	8	9	79

Mathewson's Shutouts by Team Finish

1	2	3	4	5	6	7	8	Total
4	11	8	11	10	11	12	12	79

Cy Young
So Great They Named an Award After Him

In 1956, a year after Cy Young's death the baseball writers decided to make a special award just for pitchers to recognize their outstanding achievements. The Most Valuable Player Award usually went to an offensive player who exhibited outstanding statistical accomplishments. Pitchers were usually handicapped because they would only appear in about ¼ of their team's games, even though there were 11 occasions where pitchers did win the award prior to 1956. It was necessary to make an award that would honor pitching excellence for the past year. Therefore, the Cy Young Award was born with the legendary pitcher having the honor of having his name etched in immortality.

Young was the pacesetter for all pitching records, some that have been broken numerous times (strikeouts, shutouts, and games pitched). Others such as games won, innings pitched, and complete games will never be approached. So, it was only fitting that the award be named after him.

When he made his debut with the Cleveland Spiders on August 6, 1890, versus the Chicago Colts, they won 3–1. He was so impressive that Chicago's player/manager "Cap" Anson offered the Cleveland owners $1,000 (a huge sum in those days) for the talented rookie. During Young's first three years in the majors, he pitched at the distance of 50'.

Before going on with Young, it's important to understand the complexities of the major league makeup at the time. During the years 1882 and 1890, the National League had a rival with the American Association. Those years saw a World Series between the two leagues. Another league called the Players League appeared and became the death knell to the American Association because of its financial instability. The Association could not compete against two leagues, which led to its demise in 1891. Because of this, the National League absorbed four of the Association's eight teams forcing them to expand to twelve clubs.

Young did not pitch a shutout during his first two years in the majors, but he started to emerge as a future star by posting a 27–20 record in his first full year. Cleveland was not a winning team during this period, but Young had become their ace. In 1891, which was the last year of the American Association, there was no World Series due to the lack of financing by the Association.

The year 1892 saw a revamping of the league championship season. To fill the void in post-season, the league set up an arrangement where there would be a first-half winner and a second-half winner with the two playing a series at the end of the regular schedule. Boston won the first half while Cleveland came out on top in the second. Young had an outstanding year winning 36 games with nine of them being shutouts. Cy fashioned a league-leading E.R.A. of 1.93! Two of these shutouts were abbreviated five-inning stints which were curtailed by darkness. Young did complete both games and received credit for a shutout each time. His game on August 31 was a 0–0 tie versus Baltimore. Young was the solidifying force for the Spiders as they met the Boston Beaneaters in the playoffs. The only bright spot for Cleveland in the series of games was in the first game when Cy pitched an 11-inning 0–0 tie against John Stivetts. After that it was all Boston as they walloped Cleveland four straight.

In 1893, drastic changes in pitching occurred in order to improve the hitting portion of the game. The pitching box was changed to a mound with a rubber slab as the pitcher's position for throwing to the batter. The distance was pushed back to 60'6" making it more difficult for the pitcher to duplicate the statistical accomplishments of previous years. E.R.A.s skyrocketed with the league leader being Ted Breitenstein at 3.19; Cy logged in at third with 3.36. It would be a few years before adjustments to the longer distance would show up in the statistics.

In 1893, Cy shut out Brooklyn 6–0. It took him until September to achieve this feat at the new distance. Despite the extended length, he again broke in the 30-win column by notching 32 decisions. He had now cemented his status as one of the league's top pitchers. The year 1893 again left a vacuum in post-season play as the 1892 split season was discarded due to fan displeasure.

During the 1890s, two teams dominated the league championships. The Boston Beaneaters won five while the Baltimore Orioles won the next three. Both Boston and Baltimore had a string of three consecutive pennants. Brooklyn took the flag in the first and last year of the decade. Cleveland, with Young as the mainstay of the staff, did have some challenging years. In 1894, Cy slipped to a 25–22 record with two 1–0 shutouts. The league leader had only three. His E.R.A. was a lofty 3.94 which seemed to indicate that the 60'6" distance was still favoring the hitters throughout the league. Also, at the end of the year, the Temple Cup was introduced as the first-place finisher would challenge the second-place team. Baltimore, the pennant winner, would succumb to the New York Giants 4–0.

In 1895, the Spiders made their most impressive run for the championship and that would be attributed to Young regaining some of his lost form in 1894. He was the league's winningest pitcher with 35 victories including four shutouts. Two of those were scores of 1–0. This gave him the league lead in shutouts tying him with four others. His E.R.A. was slightly lower than 3.24. In the Temple Cup he excelled by defeating the Orioles three times. This was the second consecutive year Baltimore would be defeated after copping the league championship. This fabled Oriole team innovated many of the strategies that are used today such as the hit and run and "Baltimore chop." They were loaded with five future Hall of Famers (John McGraw, Huey Jennings, Wilbur Robinson, "Wee" Willie Keeler, and Joe Kelley).

During the year of the pennant race going down to the wire, Young was called on to relieve on a Sunday. But it was stated in his contract that he would not pitch on a Sunday (because of his religious convictions). This occurred during the second game of a doubleheader against the St. Louis Browns. Cy volunteered to pitch and got the save in a shortened seven-inning game due to darkness.

In 1896, Cleveland finished second again to Baltimore but not as close as the previous year. They were outdistanced by 9½ games.

They did have a close race for second with Cincinnati beating them out by 2½ games which again gave them the right to compete for the Temple Cup.

Young's stats for 1896 were impressive as he finished with a 29–16 record. He was one victory short of league leaders "Kid" Nichols of Boston and Frank Killen of Pittsburgh. Cy did tie with Killen for the league lead in shutouts at five. He didn't pitch his first shutout until July when the heat of summer seemed to give him an extra boost as he threw three that month. Two of them were consecutive starts against Louisville and Philadelphia. His game versus Philadelphia was a stunning game in which he pitched a one-hitter spoiled by Ed Delahanty in the ninth with two outs. As of now Delahanty is the only man to win a batting title in both leagues.

In the Temple Cup, Baltimore finally came out on top sweeping the Spiders in four straight. Cy lost the first game.

In 1897, the Spiders fell to fifth place and Young struggled with a 21–18 record. By today's standards that would be good, but not for the all-time winner. His E.RA. balloned to 3.79. He had only two shutouts, but he was only one off the league lead of three. His shutout of Cincinnati on September 18 was a masterpiece as he pitched a 6–0 no-hitter against the Reds. This was the first of three that tied a record with Larry Corcoran and later Bob Feller. Sandy Koufax broke this record in 1965. Nolan Ryan later shattered it.

In 1898, Cy improved his record to 25–14 and was credited with one shutout versus Boston defeating them 2–0 and giving up seven hits. His 2.53 E.RA. was impressive and the first time since the 60'6" distance that he was below the 3.00 E.RA. mark. This was his last year with Cleveland.

In 1899 the owner of the Cleveland Spiders also owned the St. Louis Browns. It seemed that the National League was not able to sustain a 12-team league and was going to cut back to eight clubs in 1900. Cleveland's owner decided to strengthen his St. Louis franchise since that was going to be one of the eight teams selected. He transferred the bulk of the Spider team to St. Louis, which gave them a formidable entry that placed fifth. Because of the demolition of the Spiders, they became the worst ball club in major league history winning 20 games while losing 134! Among the Spiders transferred were Cy Young, Jesse Burkett, and Bobby Wallace—all future Hall of Famers.

The move to St. Louis did not hamper Young. He logged a 26–15 record with a splendid 2.58 E.R.A. which placed him third. He also threw four shutouts to place one behind the league leader, Vic Willis.

The dawning of a new century didn't shine brightly on the St. Louis franchise who were now known as the Perfectos; they fell below the .500 mark to sixth place. Young struggled with a 21–18 record with his E.R.A. an even 3.00. This was with the aid of four shutouts which placed him in a four-way tie for the league lead. His co-leaders were an elite class that included "Kid" Nichols, Clark Griffith, and Frank Hahn. His 1–0 shutout of Pittsburgh on September 4 was a harbinger of things to come, for the man he defeated was "Rube" Waddell. Further down the road, they would have some legendary duels.

This was his last year with St. Louis. In 1901 the newly founded American League would beckon him and many others with the lure of the dollar.

The newly founded American League emerged from the Western Association of 1900. Spurned on by Ban Johnson's endeavors, they raided the National League teams in the first two years. There was outright war between the two leagues. Outstanding players such as Nap Lajoie, Ed Delahanty, Jack Chesbro, Elmer Flick, Clark Griffith, and Cy Young would solidify the foundation of the fledgling new league.

Cy joined the Boston Somersets in his first years in the American League. The Somersets were named after their owner, Charles Somers. In 1903 they became the Pilgrims and officially adopted the name Red Sox in 1907. Young was an instant success in the new league as he dominated the pitching stats at the age of 34. His stellar 33–10 record proved that there was life left in his durable right arm as he captured the triple crown of pitching.

He twirled five shutouts, which gave him the league lead in that department. His blanking of Washington 7–0 on July 6 was his first American League shutout as he scattered seven hits. His efforts were not enough. Boston finished four games behind the Chicago White Sox, giving that team the distinction of winning the league's first pennant.

In 1902, he again had another remarkable year posting a 32–11 record. He outdistanced the runner up, Rube Waddell, by eight wins. In fairness to Waddell, he didn't start pitching for the Philadelphia A's until July when he garnished 24 wins! Because of Waddell's stupendous effort, Philadelphia was able to cop the pennant over St. Louis by 5 games and Boston by 6½. Cy did pitch three shutouts that year which made his E.R.A. a respectable 2.15 as he finished fourth behind Ed Siever.

The year 1903 saw a cooling of the war between the two leagues as they ceased raiding each other's teams. An agreement prevailed and they decided to stage a World Series between the two pennant winners.

Young slipped to 28 victories, but the Pilgrims were so good that they walked to the pennant by 14½ games over the As. Cy whitewashed the opposition seven times with three consecutive shutouts (all 1–0) within an eight-day span. His seven shutouts made him the league leader for the second time in three years. The Pilgrims met the Pittsburgh Pirates, who had annexed their third straight flag, in the first modern-day World Series in the best of nine games. This was a good Buc team that sported the likes of Honus Wager and player manager Fred Clark. The Pirates were short in their pitching rotation due to the loss of Ed Doheny who had a nervous breakdown. The bulk of the pitching fell on Charles "Deacon" Phillippe.

The first modern World Series game pitted Phillippe against Young. Cy was tagged for four runs in the first inning giving him the first loss (7–3) in World Series play. He also gave up the first home run to Jimmy Sebring in the seventh inning. Because of the excessive burden placed on Phillippe, Pittsburgh blew a 3–1 game advantage and lost the last three games played at their home field. Young was the beneficiary of two of these winning games (5 and 7). Phillippe and Bill Dinneen won three games each with Cy getting the other two victories. The Series seemed to solidify the American League to the older circuit.

In 1904, the American League had its first down-to-the-wire dogfight between the Pilgrims and the New York Highlanders. The Highlanders who would eventually become the Yankees, migrated from Baltimore in 1903. This was the same Baltimore team that John McGraw quit as manager to take over the reins of the New York Giants.

The Giants walked away with the National League flag, and it seemed the Highlanders had a strong chance to become the American League champions. McGraw refused any post-season play against the American League champions, therefore putting a damper on what could have been an exciting confrontation for New York baseball.

The 1904 pennant went down to the final day when Boston and New York met in a doubleheader. The Highlanders had to win both games to capture the title. Jack Chesbro unleashed a wild pitch in the ninth inning of the first game that enabled Boston to score the tie-breaking run from third. It was highly disheartening because Chesbro won 41 games during the regular season! Boston, with Young still pitching brilliantly along with Bill Dinneen and Jessie Tamnehill, were able to offset New York's ace.

Young posted 26 victories with ten shutouts, the most he had in one season. Every team in the league felt the brush of his whitewashing. His E.R.A. was a stunning 1.97.

His first shutout that year was his most stellar single-game performance on May 5 defeating the Philadelphia A's 3–0. The A's started Rube Waddell versus Cy that day. Six days later he tossed his second shutout, a 1–0 victory versus Detroit. He went 15 innings giving up only five hits as he defeated Ed Killeen.

To show his tenacity in the pennant race in October, he pitched three consecutive shutouts (two of them on the road). On October 2, St. Louis felt his sting 2–0. On October 5, he defeated Chicago 3–0 for his 56th career shutout. On October 8 he pitched his most crucial game of the season when he defeated the Highlanders and Jack Powell. This game also gave him a share of the major league record for shutouts. His performance kept Boston in first place and they increased their lead over New York to 1½ games. This put the pressure on the Highlanders to win the season-ending doubleheader, which they didn't. Cy was 37 years old and still one of the dominant pitchers in the league.

In 1905 the Pilgrims fell to fourth place, 15 games behind pennant-bound Philadelphia. Cy started to show his age by recording his first losing season with an 18–19 record. His E.R.A. was an outstanding 1.82 based on four shutouts.

One game against Philly and the eccentric Rube Waddell wasn't a shutout but was nevertheless an extraordinary pitching duel. This game took place on July 4 at Boston. It was a 20-inning struggle. Boston touched Waddell for two runs in the first; Rube shut out the Pilgrims for the next 19 innings (more than two complete shutout games)! Cy gave up two runs in the sixth and held the A's at bay until the top of the 20th when Philadelphia broke through for two runs and a 4–2 victory. Young went 13 consecutive innings without giving up a run only to fall short. At the time it was the longest game in Boston history, and it was a classic.

The Pilgrims hit the cellar in 1906 with a resounding thud. They lost 105 games with injuries and age being contributing factors. Cy hit rock bottom with the rest of his teammates with a 13–21 record. He did not pitch a shutout during the season which caused his E.R.A.

to swell at 3.19. It looked like Cy was at the end of the trail. In 1907, Boston rose to seventh and Cy had a reversal of fortune as he improved his record to 22–15 with six shutouts, only two behind league-leader Eddie Plank. His E.R.A. was an outstanding 1.99! The game against the A's on September 9, 1907, was another nail-biting marathon against Rube Waddell. Philadelphia was in a pennant struggle with the Detroit Tigers who were emerging as a force to be reckoned with. With Ty Cobb as the catalyst for Detroit, every game was crucial.

The game was played at Boston, went 13 innings, and the final score was 0–0. Darkness set in and play could not continue. Young doled out four hits while Waddell scattered a mere six. The outstanding feature of the game was that neither moundsman yielded a base on balls.

Cy was now 40 years old and somehow was resurrected for some more productive years. Cy proved that 1907 wasn't a fluke year as he joined the 20-win circle again with a 21–11 record. Included in those victories were three shutouts, one being a one-hitter. This was against Washington with Jerry Freeman getting the only hit and being the only base runner for the Senators. This spoiled his bid for a third no-hitter, but on June 30 he pitched a no-hitter versus the Highlanders, defeating them 8–0. This was his third, which now tied him for the major league record. All of them were performed from the 60'6" distance. His E.R.A. was an outstandingly low 1.26, placing him second behind Cleveland's Addie Joss.

In 1909, Boston sold Cy to the Cleveland Naps for the waiver sum of $12,500 dollars, a large amount back then. The Naps just missed winning the pennant by half a game and felt that the 42-year-old Young would still be a good investment for pennant insurance.

Cleveland did not duplicate their fine season of 1908 as they fell under .500 tumbling to sixth place (27½ games behind Detroit). Cy did not falter in his effort as he led the Cleveland staff with a 19–15 record. He threw three shutouts, all during the month of July which gave him a highly respectable E.R.A. of 2.26. He defeated Detroit 6–0 as they were going for their third consecutive pennant.

In 1910, at the age of 43, he witnessed his third losing season at 7–10. It was now evident that he was near the end of the line. He managed one shutout against St. Louis where he meted out only two hits. This was his last American League shutout. His E.R.A. was a commendable 2.54, which indicated that he was still competitive on the mound.

All things must come to an end, even a great career such as Young's. He struggled with a 3–4 record when Cleveland released him. He was picked up by the Boston Rustlers who became the Braves in 1912.

Cy strove to give every indication that he still had something left as he squeezed out of his aging arm the last two shutouts of his career. Both of these were against Pittsburgh, who still possessed Wagner and Clarke in their lineup. The Rustlers were deeply embedded in the cellar when Cy joined them.

One game he pitched on September 7 versus the Phillies and their outstanding rookie, Grover Cleveland Alexander, was a picture of the old guard versus the new as Father Time was giving way to the New Year's baby. Alexander prevailed in a 1–0 decision as Cy went the distance, still showing that he could pit himself against the stiff competition.

Cy decided that 1911 was to be his last year as a player because his age was taking its toll. Teams did not seek 45-year-old part-time players. After 22 seasons, he wore the cloak of victory 511 times. His greatness will endure as long as there is a national pasttime.

Cy Young

Date	Team	Score	Hits	S.O.	Walks	Loser
4/15/92(A)	Cin.	2–0	4	4	1	Mullane
5/6/92(H)	Bal.	1–0	3	5	3	Healy
5/17/92(H)	Lou.	9–0	2	7	1	Jones
5/24/92(H)	Stl.	2–0	8	5	2	Dwyer
8/12/92(A)	Chi.	2–0	3	0	3	Hutchinson
8/31/92(H)	Bal.	0–0	4	3	1	McMahon
9/5/92(A)	Phi.	6–0	5	3	2	Knell
10/3/92(H)	Chi.	15–0	3	1	1	Hutchinson
10/5/92(H)	Cin.	6–0	5	5	0	Chamberlain
9/2/93(A)	Brk.	6–0	6	4	1	Sharrott
4/24/94(A)	Cin.	1–0	2	3	5	Parrott
8/14/94(A)	Wash.	1–0	4	1	1	Mercer
6/14/95(A)	N.Y.	1–0	5	7	3	Clark
7/16/95(H)	Bal.	1–0	4	4	1	Esper
8/17/95(H)	Cin.	6–0	6	0	0	Pattott
9/17/95(H)	Cin.	7–0	3	2	0	Foreman
7/9/96(H)	Bal.	7–0	7	3	3	Pond
7/19/96(A)	Lou.	7–0	9	6	0	Hill
7/23/96(H)	Phi.	2–0	1	3	1	Keener
8/20/96(A)	Wash.	2–0	6	1	1	Norton

48   The Great Shutout Pitchers

Date	Team	Score	Hits	S.O.	Walks	Loser
9/14/96(H)	Chi.	2–0	6	5	0	Friend
8/19/97(A)	Bal.	3–0	5	0	0	Amole
9/18/97(H)	Cin.	6–0	0	3	1	Rhines
6/6/98(A)	Bos.	2–0	7	4	0	Lewis
8/18/99(A)	Phi.	8–0	5	2	0	Platt
8/21/99(H)	Chi.	2–0	7	3	0	Callahan
8/24/99(H)	Phi.	5–0	3	2	0	Fraser
9/16/99(A)	N.Y.	6–0	4	5	1	Gettig
4/19/00(H)	Pitt.	3–0	5	9	0	Waddell
7/4/00(H)	Brk.	9–0	7	2	2	McGinnity
8/25/00(H)	Chi.	1–0	4	4	0	Garvin
9/24/00(H)	Pitt	1–0	4	2	0	Waddell
7/6/01(H)	Wash.	7–0	7	3	1	Lee
8/2/01(A)	Phi.	13–0	7	1	1	Bernhard
8/20/01(H)	Mil	6–0	7	3	0	Hawley
9/11/01(A)	Wash.	9–0	3	4	0	Mercer
9/17/01(H)	Cle.	5–0	8	1	1	Dowling
5/30/02(H)	Det.	12–0	5	2	4	Mercer
7/19/02(H)	Chi.	2–0	5	3	1	Garvin
8/8/02(A)	Stl.	8–0	4	2	1	Harper
5/24/03(A)	Chi.	7–0	4	3	1	Flaherty
5/30/03(H)	Wash.	4–0	3	6	1	Patten
6/13/03(H)	Stl.	7–0	4	3	1	Powell
6/23/03(A)	Det.	1–0	7	5	1	Donovan
6/28/03(A)	Stl.	1–0	5	4	1	Donahue
7/1/03(A)	Chi.	1–0	6	1	0	Flahery
9/10/03(H)	Wash.	3–0	3	6	0	Orth
5/5/04(H)	Phi.	3–0	0	8	0	Waddell
5/11/04(H)	Det.	1–0	5	5	5	Killian
6/6/04(A)	Det.	3–0	3	2	0	Killian
7/6/04(A)	Wash.	3–0	7	3	0	Jacobsen
8/1/04(A)	Cle.	8–0	5	10	0	Bernhard
8/22/04(H)	Stl.	8–0	7	1	0	Glade
8/30/04(H)	Det.	13–0	6	1	2	Kitson
10/2/04(A)	Stl.	2–0	3	1	0	Peity
10/5/04(A)	Chi.	3–0	6	8	0	Altrock
10/8/04(H)	N.Y.	1–0	7	4	0	Powell
5/30/05(A)	Wash.	2–0	5	9	1	Townsend
8/29/05(A)	Stl.	2–0	6	9	1	Howell
9/19/05(A)	Wash.	1–0	2	11	0	Townsend
9/23/05(H)	Stl.	5–0	2	12	0	Glade
5/3/07(A)	Wash.	3–0	4	5	1	Falkenberg
5/19/07(A)	Chi.	4–0	6	2	2	White
5/24/07(A)	Stl.	4–0	5	1	0	Powell
6/1/07(H)	N.Y.	2–0	7	6	1	Keefe
7/30/07(H)	Cle.	3–0	3	7	0	Clarkson
9/9/07(H)	Phi.	0–0	6	8	0	Waddell

Date	Team	Score	Hits	S.O.	Walks	Loser
4/24/08(A)	Wash.	7–0	4	4	1	Falkenberg
5/30/08(H)	Wash.	6–0	1	7	0	Burns
6/30/08(A)	N.Y.	8–0	0	2	1	Manning
7/6/09(H)	Det.	6–0	5	3	0	Summers
7/10/09(H)	Wash.	4–0	4	4	2	Groom
7/24/09(H)	N.Y.	2–0	3	2	1	Lake
6/30/10(H)	Stl.	5–0	2	5	1	Ray
8/30/11(H)	Pitt.	6–0	5	2	2	Hendrix
9/22/11(A)	Pitt.	1–0	9	3	0	Adams

Year	Home	Away	Total
92	6	3	9
93	0	1	1
94	0	2	2
95	3	1	4
96	3	2	5
97	1	1	2
98	0	1	1
99	2	2	4
00	4	0	4
01	3	2	5
02	2	1	3
03	3	4	7
04	5	5	10
05	1	3	4
07	3	3	6
08	1	2	3
09	3	0	3
10	1	0	1
11	1	1	2
	42	34	76

Young's Shutouts by Team

National League

Bal.	Bos.	Brk.	Chi.	Cin.	Cle.	Lou.	N.Y.	Phi.	Pit.	Stl.	Wash.	Total
5	1	2	5	6	0	2	2	4	4	1	2	34

American League

Bos.	Chi.	Cle.	Det.	Bal. N.Y.	Phi.	Mil. Stl.	Wash.	Total
0	5	3	6	4	3	9	12	76

Young's Shutouts by Team Finish

National League

1	2	3	4	5	6	7	8	9	10	11	12	*Total*
4	3	4	2	3	1	2	5	2	4	2	2	34

American League

1	2	3	4	5	6	7	8	*Total*
1	3	2	4	4	7	11	10	42

Eddie Plank
The First Great Left-Hander

Eddie Plank was not an average rookie when he hit the major leagues in 1901. There was no minor league preparation to groom him along the way to the big time. He started his career later than most players. Walter Johnson was 19 and Christy Mathewson was 20 when they made their debuts. Cy Young and Grover Alexander were both 23, but Plank started his career at 25. Like another left-hander who would rise to greatness 40 some years later (Warren Spahn) at 25, Plank would set records that southpaws would aim to break. Some of his records such as career shutouts by a left-hander still endure.

It seems he didn't have a timetable for his life when he started at Gettysburg College at age 21. It was there he began to pitch. Four years later he was recommended to Connie Mack, the manager/owner of the Philadelphia Athletics. From there on, it's a matter of record how he performed for the "Tall Tactician."

Plank debuted versus the Baltimore Orioles in a relief stint on May 13 giving up three runs in four innings. He made his first start (a winning one) on May 18, 1901, against the Washington Senators. He pitched his first shutout against the Milwaukee Brewers, defeating them 6–0 while giving up only two hits. This Brewer team was the forerunner of the St. Louis Browns who in 1954 became the Baltimore Orioles. Plank finished with a record of 17–13 and an E.R.A. of 3.31.

In 1902, Eddie was joined by George "Rube" Waddell who came to the A's at the end of June. Together they pitched the "Mack Men" to their first pennant. After Waddell was acquired, he blazed his way to 24 victories. Plank broke into the 20-game circle with a 20–15 mark. Eddie's E.R.A. was high at 3.30 (a point above the staff's mark). He and Waddell established themselves as a duet for another five years. Eddie did manage one shutout versus Washington, defeating them 11–0 on only four hits.

In 1903, the A's added Albert "Chief" Bender to their staff, which, along with Plank and Waddell, would give Philadelphia a contending team for years to come. Plank and Bender would be together through 1914 when Connie disassembled his clubs due to financial problems. The Athletics mound corps consisted of three future Hall of Famers. By 1908, Waddell was sold to St. Louis because of his continuous eccentricity that frayed the patience of the placid "Mack." Eddie joined the 20-win club again in 1903 notching a 23–16 mark that included three shutouts. His E.R.A. finally dwindled under the 3.00 level at 2.38. On May 2, he blanked Boston and Cy Young giving up four hits. This he did against a team that would become the first world champions.

Philadelphia fell to fifth place in 1904. They had a good record at 81–70 but finished 12½ games behind the Boston Pilgrims. This pennant race was decided on the final day. Jack Chesbro of the New York Highlanders threw a wild pitch in the ninth inning versus the Boston Pilgrims.

Plank and Waddell had identical records of 26–17. They together compiled two-thirds of the team's victories. Waddell had a superior E.R.A. to Plank's (1.62 versus 2.14). Rube had eight shutouts while Eddie forged seven, which placed him third behind league-leader Cy Young's. Eddie did manage to shut out six of the seven opponents— the Washington Senators escaped his whitewashing. His last two shutouts of the year were against New York and Boston, who were in need of victories to keep pace with each other. He bested the Highlanders and Jack Powell 3–0 scattering six hits. Just three days later, he stopped the Pilgrims and their ace, Cy Young, 1–0 on just seven hits. He kept the pennant contenders at an even level with each other as if they were two thoroughbreds charging toward the finish line.

The Philadelphia's A's emerged as the league champions in 1905. This was another close finish as they edged the Chicago White Sox by two games. They were joined in the rotation by Andy Coakley who contributed 19 victories. Coakley, like Eddie, was a college graduate from Holy Cross and fitted into the image that the tacit "Mac" wanted his players to portray. "Chief" Bender was from Carlysle Indian College, the same one that Jim Thorpe would make famous a few years later.

Regarding Coakley's record, there is some dispute if he had 19 or 20 victories. Most historians credit him with 19, therefore depriving the A's as one of a handful of modern teams to have had three 20-game winners. The Philadelphia pitching staff was well armed with Coakley, an added asset during the season because runner-up Chicago was well fortified in the pitching department. Plank had an outstanding year with a 25–12 record. He threw four shutouts, winning three of them 1–0.

In the World Series, Eddie pitched the opening game versus the New York Giants and their ace Christy Mathewson. It was the first Series game that two future Hall of Famers dueled on the mound. He matched Matty for four innings until the Giants broke through for two runs in the top of the fourth. He allowed ten hits as he fell to the New Yorkers 3–0. His teammates did not give him much support offensively as they scrounged only four hits off the Giants' ace.

In the fourth game, he was matched against the Giants' other phenom, "Ironman" Joe McGinnity, and lost 1–0 with an unearned run in the fourth inning, the only blemish against him that day. He out-pitched McGinnity, giving up four hits where the Ironman allowed five.

In 1906, the Chicago White Sox won their second pennant edging the Highlanders by three games. Philadelphia was a distant fourth 12 games back. Part of the A's fall could be traced to losing Andy Coakley to illness and the lack of commitment by the eccentric Rube Waddell who finished with a 16–16 record. Plank provided a steadiness on the staff. His 19–5 mark led the league in winning percentage. He blanked the opposition five times. One of those was a 1–0 victory over the pennant-bound Chicago White Sox and Nick Altrock. Eddie's E.R.A. was a respectable 2.25 (more than a half run below the staff's).

In 1907, there was another down to the wire dog fight involving the A's and the Detroit Tigers. This year Ty Cobb emerged as the offensive leader for Detroit and won the first of his 12 batting titles. Detroit edged out Philadelphia by 1½ games, but the A's had one less loss than the Tigers. During the early years of the American League, they didn't make up postponed games at the end of the season. This would change after the close race in 1908 when Cleveland lost by half a game because Detroit would not have to make up a rained-out game. Eddie had another fine season, leading the team in victories with 24. He carved out eight shutouts which gave him the league lead in the department, and his E.R.A. was a solid 2.20. Three of his shutouts were against Detroit. He beat them on May 20 by the score of 1–0; on June 20 by 4–0 and on August 13 by 3–0. His blanking of Detroit on August 13 was the 25th shutout of his career. He was the mainstay of the staff down the stretch pitching six shutouts after August 1. Three of these were in September. When he defeated Boston on September 10 by a score of 3–0 going seven innings. This was a complete game thus he received credit for a shutout.

If one could reflect back on the 1907 race and why the A's lost the pennant, the cause could be traced to Rube Waddell and his inconsistent behavior. Disappearing for days he would put a strain on the pitching staff. At the end of the season, the patient Connie Mack sold him to St. Louis.

If 1907 was a highly-frustrating year for the A's, 1908 was even more disappointing as they tumbled into sixth place, the first losing season in club history. Eddie witnessed his first losing season and finished 14–16 with a 2.17 E.R.A. which shows he pitched convincingly. He had four shutouts during the year; one of them was against Detroit who were on their way to a second consecutive pennant. He defeated them 3–0, scattering four hits.

A combination of age and poor seasons by Dygert and Bender, who accounted for a combined 36–17 record in 1907, cashed in with a 19–24 total in 1908. The departure of Waddell, who could have contributed 20 wins, might not have hurt, as much because of the negative effect he would have had on his teammates.

The A's like the mystical Phoenix, rose from the ashes in 1909 and made a strong showing against Detroit, who copped their third pennant in as many years. The Mack Men finished only 3½ games behind the Tigers. The rejuvenation in Philadelphia could be traced to the revamping of the infield with Eddie Collins at 2nd base and Frank "Home Run" Baker (both who were future Hall-of-Famers).

As the team rebounded, so did Plank. He showed a 19–10 record with a stunning E.R.A. of 1.70. He finished fourth behind teammate Harry Krause. Eddie blanked the opposition three times including the champion Tigers at their home field by the score of 2–0. Better days lay ahead for Philly as the final pieces would be fitted together by Connie Mack in 1910.

The initial phase of Mack's first dynasty took place in 1910. The A's romped to the pennant by 14½ games over the New York Highlanders. This Athletics were outstanding as they won 102 games, becoming the first American League club to reach the century mark. The staff was anchored by Jack Coombs whose season was a glowing 31–9. Coombs was also a college man from Colby College and was frequently referred to as "Colby Jack." Chief Bender also had his career year with a 23–5 total, and he led the league in pitching percentage.

Eddie was the number-four man in the rotation coming in at 16–10 with a sparkling 2.02 E.R.A. He pitched only one shutout that year against Detroit, beating them 5–0. He always seemed to be at his best versus the Tigers.

In the World Series versus the Chicago Cubs, Eddie did not make an appearance as the A's swept past the Cubs in five games. This was still the famous Tinkers to Evers to Chance club and Mack decided to use Coombs and Bender in all of the starts. Coombs won three games in the Series. This was the first time two teams with at least 100 wins met in the world championship. In the fourth game of the Series, player/manager Frank Chance was ejected for vehemently disputing a call on a fair ball. This was the second time a manager was ejected in a World Series game.

The following year, 1911, Philadelphia waltzed to their second consecutive pennant with a 13½ game bulge over Detroit. Plank was the number-two man behind Coombs, who posted 28 wins. Eddie finished with a 22–8 log. It would be his first 20-win season since 1907. He also threw six shutouts, tying with Walter Johnson for the league lead. Three of them were against St. Louis. His E.R.A. was a magnificent 2.10, almost 1.5 runs less per game than Coombs.

The Series pit Philly against the New York Giants, whose Mathewson stung the A's with humiliation in the 1905 Series. In 1905 Eddie was tagged with two losses in that Series. Eddie performed much better in 1911. He won the second game defeating "Rube" Marquard 3–1. This was a crucial game for the A's as they lost the first game and another loss would have put them behind 0–2. Plank was the loser in the fifth game. He entered the game as a relief pitcher in the 10th and gave up the winning run in the top of that inning. The A's captured the Series in the sixth game and routed the Giants 13–2.

In 1912, Philadelphia stumbled into third place, 15 games behind the pennant-winner Boston Red Sox. The A's didn't collapse, rather the Red Sox had a phenomenal year riding the crest of the wave of success on the right arm of "Smoky" Joe Wood.

Wood had a 34–5 record with ten shutouts. Philly finished one game behind the Senators because Walter Johnson also broke the 30-game mark. While the aces for the Red Sox and the Senators were having superhuman years, Eddie Plank was having a career year with a 26–6 record, which tied his high for wins, and his highest winning percentage of .813. His E.R.A. was a polished 2.21 built on five shutouts. He did this at the age of 36. His shutout on August 14 versus Cleveland, beating them 2–0 for the American League record for shutouts by a left-hander, tied him with Rube Waddell at 47. He scattered four hits in that game. Five weeks later on September 16 also versus Cleveland, he set the American League record for shutouts by left-handers, blanking them 8–0. He also doled out four hits in that contest.

The A's again became champions in 1913, but this time it was Boston that collapsed. The Red Sox lost Joe Wood for a good deal of the season as they plummeted to fourth place. Philly lost the services of Jack Coombs but that did not slow them down as they topped Washington by 6½ games.

Eddie had another good year finishing up at 18–10 while Chief Bender led the staff with 21 victories. Plank had seven shutouts which was almost half of the staff's 15. His shutout on May 22 was the 50th of his career and tied him with the major league record for left-handers along with Rube Waddell. In this game, he defeated the Cobb-led Tigers, meting out only three hits. In his next start, he blanked the Washington Senators on two hits to set the major league record for shutouts by a left-hander.

In the Series, Philly subdued the New York Giants in five games. In the second game Eddie fell to Christy Mathewson in a 3–0 whitewashing (Matty's fourth Series shutout—a record). Eddie battled the Giants' legend for nine innings when he weakened in the 10th by giving up three runs.

It was a measure of sweet revenge as Plank clinched against Matty defeating him 3–0. He stymied the Giants with only two hits. It was a fine year for the aging lefty.

The A's continued winning in 1914 by annexing their fourth pennant in five years. They finished comfortably in front of the Red Sox by 8½ games. Their pitching staff was loaded and seven pitchers won ten or more games. Eddie recorded a 15–7 mark with four shutouts. His E.R.A. rose to 2.87, his highest since 1902 when he was over the 3.00 barrier. When Plank shut out St. Louis on May 28th by a score of 3–0, it tied him with Ed Walsh for the American

League record for shutouts at 57. He set the league record at 58 on June 22, against the Browns by the score of 3–0.

Little did anyone know at the time this A's team would be disassembled by Connie Mack at the end of the year. This was because of the financial burden that fell on the team with the emergence of the newly formed Federal League at the start of the 1914 season. Because of the lure of money, many top-notch stars would be enticed to come over to the new circuit. Walter Johnson almost made the exodus from the establishment.

The 1914 World Series was an indication that Connie's first dynasty had reached its apex. The A's faced the miracle Braves for Boston that year. The Braves, who were 17 games behind the first-place Giants on July 4, made a meteoric run in the second half and captured the pennant by 10½ games. They continued their momentous drive into the Series versus Philly. They swept the talent-laden A's contingent in four games.

In the second game of the Series, Eddie pitched the best game for the A's. He lost 1–0 to Bill James as the Braves pushed a run across in the top of the ninth. Eddie gave up eight hits while his teammates struggled to get only two safeties off of the starter.

The first dynasty of Connie Mack came to a sudden end with the Series final. Mack sold his stars to stay afloat due to the bidding war caused by the Federal League. Plank, at the age of 39, was in the twilight of his career. Mack wasn't about to offer any substantial raise to keep him. The call of the Federal League gave Eddie a chance to make more money.

Certain historians do not recognize the Federal League as a major league. Therefore, all statistical achievements are not included in the career records of those who participated during the two years of the Fed's existence. *The Sporting News* still does not acknowledge the Federal League's records and refused to run any box scores and accounts of the Federal League. For years the Hall of Fame followed *The Sporting News* by ignoring records compiled by the short-lived league.

The Federal League was a closely competitive circuit as indicated in 1914, their first year when the Indianapolis Hoosiers edged the Chicago Chi-Feds by 1½ games. The second year would even be closer as the Chicago Whales eked out the St. Louis Terriers by .001 of a percentage point (.556 versus .555)! The Terriers won more games than the Whales (87 to 86), but an extra loss by St. Louis gave Chicago the flag.

Plank was a member of the Terrier staff, which was comprised of three 20-game winners who came from two established leagues. Dave Davenport (St. Louis Browns), "Doc" Crandall (New York Giants), and Eddie were the stellar trio. They together garnered almost three-quarters of the team's victories.

Eddie did yeoman's duty starting and relieving as he saved three games along with his 21 victories. He pitched six shutouts, his first against the Newark Peppers on May 2, defeating them 1–0 on three hits. Parity was well illustrated in the league, as Newark finished fifth only five games back. Only the Baltimore Terrapins were completely out of it, finishing 40 games in the rear. Eddie blanked the Terrapins three times during the season which lowered his E.R.A. to an outstanding 2.08.

The Federal League folded after the 1915 season due to financial problems by a majority of the owners. Players were sold back to the American and National leagues. One of these was Eddie himself. He become a member of the St. Louis Browns and finished his career with them.

He was sold by the Terriers with many of his teammates. The owner of the St. Louis Terriers eventually bought the St. Louis Browns which caused the mass selling of the best ball players.

The addition of Plank, along with Bob Groom and Dave Davenport, made the Browns competitive as they finished fifth with a 79–75 record, only one game out of the first division. Eddie chipped in with a 16–15 ledger and a 2.33 E.R.A. He chalked up three shutouts with his first versus Washington, beating their ace, Walter Johnson, 5–0. He was still productive at the age of 40.

In 1917, Plank slowed to a 5–6 mark with only one shutout, his last career one as he defeated Washington 4–0. At the end of the season, Eddie, along with Del Pratt, was sold to the Yankees. Eddie decided to call it a career realizing that there were just so many pitches in one arm. The aches and pains he frequently complained about throughout the years were now a reality.

When looking back at the early years of baseball, it can be assuredly stated that he was truly the first great left-hander.

Eddie Plank

Date	Team	Score	Hits	S.O.	Walks	Loser
6/13/01(H)	Mil.	6–0	2	1	4	Garvin
5/6/02(H)	Wash.	11–0	4	3	1	Carrick
5/2/03(A)	Bos.	3–0	4	6	2	Young

Eddie Plank

Date	Team	Score	Hits	S.O.	Walks	Loser
5/13/03(A)	Chi.	3–0	3	6	1	Flaherty
9/7/03(H)	Wash.	6–0	4	5	1	Orth
5/21/04(H)	Cle.	7–0	5	9	1	Bernhard
6/11/04(A)	Cle.	1–0	4	5	0	Rhodes
7/20/04(H)	Stl.	2–0	5	5	1	Howell
7/29/04(H)	Det.	2–0	5	3	4	Mullin
8/31/04(H)	Chi.	1–0	5	4	3	Owen
9/7/04(H)	N.Y.	3–0	6	5	1	Powell
9/10/04(H)	Bos.	1–0	7	1	2	Young
6/27/05(A)	Wash.	1–0	6	10	0	Patten
7/23/05(A)	Chi.	1–0	2	8	3	Owen
8/4/05(H)	Det.	8–0	9	2	1	Donovan
9/13/05(H)	Bos.	1–0	2	3	0	Tannerhill
4/27/06(H)	Bos.	3–0	3	1	2	Young
5/15/06(H)	Chi.	1–0	5	3	2	Altrock
6/9/06(A)	Stl.	2–0	5	5	4	Glade
6/23/06(H)	Bos.	8–0	5	6	0	Harris
6/27/06(A)	Wash.	5–0	3	4	4	Hughes
5/20/07(A)	Det.	1–0	5	8	2	Enbank
6/20/07(H)	Det.	4–0	4	7	0	Enbank
8/1/07(H)	Stl.	2–0	4	6	3	Dinneen
8/13/07(A)	Det.	3–0	3	3	3	Mullin
8/23/07(A)	Stl.	1–0	6	2	1	Powell
9/10/07(A)	Bos.	3–0	7	4	2	Glaze
9/21/07(H)	Stl.	6–0	8	5	1	Dinneen
9/25/07(H)	Chi.	5–0	2	11	2	Smith
6/6/08(A)	Stl.	2–0	3	4	0	Howell
6/25/08(H)	N.Y.	3–0	6	4	1	Orth
7/28/08(A)	Chi.	2–0	5	5	1	Walsh
8/7/08(A)	Det.	3–0	4	3	0	Donovan
7/9/09(A)	Det.	2–0	7	7	2	Works
8/30/09(A)	Chi.	5–0	3	6	3	Scott
9/11/09(H)	Bos.	1–0	7	3	1	Cicotte
7/9/10(H)	Det.	5–0	5	4	2	Donovan
4/17/11(H)	Bos.	1–0	7	7	4	Karger
5/5/11(A)	Wash.	9–0	7	5	1	Otey
5/13/11(A)	Stl.	7–0	4	5	4	Lake
6/13/11(H)	Stl.	6–0	6	10	5	Lake
7/15/11(A)	Stl.	2–0	6	5	3	Powell
9/13/11(A)	N.Y.	2–0	3	5	2	Ford
4/24/12(A)	N.Y.	7–0	4	2	2	Warhop
6/20/12(H)	Wash.	5–0	5	5	2	Engle
8/10/12(A)	Chi.	8–0	4	3	1	Benz
8/14/12(H)	Cle.	2–0	8	6	3	Steen
9/16/12(A)	Cle.	8–0	4	0	4	Mitchell
4/25/13(H)	N.Y.	4–0	3	10	0	Ford
5/22/13(A)	Det.	7–0	3	4	5	Hall

Date	Team	Score	Hits	S.O.	Walks	Loser
5/27/13(H)	Wash.	8–0	2	4	3	Engle
6/30/13(A)	N.Y.	6–0	3	7	3	Schultz
7/15/13(A)	Det.	7–0	9	5	1	Hall
7/20/13(A)	Stl.	8–0	6	9	2	Leverenz
8/25/13(A)	Stl.	3–0	5	11	5	Leverenz
5/14/14(H)	Cle.	1–0	6	9	1	Hagerman
5/28/14(H)	Stl.	3–0	6	8	2	Baumgardner
6/22/14(A)	Stl.	3–0	9	3	4	Leverenz
7/8/14(H)	Det.	3–0	3	6	3	Dauss
5/2/15(A)	New.	1–0	3	2	1	Falkenberg
5/29/15(H)	Brk.	11–0	3	5	2	Seaton
6/26/15(A)	Bal.	2–0	3	9	0	Bender
8/5/15(A)	Bal.	1–0	6	9	2	Johnson
8/9/15(A)	Bal.	3–0	4	2	1	Quinn
9/26/15(H)	Buf.	5–0	3	8	0	Bedient
7/7/16(A)	Wash.	5–0	5	4	4	Johnson
7/30/16(H)	N.Y.	2–0	4	5	0	Fisher
8/12/16(H)	Cle.	11–0	2	2	0	Morton
7/22/17(H)	Wash.	4–0	7	1	2	Shaw

American League

Year	Home	Away	Total
01	1	0	1
02	1	0	1
03	1	2	3
04	6	1	7
05	2	2	4
06	3	2	5
07	4	4	8
08	1	3	4
09	1	2	3
10	1	0	1
11	2	4	6
12	2	3	5
13	2	5	7
14	3	1	4
16	2	1	3
17	1	0	1
	33	30	63

Federal League

15	4	2	6
	37	32	69

Eddie Plank

Date	Team	Score	Hits	S.O.	Walks	Loser
5/13/03(A)	Chi.	3–0	3	6	1	Flaherty
9/7/03(H)	Wash.	6–0	4	5	1	Orth
5/21/04(H)	Cle.	7–0	5	9	1	Bernhard
6/11/04(A)	Cle.	1–0	4	5	0	Rhodes
7/20/04(H)	Stl.	2–0	5	5	1	Howell
7/29/04(H)	Det.	2–0	5	3	4	Mullin
8/31/04(H)	Chi.	1–0	5	4	3	Owen
9/7/04(H)	N.Y.	3–0	6	5	1	Powell
9/10/04(H)	Bos.	1–0	7	1	2	Young
6/27/05(A)	Wash.	1–0	6	10	0	Patten
7/23/05(A)	Chi.	1–0	2	8	3	Owen
8/4/05(H)	Det.	8–0	9	2	1	Donovan
9/13/05(H)	Bos.	1–0	2	3	0	Tannerhill
4/27/06(H)	Bos.	3–0	3	1	2	Young
5/15/06(H)	Chi.	1–0	5	3	2	Altrock
6/9/06(A)	Stl.	2–0	5	5	4	Glade
6/23/06(H)	Bos.	8–0	5	6	0	Harris
6/27/06(A)	Wash.	5–0	3	4	4	Hughes
5/20/07(A)	Det.	1–0	5	8	2	Enbank
6/20/07(H)	Det.	4–0	4	7	0	Enbank
8/1/07(H)	Stl.	2–0	4	6	3	Dinneen
8/13/07(A)	Det.	3–0	3	3	3	Mullin
8/23/07(A)	Stl.	1–0	6	2	1	Powell
9/10/07(A)	Bos.	3–0	7	4	2	Glaze
9/21/07(H)	Stl.	6–0	8	5	1	Dinneen
9/25/07(H)	Chi.	5–0	2	11	2	Smith
6/6/08(A)	Stl.	2–0	3	4	0	Howell
6/25/08(H)	N.Y.	3–0	6	4	1	Orth
7/28/08(A)	Chi.	2–0	5	5	1	Walsh
8/7/08(A)	Det.	3–0	4	3	0	Donovan
7/9/09(A)	Det.	2–0	7	7	2	Works
8/30/09(A)	Chi.	5–0	3	6	3	Scott
9/11/09(H)	Bos.	1–0	7	3	1	Cicotte
7/9/10(H)	Det.	5–0	5	4	2	Donovan
4/17/11(H)	Bos.	1–0	7	7	4	Karger
5/5/11(A)	Wash.	9–0	7	5	1	Otey
5/13/11(A)	Stl.	7–0	4	5	4	Lake
6/13/11(H)	Stl.	6–0	6	10	5	Lake
7/15/11(A)	Stl.	2–0	6	5	3	Powell
9/13/11(A)	N.Y.	2–0	3	5	2	Ford
4/24/12(A)	N.Y.	7–0	4	2	2	Warhop
6/20/12(H)	Wash.	5–0	5	5	2	Engle
8/10/12(A)	Chi.	8–0	4	3	1	Benz
8/14/12(H)	Cle.	2–0	8	6	3	Steen
9/16/12(A)	Cle.	8–0	4	0	4	Mitchell
4/25/13(H)	N.Y.	4–0	3	10	0	Ford
5/22/13(A)	Det.	7–0	3	4	5	Hall

Date	Team	Score	Hits	S.O.	Walks	Loser
5/27/13(H)	Wash.	8–0	2	4	3	Engle
6/30/13(A)	N.Y.	6–0	3	7	3	Schultz
7/15/13(A)	Det.	7–0	9	5	1	Hall
7/20/13(A)	Stl.	8–0	6	9	2	Leverenz
8/25/13(A)	Stl.	3–0	5	11	5	Leverenz
5/14/14(H)	Cle.	1–0	6	9	1	Hagerman
5/28/14(H)	Stl.	3–0	6	8	2	Baumgardner
6/22/14(A)	Stl.	3–0	9	3	4	Leverenz
7/8/14(H)	Det.	3–0	3	6	3	Dauss
5/2/15(A)	New.	1–0	3	2	1	Falkenberg
5/29/15(H)	Brk.	11–0	3	5	2	Seaton
6/26/15(A)	Bal.	2–0	3	9	0	Bender
8/5/15(A)	Bal.	1–0	6	9	2	Johnson
8/9/15(A)	Bal.	3–0	4	2	1	Quinn
9/26/15(H)	Buf.	5–0	3	8	0	Bedient
7/7/16(A)	Wash.	5–0	5	4	4	Johnson
7/30/16(H)	N.Y.	2–0	4	5	0	Fisher
8/12/16(H)	Cle.	11–0	2	2	0	Morton
7/22/17(H)	Wash.	4–0	7	1	2	Shaw

American League

Year	Home	Away	Total
01	1	0	1
02	1	0	1
03	1	2	3
04	6	1	7
05	2	2	4
06	3	2	5
07	4	4	8
08	1	3	4
09	1	2	3
10	1	0	1
11	2	4	6
12	2	3	5
13	2	5	7
14	3	1	4
16	2	1	3
17	1	0	1
	33	30	63

Federal League

15	4	2	6
	37	32	69

Eddie Plank's Shutouts by Team

American League

Bos.	Chi.	Cle.	Det.	Bal. N.Y.	Phi.	Mil. Stl.	Was.	Total
8	8	6	11	7	0	14	9	63

Federal League

Bal.	Brk.	Buf.	Nwk.	Total
3	1	1	1	6

Total Both Leagues 69

Shutouts by Team Finish

American League

1	2	3	4	5	6	7	8	Total
8	4	6	8	7	9	9	12	63

Federal League

5	6	7	8	Total
1	1	1	3	6

Warren Spahn
The Greatest Left-Hander Ever

When historians ponder who the greatest was at each position, there is always an excellent chance of debate over several positions. If one had to choose who the starting left-hander would be on the all-time greatest team, several names such as Eddie Plank, Steve Carlton, Sandy Koufax, Whitey Ford, and Warren Spahn should be considered. In sifting through the records of each, Spahn would come out on top in victories (363), and most years of 20 games won in modern times (13). He was second in shutouts for a left-hander (63) which places him in elite company.

Recently, *Baseball Digest* took a poll of the top ten at each position. Spahn was overwhelmingly selected as the top left-hander. If I had to select my number-one southpaw, I would definitely tap Warren. I could still see his hawk-like profile and a high leg kick enticing hitters to hit his pitch. I followed "Spahnie" his whole career except when he came up in 1942 at the tender age of 21.

When Spahn started his career in 1940, the minors were classified from Triple A all the way down to class D. That was as low as one could start. Warren broke in with Bradford in the class D Pony League (Pennsylvania, Ohio, New York). His 5–4 record earned him a rise to class B Three I League pitching for Evansville in 1941. I'll leave it to the geographical trivial experts to determine what three states that league encompassed.

Spahn excelled at Evansville, leading the league in wins and E.R.A. at age 20. The following year he was promoted to Hartford in the class A Eastern League. There he logged in with a 17–12 mark, which was good enough to be called up by the parent club, the Boston Braves. There he started his major league career under the tutelage of Casey Stengel. He appeared in four games with two starts getting no decisions.

Because of World War II, many of the ballplayers were drafted and their military obligations were primary and their baseball careers were interrupted. Spahn was no exception. He went off to war and was decorated with a Purple Heart and Bronze Star. Although he was not an established star at the time, baseball historians wonder what his career totals could've been if it wasn't for the war. Men like Joe DiMaggio, Ted Williams, Hand Greenberg, and Bob Feller would've achieved more stellar statistics if there wasn't a national emergency. Spahn lost three years in the army. He might have reached his milestones at an earlier age if it hadn't been for the war.

After the war, the ball players returned to their respective teams. Spahn came back to the Braves in the middle of 1946 and posted an 8–5 record with a 2.93 E.R.A. He was now under the watchful eye of Manager Billy Southworth who handled the St. Louis Cardinals to three consecutive pennants and two World Championships from 1942 to 1944. Each year the Cardinals would manage 100 or more wins for those three years (being only the second team to accomplish that feat). Southworth's managerial magic continued in Boston as he led the Braves to fourth place, the first time they made the first division since 1934. The 1946 Braves were not much of an offensive threat, so their rise would have to be attributed to Southworth's managerial skills and his handling of the pitching staff.

The 25-year-old Spahn rejoined the Braves, and for the next few years he teamed up with Johnny Sain as a lefty-righty tandem. The duo became a formidable entry for Boston, raising the well-known cry, "Spahn and Sain; pray for rain!"

In 1947 the color barrier in baseball was broken, and the Brooklyn Dodgers promoted Jackie Robinson to the parent club. Little did anyone think that the advent of Robinson would have such a revolutionary effect on the major leagues since the inception of league play in 1871. The same year, Spahn emerged in the National League where he went 21–10. He spun seven shutouts to lead the league in that department and also led in E.R.A. with a 2.33 mark.

His first shutout was on April 29 when he four-hitted the Cincinnati Reds 4–0 defeating Joe Beggs. His control was off as he walked five men, but he didn't let that pose a problem. That also was the Braves' first shutout of the year, and at year's end, Warren pitched one half of the team's 14 shutouts.

The shutout that he threw versus Brooklyn on September 2 at Ebbetts Field would be a rarity because the Dodgers, whether in Brooklyn or Los Angeles, were Spahnie's nemesis throughout his career. He would often be passed by in a scheduled start versus the Dodgers in their home park.

The year 1948 saw the Braves break fast from the gate and win their first pennant since 1914. This was Johnny Sain's career year as he posted 24 wins. Spahn struggled in the beginning of the year, but down the stretch he mustered up enough consistency to finish with a 15–12 record. He pitched only three shutouts with a high ERA of 3.71.

He did shut out Brooklyn at Ebbetts Field on four hits 1–0 where a homerun by Jimmy Russell in the first was all he needed. On August 25 he defeated St. Louis 2–0 as the Cardinals made a late-season run at the Braves. Spahnie defeated them at their home in Sportsmen Park by defeating one of their ace left-handers, Howie Pollett.

In the World Series, the Cleveland Indians met the Boston Braves after they won the first American League playoff versus the Boston Red Sox. Cleveland was successful in six games versus the Braves. Warren started the second game against another future Hall of Famer, Bob Lemon, and lost 4–1. He was relieved by Barrett in the fifth. After four games, Cleveland had a 3–1 lead and were looking to clinch the Series the next day. Boston started Nelson Potter and he was driven out in the fourth inning. Southworth, fighting elimination, went with Spahn in relief who didn't disappoint his manager. He battled Bob Feller evenly into the seventh inning when the Braves erupted for six runs to take an 11–5 lead. Spahnie kept the door closed the rest of the way and came out with his first World Series victory. The Braves only prolonged the inevitable and lost the Series in the sixth game to Bob Lemon.

After tasting victory in 1948, the Braves collapsed below .500 in 1949 but managed to salvage fourth place. Spahn rebounded back into the 20-game victory circle (21–14). He threw four shutouts with a 3.07 E.R.A. Each shutout was against the three top teams. He defeated the Phillies twice, both times besting future Hall of Famer, Robin Roberts. During August, he blanked the Dodgers 4–0, but there would be leaner days ahead versus Brooklyn.

The dawning of the '50s saw the Philadelphia "Whiz Kids" take what seemed an insurmountable lead but almost blow it to the charging Dodgers in the first week of the 1950 season. The last game of the season pitted the Phils versus the Dodgers, and only Dick Sisler's home run against Don Newcombe in the top of the tenth sealed the pennant for Philadelphia.

The Braves improved to an 83–71 record with Spahn notching a 21–17 mark. Warren had a 3.16 E.R.A. accounting for only one shutout versus St. Louis on September 21. This was his last win of the season, which gave him the league lead in victories. He had established himself as the league's top left-hander.

In 1951, Warren continued in his splendor as the top southpaw winning 22 games against 14 losses. This was the year of the famous Thomson home run that snatched the pennant from Brooklyn in the emotionally draining playoffs. This was also the year of the arrival of Willie Mays. Warren will always be known for giving up "Say-Hey's" first hit, which was a homer after Willie went 0–21 and begged to be returned to the minors. The hit off Spahnie opened the floodgates to 3,288 hits and 660 home runs by the legendary Willie.

During 1951, Spahn dealt out seven shutouts tying him for the major league with the Yankees' Allie Reynolds. He pitched consecutive shutouts on May 2 and 6. The one on May 6 was against Pittsburgh in the first game of the doubleheader. In the second game the Pirates turned the tables on Boston when Cliff Chambers not only shut them out, but threw a no-hitter. On September 13 Spahn tossed his seventh shutout of the season versus St. Louis and that was a one-hitter. Losing pitcher Al Brazle dimmed the spotlight on the Braves' lefty by getting the only hit.

Another oddity about that game was that it became the second game of a doubleheader in which the Cardinals played the New York Giants in the first game! The Giants had to make up a game versus the Cardinals because it was the last time the Giants would meet St. Louis and the game was necessary because of the closeness of the pennant race. The night-game victory by the Braves was Spahn's 20th of the season. During the season, Manager Southworth retired and the team was taken over by Tommy Holmes.

During 1951 Spahn pitched a game on his birthday, April 23. He pitched 16 innings against Brooklyn in Ebbets Field and lost 2–1. This would be typical of his frustrations versus the Dodgers.

The following year, 1952, Boston's National League entry fell into the second division after six consecutive years as tenants of the first division. The only thing that kept them out of the cellar was the

Pittsburgh Pirates who lost 112 games. Tommy Holmes was replaced as manager by Charley Grimm early in the season, but the Braves still floundered. The introduction of a young rookie by the name of Eddie Matthews during the season indicated that there was a future for the team, but not in Boston.

Spahnie endured his first losing season as he won 14 games versus 19 losses. He pitched competitively as his E.R.A. of 2.98 would testify. He mastered five teams by the shutout route with four of them coming after August 9. These were his last four wins of the season. His shutout of Cincinnati on August 26 was his 25th career shutout. On September 13 he shut out the Pirates, striking out 13 batters in the game with six coming consecutively.

The year 1953 saw the first franchise shift in 50 years when the Braves abandoned Boston for the friendly confines of Milwaukee. The last team that moved was the Baltimore Orioles who transferred to New York to set the roots for the present-day Yankees.

The Braves were overwhelmingly accepted and it seemed to interject a new vitality as well as a new spirit for winning. They surpassed their last year in Boston by 28 more victories. For a while they looked like pennant contenders as they battled the Dodgers into July. They finally settled in second place, 13 games behind Brooklyn but 9 games ahead of St. Louis and Philly.

The improvement came in the additions of Joe Adcock and Andy Pafko through trades and the return of Del Crandall and Johnny Antonelli from military service. The emergence of Eddie Matthews as a superstar and rookie Bill Bruton patrolling center field with assurance were dominant factors in the Braves' rise in the standings.

Warren Spahn also played an extremely important part when he posted his best season at 23–7 with a league-leading 2.10 E.R.A. His 23 victories tied Robin Roberts in that department, while his five shutouts fell one short of Harvey Haddix's top mark of six. One of his shutouts was on August 1 versus Philly when Spahnie threw a one-hitter. A single by Richie Ashburn spoiled the pitching gem as only 28 Phillies trekked to the plate. With Spahn the dominant member of the pitching staff, the Braves were contenders for their entire stay in Milwaukee. They never witnessed a losing season and finished out of the first division only once (that being 1963 when they fell to sixth place).

In 1954 the Braves proved that 1953 was no fluke. They tried to strengthen their new status as contenders by trading Antonelli, Don Liddle, and Ebba St. Clair to the New York Giants for the renowned Bobby Thomson. The former Giant broke his ankle during spring training which gave the Braves the opportunity to try a rookie named Henry Aaron.

The Braves stayed in contention until the last week of the season and failed to close the gap on the Giants and Dodgers during their last eastern trip. The Giants rode the left arm of Johnny Antonelli (whom they secured from Milwaukee) to the pennant. He was greatly aided by Willie Mays, who returned from the military service and sparked the Giants throughout the year while gaining an MVP award.

Spahnie contributed 21 victories with only one shutout and an E.R.A. of 3.15. He threw his one shutout versus Pittsburgh winning by a score of 7–0. He was the pillar of strength on this pitching staff.

In 1955, the Dodgers made a shambles of the National League pennant when they won 22 of their first 25 games. They built up a substantial lead that no one could put a dent in to bring them back to the pack. Milwaukee did finish second (13 lengths back). Spahn could only forge a 17–14 record with a high 3.26 E.R.A. He again threw one shutout, also versus the Pirates. This shutout was pitched on June 22 which oddly was the first Milwaukee shutout of the season (the Braves were noted for their superior pitching). In that game Warren aided his cause by hitting a two-run homer.

Baseball would hear a phrase never before stated in its history—"The World Champion Brooklyn Dodgers." "Wait 'til next year" finally become a reality. The Dodgers were now defending champs of the sport's most glorious title. The hated Yankees gave them that long-awaited achievement in the 1955 World Series. Now the rest of the National League would be gunning for Brooklyn.

The 1956 race was a nail-biter down to the last day of the season. The Braves, Dodgers, and Cincinnati Reds jockeyed for position throughout the year. The Braves at one time sported a seven-game lead, but Brooklyn persevered and kept it close. On the last weekend of the season, Milwaukee lost two of three games to St. Louis, which enabled Brooklyn to slide past the Braves and capture the pennant.

Spahnie had another outstanding year. He again chalked up another 20 wins, coming in at 20–11. He pitched three shutouts with his first on May 8 versus Pittsburgh. This also was his first win of the season. On July 6, he pitched his third shutout to even his record at 7–7. From then on he was superlative as he tried to keep the Braves on top by going 13–4 in the last half of the season.

The Braves didn't let the near miss of 1956 dampen their spirits in 1957. They started strong and despite injuries managed to find the right replacements through promotion in the farm system or by trades. The acquisition of Al "Red" Schoendienst solidified the infield and gave them a needed leader down the stretch. This team was solid and had four men destined for Cooperstown (Aaron, Matthews, Schoendienst, and Spahn).

The Braves led in hitting homers (199) with Hank Aaron emerging as a rival to the amazing Willie Mays. He led the league in homers (44) and captured the MVP. In the pitching department, Warren was again dominant as he led the league in wins (21) and complete games (18). He blanked the opposition four times with his E.R.A. at 2.69.

His shutout on August 10 versus St. Louis defeating them 9–0 was the 40th of his career. This tied him with Larry French, for most career shutouts in the National League for a lefthander. On September 3, he established the record at 41 when he whitewashed the Cubs 8–0. His steadiness throughout the year won him the second Cy Young Award. He became the first left-hander to win the prestigious award.

In the World Series versus the New York Yankees he was matched against Whitey Ford in the opener losing 3–1 as the Yanks KO'd him in the sixth. This was the Series in which Lew Burdette won three games (two by shutouts). Warren came back in game four defeating the New Yorkers in ten innings. He was sailing along winning 4–1 when the Yankees exploded for three runs in the top of the ninth. In the top of the tenth, the Bronx Bomber took the lead and it looked like it was over for Milwaukee. But the Braves rebounded with three runs in the bottom of the tenth on the strength of Matthew's homer. This game tied the Series at 2–2. In the deciding seventh game, Spahn was scheduled to start but came down with the flu. On two days rest, Burdette came back and shut out the Yankees to win the world championship.

The Braves were defending World Champions in 1958 and set out to prove their worth. This was the first year Major League ball was played on the West Coast due to the Dodgers and Giants who defected from the New York-Metropolitan area. The Dodgers would collapse into seventh place, a mere two games ahead of the last-place Phillies. The Giants rose to third with the arrival of Orlando Cepeda, a major reason they attained those lofty heights.

Spahn was again outstanding as he led the league in victories and pitching percentage (tied with teammate Lew Burdette). He also led in complete games and innings pitched. His E.R.A. was 3.07 with two shutouts on his ledger.

The Series again matched the Braves versus the Yankees, but this time the New Yorkers would prevail. Spahn pitched his best during this Series as he defeated Ryne Duran in relief of Ford. Spahnie went the distance (ten innings) winning 4–3. In the fourth game, Spahn painted a masterpiece, blanking the Yankees 3–0 at the stadium. He doled out two hits as he edged out Whitey Ford.

In game six at Milwaukee, he battled the Yankees into the tenth when they dented the plate for two runs, knocking him out of the box. He was tagged with a 4–3 loss. The next day the New Yorkers would defeat Burdette for the championship.

In 1959 a close race ended in a playoff between the Los Angeles Dodgers and the Milwaukee Braves. The Giants stayed close but failed in the last week and settled for third place. The Braves would lose the playoffs 2–0. Spahn did not face the Dodgers as Manager Fred Haney held him back. Spahnie again managed to win 20 games and lead the league in victories (tied with Burdette and Sam Jones of San Francisco). His E.R.A. was 2.96 on the strength of four shutouts.

In 1960, the Pirates won the pennant for the first time in 33 years. The Braves followed seven games back in second place. Warren again notched 21 victories which led the league in that category. His E.R.A. was rather high at 3.49 but still lower than the staff's (3.76). In his repertoire of victories were four shutouts. The one he pitched on July 7, his first of the season, he retired 21 Phillies in a row. He ran into trouble in the ninth inning, but a double-play ball preserved his shutout. On August 30 he chalked up his 50th career shutout with a 10–0 drubbing of St. Louis. He scattered five hits in that game.

Finally on September 16 he realized a dream that every pitcher cherishes when he no-hit the Phillies 4–0. To show how close Spahnie came to losing his gem, the ninth inning must be recreated. He fanned the first two batters in the inning (Bobby Gene Smith and Bobby DelGreco). Bob Malkmus was the next hitter and he nubbed a ball past the mound. Warren deflected the ball, which looked like it was going to be beaten out for a hit. Johnny Logan, who was a deft shortstop, anticipated perfectly and threw to first baseman Joe Adcock, who stretched his 6'4" frame and nipped Malkmus to preserve the gem. Warren had achieved this no-hitter at the age of 39. For a point of information, Warren's roommate, Lew Burdette, fashioned a no-hitter on August 15 versus the Phillies. This was the sixth time that teammates would pitch no-hitters in the same year. His no-hitter was his 20th win of the season, making that the 11th time he accomplished that feat.

The next year, 1961, the Cincinnati Reds won the pennant after a long drought of failure. After 20 years, they finally secured the top perch. The Braves wound up fourth, ten games back. For the 12th time, Spahnie managed another 20-game win season (21–13). He led the league in victories, shutouts, and E.R.A.—at the age of 40.

His first shutout of the year was April 28 versus the San Francisco Giants. Not only was it a shutout, but it was also a no-hitter. He was masterful in making a first-inning run stand up while only walking two batters. This made him the first National League pitcher to toss a no-hitter after age 40. Cy Young pitched his third no-hitter at 41 in the American League. Later on in 1990 and in 1991, Nolan Ryan accomplished the same feat.

Another distinction was being the only pitcher to win the E.R.A. title in three different decades (1947, 1953, and 1961). In September he pitched three of his four shutouts. Versus the Los Angeles Dodgers, he doled out two hits in that game defeating Sandy Koufax. It seemed the old master did not want to concede his crown to the young upstart. The next year, in 1962, the National League followed the junior circuit's lead by expanding. They placed two new franchises in New York and Houston. Warren still showed that he could win by compiling an 18–14 record. He failed to attain the 20-win club for the first time after six consecutive years and did not pitch one shutout.

Little did he know that 1963 would be his last hurrah as he boomed back with a 23–7 record. At 42 he was making heads shake in disbelief. Included in these victories were seven shutouts. His shutout on April 16 versus the Phils was highlighted by Eddie Matthews hitting his 400th career homer. He shut out Houston 4–0 on July 7. There was nothing significant about that except that in his prior start he went 15⅓ innings on July 2 losing 1–0 to Juan Marichal. This was at the age of 42! His seven shutouts placed him second behind Koufax, the unanimous Cy Young winner. If Sandy didn't have his first outstanding year, Warren might have had the award.

The following year, 1964, Spahn seemed to come to the end of the road when his record plummeted to 6–13. His E.R.A. rocketed to 5.28 with only one shutout against the hapless New York Mets on May 5. He blanked them 6–0. The losing pitcher was Tracy Stallard. Stallard will always be known for giving up Roger Maris' 61st homer and also being the losing pitcher in Jim Bunning's perfect game. Stallard always seemed to be the opponent in milestone games. This would be Warren's last career shutout.

In 1965, Spahnie was sent to the Mets where he compiled a 4–12 record for a horrendous team. San Francisco needed pitching help and secured him for pennant insurance for a stretch run versus Los Angeles. He finished with a 3–4 mark and a 3.38 E.R.A. The end of the season he was released.

Like the true competitor, he felt he could still pitch as he made his way back to the minors. His last year in pro ball was in the Mexican League. That was when he decided to forego another season. His legacy of brilliance is the benchmark all left-handed pitchers strive for, as he was truly the best southpaw ever.

Warren Spahn

Date	Team	Score	Hits	S.O.	Walks	Loser
4/29/47(H)	Cin.	4–0	4	3	5	Beggs
6/7/47(H)	Cin.	9–0	3	7	2	Erautt
7/12/47(H)	Cin.	4–0	4	1	2	Vandermeer
7/16/47(H)	Stl.	3–0	6	1	2	Dickson
9/14/47(A)	Chi.	1–0	9	4	2	Erikson
9/21/47(A)	Brk.	4–0	6	5	6	Branca
9/26/47(H)	N.Y.	2–0	7	0	2	Poat
4/28/48(H)	Phi.	7–0	2	4	0	Donnelly
5/15/48(A)	Brk.	1–0	4	4	1	Barney
8/25/48(A)	Stl.	2–0	7	3	2	Pollett
4/27/49(A)	Phi.	2–0	3	5	3	Roberts
5/11/49(H)	Stl.	7–0	3	6	4	Munger
8/20/49(H)	Brk.	4–0	7	6	0	Roe
9/10/49(H)	Phi.	1–0	6	11	4	Roberts
9/21/50(H)	Stl.	5–0	2	3	0	Staley
5/2/51(H)	Stl.	5–0	6	2	4	Staley
5/6/51(H)	Pitt.	6–0	8	4	2	Dickson
6/16/51(A)	Cin.	3–0	4	4	2	Raffensberger
6/20/51(A)	Chi.	9–0	5	8	2	Minner
7/15/51(H)	Chi.	7–0	5	3	3	Hiller
8/15/51(A)	Phi.	9–0	8	5	3	Johnson
9/13/51(A)	Stl.	2–0	1	2	1	Brazle
5/22/52(H)	Chi.	5–0	9	7	0	Klippstein
8/9/52(H)	N.Y.	2–0	3	10	1	Hearn
8/26/52(A)	Cin.	2–0	5	5	2	Podbielan
9/9/52(H)	Cin.	1–0	3	6	0	Nuxhall

Date	Team	Score	Hits	S.O.	Walks	Loser
9/13/52(H)	Pitt.	8–0	7	13	4	Kline
5/26/53(H)	Cin.	6–0	4	3	2	Judson
7/5/53(H)	Stl.	4–0	3	2	0	Staley
7/27/53(H)	N.Y.	13–0	7	7	2	Hearn
8/1/53(H)	Phi.	5–0	1	8	0	Konstanty
8/15/53(A)	Chi.	2–0	5	4	3	Church
6/5/54(H)	Pitt.	7–0	6	6	0	O'Donnell
6/22/55(H)	Pitt.	6–0	6	5	3	Surkont
5/8/56(H)	Pitt.	5–0	3	10	1	Friend
5/13/56(A)	Cin.	15–0	9	7	1	Fowler
7/6/56(H)	Chi.	5–0	4	4	1	Kaiser
5/28/57(H)	Cin.	1–0	8	3	0	Gross
6/7/57(A)	Pitt.	5–0	7	2	1	Purkey
8/10/57(A)	Stl.	9–0	5	3	1	V. McDaniel
9/3/57(A)	Chi.	8–0	6	5	1	Littlefield
4/19/58(A)	Phi.	5–0	5	4	5	Simmons
8/3/58(H)	S.F.	6–0	4	3	2	Gomez
4/10/59(A)	Pitt.	8–0	7	4	2	Friend
4/30/59(H)	Stl.	1–0	6	4	0	Kellner
7/13/59(H)	S.F.	3–0	6	3	0	Jones
7/26/59(H)	Pitt.	4–0	5	4	3	Friend
7/7/60(H)	Phi.	2–0	5	10	1	Short
7/20/60(H)	Stl.	3–0	7	2	1	Broglio
8/30/60(H)	Stl.	10–0	5	2	2	Broglio
9/16/60(H)	Phi.	4–0	0	15	2	Buzhardt
4/28/61(H)	S.F.	1–0	0	5	2	Jones
9/2/61(H)	L.A.	4–0	2	3	0	Koufax
9/6/61(H)	Phi.	1–0	3	6	1	Buzhardt
9/24/61(H)	Chi.	8–0	2	7	1	Cardwell
4/16/63(H)	Phi.	8–0	4	7	4	McLish
6/14/63(H)	Phi.	3–0	3	3	1	Culp
6/28/63(A)	L.A.	1–0	3	2	0	Drysdale
7/7/63(A)	Hou.	4–0	5	4	1	Umbricht
9/4/63(H)	Pitt.	1–0	4	4	2	Friend
9/21/63(A)	Chi.	4–0	3	4	0	Jackson
9/29/63(H)	Chi.	2–0	4	6	1	Buhl
5/5/64(H)	N.Y.	6–0	4	2	2	Stallard

Year	Home	Away	Total
47	5	2	7
48	1	2	3
49	3	1	4
50	1	0	1
51	3	4	7
52	4	1	5
53	4	1	5

Year	Home	Away	Total
54	1	0	1
55	1	0	1
56	2	1	3
57	1	3	4
58	1	1	2
59	3	1	4
60	4	0	4
61	4	0	4
63	4	3	7
64	1	0	1
	43	20	63

Spahn's Shutouts by Team

Chi.	Cin	Hou.	Brk. L.A.	Bos. Mil.	N.Y.	Phi.	Pit.	N.Y. S.F.	Stl.	Total
10	9	1	5	0	1	11	9	6	11	63

Spahn's Shutouts by Team Finish

1	2	3	4	5	6	7	8	9	10	Total
3	6	13	6	7	6	9	11	1	1	63

Tom Seaver
The Franchise

If any pitcher of the last half of this century could be compared to a pitcher of the first half of the century, it would be Tom Seaver with Walter Johnson. Statistically, Seaver falls short of the numbers that the "Big Train" compiled relative to wins, complete games, and E.R.A. The similarity is that both pitched for extremely weak teams in the early part of their careers and were still winners. If both had been with pennant contenders, their records would be even more impressive. In fact, Seaver could probably have pitched during Johnson's era and duplicated what he had achieved in the 1960s through the 1980s. He was a truly a titan among his peers.

It was unique how the New York Mets obtained Tom Seaver. He was originally signed by the Atlanta Braves, but through some illegality (they signed him while he was still in college), the deal with the Braves was voided by the commissioner's office. Since the Mets and the Cleveland Indians both showed an interest in Tom, his name was thrown into a hat, and the Mets were the fortunate team to obtain his services. He was to the Mets what Johnson was to the Washington Senators.

In 1967, the Mets were only in their sixth year when Seaver started pitching and setting records for victories, E.R.A., and strikeouts. The previous year the team was coming off its best performance when they finished ninth. Prior to that, they had occupied the basement by losing 100 or more games for five consecutive years. This same year they returned to the cellar again as they lost over 100 games. Seaver, as a rookie with 16 victories, had over 25 percent of the team's wins. Without him they probably would have come close to their first year of futility when they established the modern-day record of 120 losses!

When viewing him on the mound, one could see he was of classic vintage, especially his mechanics. He was a thinking machine and knew how to set up hitters with precision. His follow-through never deviated. His left knee always scraped the ground, indicated by the dirty mark staining his uniform pants.

His first year he gained his initial victory against the Chicago Cubs on April 24, 1967, defeating them 6–1. That was the first of 311 victories. His E.R.A. of 2.76 was the first time a Mets starter scored below the 3.00 mark. He struck out 170 batters to surpass the team record by 28. He tossed two shutouts that initial year. The first came against the Pirates, defeating them 3–0 on August 13. He doled out four hits and walked three; he was on his way as a superstar.

In 1968, the Mets saw the arrival of a left-hander named Jerry Koosman who temporarily broke Seaver's records of victories and E.R.A. in a season. Koosman supplemented Tom on the mound as a fearsome duo that gave the Mets credibility for almost a decade. They made other teams cognizant that the days of the soft touch were over in New York.

Seaver improved his record to 16–12 and lowered his E.R.A. to 2.20 with the aid of five shutouts. In June he tossed three of them with the first coming on June 10 as he blanked the Los Angeles Dodgers 1–0. He went ten innings, besting Don Sutton. He gave up only four hits and walked one. He also won 1–0 on June 30 beating Houston and Mike Cuellar.

As 1969 drew the turbulence of the decade to a close, two more outstanding events emerged. In July, Neil Armstrong became the first man to trek on another world other than the earth as he made mankind's first giant step on the moon. The Mets not only surprised the odds makers and the sports world by winning the pennant, but they disposed the mighty Orioles in five games to win the World Series.

During the year, Tom was unbelievable. He compiled a 25–7 record and won the Cy Young Award hands down by getting 23 of the 24 votes cast. Only one Atlanta writer deprived him of the unanimous victory by casting his vote for the hometown ace, Phil Niekro.

Five of Tom's victories came by the shutout route. One game of particular interest was when he pitched against the Chicago Cubs in a night game at Shea Stadium. The Cubs were riding high in first place. The Mets were in second and on their miraculous rise were closely pursuing the Chicagoans. Tom was terrific that night, an adjective that became his moniker throughout his career. He dissected the Cubs' lineup inning by inning like he was pulling wings off flies, leaving them in a helpless state. By the end of the eighth inning, 24 Cubs went to bat and 24 Cubs returned to the dugout with bat in hand. Everyone knew that a perfect game was at stake.

In the top of the ninth, the first Cub bit the dust. Manager Leo Durocher sent up a switch-hitting pinch hitter, Jimmy Qualls. Qualls, a rookie, committed the unpardonable sin to Seaver and the N.Y. fans. He lined a clean hard single to left center field, rejecting Tom's attempt at instant immortality. A chorus of boos rang out at the Cubs' only base runner. This was Qualls only claim to fame. Tom gave up that only hit, walked none, and struck out 11 Bruins.

The year 1969 was also the first year of division playoffs. The Mets, winner of the Eastern Division, squared off against the Western Division Champs, the Atlanta Braves. Tom opened the series and received the win, but he wasn't his sharp self as he gave up five runs in seven innings. He received credit for the victory because the Mets exploded for five runs in the top of the eighth. The Mets swept the Braves in three straight games and earned the right to meet the Baltimore Orioles in the World Series. They went to the confrontation as major underdogs.

In the World Series versus the Baltimore Orioles, Tom started the opener against Mike Cuellar and lost 4–1. He came back in the fourth game and had the Orioles shut out 1–0 when Baltimore tied it in the top of the ninth. The game went into extra innings, and the Mets captured the victory 2–1 when they pushed across the winning run in the bottom of the tenth. Seaver allowed only six hits and went the distance to push the Mets ahead 3–1. The following day Koosman clinched the championship by a score of 5–3.

In 1970 the Mets returned to reality by finishing third, six games in back of the division-winning Pirates. Tom slumped to an 18–12 record but his percentage (.600) was much higher than the team's (.512). He did lead the league in E.R.A. (2.81). He pitched two shutouts against the Phillies in the early part of the year. One of these was his second one-hitter, which Mike Compton spoiled with a single. In that game, he struck out 15 men. He also led the league in strikeouts with 283.

In 1971, the Mets struggled and finished with the identical record they had in 1970, which enabled them to finish in a tie for third place with the Cubs. Seaver had his second 20-win season as he chalked up 20 wins against 10 losses. His E.R.A. was an astonishing 1.76 which gave him the league lead for the second consecutive year. The runner-up in that category, Dave Roberts of San Diego, had 2.10. The Mets were not a strong-hitting team, so Tom had to rely mostly on his talents which would keep his team in contention. He started 35 games and completed 21, a high percentage even for those days. Tom again led the league in strikeouts for the second time with 289, which marked the third time he broke the 200 mark. Included in his victory total were four shutouts. In each of those games he struck out ten or more batters. He was now, along with Ferguson Jenkins and Bob Gibson, one of the leading pitchers in the league.

In 1972, the Mets were shocked by the death of their manager, Gil Hodges, just before the season began. He was playing a round of golf when he collapsed on the course. He couldn't be revived. The leadership of the team went to Yogi Berra who led the Mets to a third-place finish.

Tom had another outstanding year with a 21–12 mark. His E.R.A. was a respectable 2.92 based on three shutouts. He again had over 200 strikeouts finishing with 209. This was the year Steve Carlton's star shone brightest as he captured the Cy Young Award unanimously on the basis of his winning the triple crown of pitching (victories, E.R.A., and strikeouts). This he did with a last-place team!

One of Seaver's shutouts was his third one-hitter by defeating San Diego 2–0. Leron Lee, with one out in the ninth, got a broken-bat single to spoil Tom's date with fame. The game of September 29 he defeated the Pirates 1–0 for his 20th victory of the season. In that game, he doled out two hits. Roberto Clemente just missed his 3000th hit when the official scorer ruled that the ball he hit was scored an error. This didn't prevent Clemente from attaining his milestone hit off Jon Matlack a few days later.

The year 1973 was a peculiar one for the teams in the Eastern Division of the National League because it seemed that no one wanted to win the division. The Pirates seemed never to recover from the death of Clemente at the end of 1972 (he was on a mercy mission to Nicaragua). This made them flounder at the end and finish at 80–82. The Mets, who were last at the end of August and well below .500, made a move to contend for the pennant. They rode the last weeks of the season on Seaver's right arm as he finished the season at 19–10. Because of him they captured the division title with an 82–79 record. Seaver led the league in strikeouts, complete games, and E.R.A. That was the third time in four years he captured the earned-run title. He fashioned three shutouts, two of them against the contending Pirates. His performance was outstanding and he was selected as the Cy Young Award winner for the second time. It was the first time a pitcher with fewer than 20 victories won that award.

In the playoffs against the Reds, Seaver pitched masterfully in the first game until the eighth inning when Pete Rose homered to tie the game at 1–1. In the ninth, Johnny Bench hit a homer to give the Reds a 2–1 victory. Tom gave up only six hits as he went the distance.

The Mets had battled Cincinnati even after four games. The fifth game pitted Seaver against Cincy's Jack Billingham. The Reds evened the game at 2–2 in the top of the fifth, but the Mets erupted for four rolls in the bottom of the fifth to ice the game and capture the pennant. Seaver received credit for the win but was relieved by McGraw in the ninth.

In the World Series, the Mets battled the defending world champion Oakland A's. Seaver pitched the third game and went eight innings, leaving with the score tied at 2. He wasn't charged with a decision as the A's triumphed in the 11th.

With the Mets ahead 3–2, Tom was given the opportunity to clinch the Series for the New Yorkers. He was again matched against Jim "Catfish" Hunter and lost 3–1, giving up only two runs as he was pinch-hit for in the eighth. The A's prevailed in the seventh game to retain their championship.

In 1974, the Mets saw their first losing season after five consecutive winning ones. The slide downward could be attributed to Seaver's sub-par season of 1–11. His E.R.A. was high at 3.20. This was the first time he went above the 3.00 mark. One bright note was he struck out over 200 batters to finish the season with 201. This made the seventh consecutive year that he struck out over 200 batters.

Out of his 11 wins, 5 were shutouts. His first shutout of the season on April 26 versus San Francisco was the 25th of his career. He scattered four hits, defeating Ron Bryant who was the runner up in the Cy Young voting.

Great ball players often rebound after a poor season and have an exceptional year. Tom had one in 1975. He showed a 22–9 mark, which helped the Mets finish above .500 and tie for third place with St. Louis. He led the league in victories and shutouts which enabled him to capture his third Cy Young Award, making him at the time the second pitcher to accomplish this (Sandy Koufax was the other who did it in 1963, 1965, and 1966).

There were five shutouts included in his 22 wins. His September 1 whitewashing of the division winner, Pittsburgh, was his 20th of the season. On September 24 Tom pitched in a duel with the Chicago Cubs. The score was 0–0 going into the bottom of the ninth. He was pitching a no-hitter with two outs when Joe Wallis singled to bleak Tom's no hit bid. The Mets eventually lost in the bottom of the 11th when reliever Skip Lockwood yielded the winning run and was charged with the loss.

The philosophy of the New York Mets at this time stressed pitching instead of hitting. The nucleus of Tom, Jon Matlack, and Jerry Koosman was the crux of the team's competitiveness. Dave Kingman was their only offensive threat in the batting order. Kingman, who was among the leaders in strikeouts and barely could hit his weight, was a model of inconsistency. Hoping for production from him was a literal hit and miss endeavor. To get results from him was like trying to grow grass in the Sahara Desert!

In 1976 Tom again had a down season even though the team had its best percentage year since 1962. He finished the year at 14–11, which included five shutouts. He shut out the Phillies, 1–0 on September 3 defeating their ace, Steve Carlton. In that game, he doled out three hits, but his control was off as he walked four. Because of his savvy, he was able to escape trouble.

The Mets' lack of offensive power would eventually lead to a confrontation with the ownership. It seemed that the consistent stress that the pitching staff was confronted with due to the poor offense was taking its toll. There was rarely an easy game for the Mets pitchers.

An eventful year arose in 1977 when in June the Mets traded Tom to the Reds for three players who weren't even starters. A tearful Seaver blamed the disintegration of the team on the ownership, which refused to seek out free agents to shore up the offense. Seaver, who still had productive years ahead of him, was crestfallen because of his deep allegiance to the team. Because the front office traded off the greatest player in their history (and one of the game's all-time greats), the Mets descended with a resounding thud into the cellar for the first time since 1967. They finished 11 games behind fifth-place Montreal.

While with the Mets in 1977, Tom performed heroically with a 7–3 record, which included three shutout victories. His last shutout for them that year was two weeks before they traded him, which was ironically against Cincinnati, the team he was dealt to. He defeated Pat Zachry, the pitcher who was part of the swap.

With Cincinnati he was outstanding and became the staff's ace immediately. Tom promptly posted a 14–3 mark with four shutouts. Combined with the three he had with the Mets, he led the league for the first tine. His seventh tied him with Frank Tanana for the Major League lead. His combined record that year was 21–6, making that the fifth time he reached the 20-victory plateau. In the early part of the year, the Dodgers built a substantial lead that the Reds couldn't cut into, even with "Tom Terrific." His strikeout totals fell below 200 for the first time since his rookie season in 1967.

The following year the National League's western race went down to the wire with Los Angeles nosing out Cincy by 2½ games. Tom's 16–14 record wasn't all that spectacular but he still was the ace of the staff. His E.R.A. was a respectable 2.87 with only one shutout, but that game was memorable as his only no-hitter. He dazzled the Cardinals 4–0, besting John Denny. Regardless of his record, he still kept the Reds competitive throughout the year. He broke the 200 strikeout barrier again with 226. This gave him ten seasons with 200 or more strikeouts which became the National League record.

The Reds in 1979 captured the National League western crown by 1½ games over the Houston Astros. Tom led and anchored the staff with a 16–6 record. His 3.14 E.R.A. was high for him despite five shutouts. That total tied him for the league lead with Steve Rogers of Montreal and Joe Niekro of Houston. At 34, he was starting to show his age as he finished 9 of his 32 starts. He had only 131 strikeouts, the lowest of his career up to that time. As the great pitcher he was, he developed new pitches (change up) to compensate for his loss of power. His game of July 20 versus St. Louis, defeating them 2–0, was his 50th career shutout when he edged John Denny again. In the playoffs versus the Pirates, he started the opener and went eight innings. In that start he issued only five hits as he battled the Bucs to a 2–2 tie.

The Reds' bullpen unraveled in the 11th and the team lost the game 5–2, wasting a splendid effort by Tom. The Pirates swept the Reds three straight games, but without Tom, Cincinnati would have been an also-ran.

In 1980, the Reds fell to third behind Houston and Los Angeles.

They were only 3½ games from the lead. The race ended in a dead heat between the first two and the first playoff for the playoffs in National League history occurred. Houston prevailed and gained the right to meet the Eastern champs, the Philadelphia Phillies.

The Reds might have done better but Tom had a shoulder injury and contributed only a 10–8 record due to his ailment. He pitched only one shutout against Atlanta. His E.R.A. was his highest ever at 3.64.

The year 1981 will go down in history as the first long enduring players' strike brought the wheels of the national pastime to a screeching halt for over 50 days. When the two warring factions decided to play, over one-third of the season was lost. The lords of baseball decided to divide the season into two halves and the leaders of each division prior to the stoppage were declared the first-half winners. The leaders at the end of the second half were declared the winners of that portion of the season. Then the "four-half" winners faced off to see who would meet in the league championship series. The oddity of the whole season was that Cincinnati had the best overall record in the Major Leagues and failed to make the playoffs! The makeshift arrangement by the club owners left a lot to be desired.

Regardless of the imperfections of the season. Tom was outstanding as he compiled a remarkable 14–2 record with a 2.55 E.R.A. He tossed one shutout against the second-half winner, Houston, defeating them and Sutton 4–0. Tom was deprived of his fourth Cy Young Award because this year Fernando Valenzuela captured all the media hype with his amazing first-half start. He also annexed the Rookie of the Year Award, making him the only person to achieve the distinction of winning the two awards in one season. Many felt that Tom had been the victim of playing before a small media market and didn't receive the publicity that Valenzuela did in Los Angeles.

The Reds fell into the cellar of the Western Division in 1982. Some of the components of the "Big Red Machine" started to show signs of age. Some vital players were not there anymore, so the process of deterioration of the team was sudden. Seaver witnessed his first losing season of his career when he finished with a 5–13 ledger. His E.R.A. was an astronomical 5.10 without a single shutout. That was the first year that happened. At the age of 37, it was obvious that his best years were now behind him and he was traded back to the Mets. In all fairness to Tom, he played in 1982 with a sore shoulder, the same one that plagued him in 1980.

In 1983 the Mets were still in the basement for the second consecutive year. As bad as the team was in the early 1980s, they were not nearly as pitiful as the Mets teams of the 1960s. Seaver's record for the Mets was 9–14 with a 3.55 E.R.A. aided by two shutouts. When the season ended, the Mets were in the process of setting up a team that would become contenders in the latter part of the decade. Tom was not put on the protected list of players because of his age (38). The team did not believe that anyone would claim him, but they were fooled when the Chicago White Sox assumed his contract. They figured if he could contribute for them in 1984 like he did for the Mets in 1983, they would have a good chance of winning the pennant in 1984.

The White Sox with Seaver finished fifth 14 games under .500, which was no fault of Tom's. At 39, Tom proved that he still was a competitor as he suddenly became the ace of the White Sox staff with a 15–11 mark. He pitched four shutouts with his first American League blanking coming at the expense of the Kansas City Royals and Bret Saberhagen. In that game, he dealt five hits and walked none. His E.R.A. for the year was 3.95 (lower than the team's 4.12).

The following year, Tom proved that his performance of 1984 was no aberration as he logged in at 16–11. His E.R.A. was much better at 3.17. Included in his victories was one shutout. No one realized that it would be the last of his career. This was a brilliant 1–0 victory over Cleveland and Bert Blylevyn. In that game, he scattered four hits and walked none.

During the year he notched his 300th career victory versus the Yankees on their home grounds on August 4, 1985. It was a tribute to the city of New York that possibly its greatest pitcher since Christy Mathewson could showcase that milestone against one of their teams. Also on that same day, Rod Carew achieved his 3000th hit against Frank Viola of the Minnesota Twins.

There are just so many pitches in a hurler's arm, and Tom "Terrific" was no exception. He started 1986 with Chicago and was traded to the Red Sox after being 2–6. The Red Sox were fighting for a division title and needed help down the stretch. Tom won 5 and lost 7 as the Red Sox went on to take the Eastern Division by 5½ over the Yankees. Seaver realized that he was only a shell of himself and retired at the end of the season.

Reviewing Tom Seaver's career, it can be assuredly stated that this man was truly one of the greatest pitchers ever. Some of his peers might have won more over a longer period of time, but none of them showed the greatness that he accomplished when pitching for poor and mediocre teams.

Tom Seaver

Date	Team	Score	Hits	S.O.	Walks	Loser
8/13/67(H)	Pitt.	3–0	4	5	3	Blass
9/23/67(H)	Hou.	1–0	3	8	3	Eiler
6/10/68(A)	L.A.	1–0	4	2	1	Sutton
6/25/68(A)	Cin.	4–0	5	4	1	Culver
6/30/68(A)	Hou.	1–0	5	8	1	Cuellar
7/18/68(A)	Pitt.	3–0	6	10	1	McBean
9/25/68(A)	Atl.	3–0	3	3	0	Pappas
5/21/69(A)	Atl.	5–0	3	2	2	Niekro
7/9/69(H)	Chi.	4–0	1	11	0	Holtzman
8/31/69(A)	S.F.	8–0	7	11	3	McCormick
9/18/69(A)	Mon.	2–0	5	9	3	Stoneman
9/27/69(A)	Phi.	1–0	3	4	2	Jackson
4/17/70(H)	Phi.	6–0	8	8	1	G. Jackson
5/15/70(A)	Phi.	4–0	1	15	3	Fryman
4/16/71(H)	Pitt.	1–0	3	14	0	Ellis
6/29/71(A)	Phi.	3–0	4	13	1	Lersch
8/16/71(A)	L.A.	6–0	7	10	4	Alexander
9/6/71(A)	Mon.	7–0	2	12	2	McAnally
4/21/72(H)	Chi.	2–0	4	9	1	Hooton
7/4/72(H)	S.D.	2–0	1	11	4	Kirby
9/29/72(A)	Pitt.	1–0	2	13	2	Briles
5/12/73(A)	Pitt.	6–0	2	3	1	Moose
8/1/73(H)	Pitt.	3–0	4	11	0	Blass
8/15/73(A)	S.D.	7–0	2	7	1	Arlan
4/26/74(A)	S.F.	6–0	4	7	0	Bryant
5/17/74(H)	Mon.	5–0	5	13	0	Moore
7/26/74(A)	Stl.	3–0	4	5	1	McGlothen
8/29/74(H)	Hou.	7–0	5	4	3	Roberts
9/13/74(H)	Chi.	6–0	4	11	4	Reuschel
6/10/75(A)	S.F.	5–0	6	9	2	Barr
6/15/75(A)	S.D.	6–0	3	4	0	Strom
8/7/75(H)	Mon.	7–0	3	7	4	Rogers
8/27/75(A)	S.D.	7–0	6	10	1	Spillner
9/1/75(H)	Pitt.	3–0	4	10	1	Candelaria
4/29/76(H)	Atl.	2–0	5	9	0	Niekro
6/4/76(A)	L.A.	11–0	3	8	1	Hooton
8/24/76(A)	S.F.	4–0	4	8	1	Barr
9/3/76(H)	Phi.	1–0	3	8	4	Carlton
9/13/76(A)	Pitt.	5–0	5	12	1	Demery
4/12/77(H)	Stl.	4–0	5	5	0	Rasmussen
4/17/77(H)	Chi.	6–0	1	6	4	Bonham
6/7/77(H)	Cin.	8–0	5	10	1	Zachry
6/18/77(A)	Mon.	6–0	3	8	0	Alcala
8/31/77(A)	Mon.	6–0	3	6	2	Twitchell
9/20/77(A)	S.D.	4–0	2	5	1	Owchinko

The Great Shutout Pitchers

Date	Team	Score	Hits	S.O.	Walks	Loser
9/25/77(A)	Atl.	4–0	3	5	3	Niekro
6/16/78(H)	Stl.	4–0	0	4	3	Denny
4/19/79(H)	Atl.	2–0	2	5	3	Niekro
6/30/79(A)	S.F.	2–0	2	5	1	Whitson
7/20/79(A)	Stl.	3–0	6	1	0	Denny
8/26/79(A)	N.Y.	8–0	4	5	0	Falcone
9/16/79(A)	L.A.	2–0	3	4	2	Sutton
9/10/80(A)	Atl.	3–0	8	3	1	McWilliams
5/8/81(H)	Hou.	4–0	6	4	6	Sutton
4/20/83(H)	Pitt.	6–0	3	9	3	McWilliams
5/11/83(A)	Hou.	3–0	5	6	2	Scott
5/14/84(H)	K.C.	2–0	5	3	0	Saberhagen
6/6/84(H)	Cal.	4–0	4	8	0	Witt
7/30/84(H)	Bos.	7–0	3	4	0	Nipper
8/25/84(A)	K.C.	3–0	3	4	2	Gubicza
7/19/85(H)	Cle.	1–0	4	4	4	Blyleven

National League

Year	Home	Away	Total
67	2	0	2
68	0	5	5
69	1	4	5
70	1	1	2
71	1	3	4
72	2	1	3
73	1	2	3
74	3	2	5
75	2	3	5
76	2	3	5
77	3	4	7
78	1	0	1
79	1	4	5
80	0	1	1
81	1	0	1
83	1	1	2
	22	34	56

American League

Year	Home	Away	Total
84	3	1	4
85	1	0	1
	4	1	5
	26	35	61

Seaver's Shutouts by Team

National League

Atl.	Chi.	Cin.	Hou.	L.A.	Mon.	N.Y.	Phi.	Pit.	Stl.	S.D.	S.F.	Total
6	4	2	5	4	6	1	5	9	4	5	5	56

American League

Bos.	Cal.	Cle.	K.C.	Total
1	1	1	2	5

Seaver's Shutouts by Team Finish

National League

1	2	3	4	5	6	7	8	9	10	Total
5	9	8	9	11	11	1	0	1	1	56

American League

1	2	3	4	5	6	7	Total
2	1	0	1	0	0	1	5

Nolan Ryan
Mr. No-Hitter

When discussing the worst trades of all times, one that will tower above the greater majority is the one made between the New York Mets and California Angels at the end of 1971. The Mets swapped their once-prized prospect, Nolan Ryan, and a few lesser players for Jim Fregosi whom the Mets believed would lead them to the pennant by solving their perennial third-base problem. Fregosi turned out to be a bust for the Mets while Ryan shed his losing image and became an instant success for California. The proverbial "one that got away" would live in Mets history when Nolan Ryan's career is discussed.

Ryan made his debut on September 11, 1966, at the age of 19 but took a loss. The Mets felt he needed more seasoning, so they farmed him out to the minors for the 1967 season.

The following year of 1968 he was back for good, finishing the season at 6–9. The most impressive thing about Nolan was his strikeouts. He fanned 133 in 134 innings pitched. His E.R.A. was a respectable 3.09. With the addition of Seaver and Koosman, the Mets seemed well on their way to the top of the standings.

In 1969 the second expansion brought the formation of divisions in both leagues. The Mets staged their miracle season and surprised everyone by making it all the way to the World Series and capturing the title.

Nolan had a 6–3 season as his contribution to the Amazin' Mets. He started in only 10 games and relieved in 15 others. A groin injury hampered his number of starts. He seemed to be the setup man for the "closer" because he showed only one save. In the playoffs versus the Atlanta Braves, he relieved Gary Gentry in the third inning and finished the game. He received credit for a 7–4 victory in which he didn't lose his poise when the Braves took the lead against him in the fifth.

In the World Series versus the Baltimore Orioles, he again relieved Gentry in the seventh inning of the third game with the Mets ahead 4–0. He shut the Orioles down the rest of the way as the "Amazin's" prevailed 5–0. He received credit for a save in that game. Little did anyone know at the time, it would be his last appearance in the Fall Classic.

Sporting the crown of world champions in 1970, the Mets seemed confident in the young arms of their pitching department. It seemed to be a bright future for Nolan.

The season turned sour for the Mets as their hopes in Ryan and Gentry diminished. With Nolan, the season looked promising as he threw his first career shutout on April 18 against the Philadelphia Phillies. In that game he gave up a single to leadoff man Denny Doyle for the Phils' only hit of the game. He walked six men, which would be a problem of his, but he also struck out 15 batters. Strikeouts would be his trademark for the remainder of his career. The total strikeouts in the game tied Jerry Koosman's club record at the time. From the fifth inning on, Ryan was spectacular as he retired 14 of the last 15 batters. He threw another shutout later that year versus the Chicago Cubs, besting them 4–0. In that game he whiffed 13 Cubs.

The Mets' hopes were still with Nolan as the 1971 season began but slowly faded as it progressed. He started 26 games but completed only three, and his E.R.A. was an unflattering 3.97 with no shutouts. He was still striking out batters but walking almost as many (137 K's to 116 BB's). He was not endearing himself to the front office, fans, or media. It might have been the pressure and demand that a country boy had to fare in the "Big Apple." The stage was set for a drastic trade that would turn out to be a blessing for Nolan. He left the Mets with a 29–37 mark.

With the Angels, Nolan joined a franchise that hadn't known much success in their brief history. He became a part of the starting rotation that included Andy Messersmith who the previous year became only the third pitcher in Angel history to win 20 or more games in a season.

With a losing team whose lineup didn't show much offensive punch and was made up of aging veterans discarded from other teams, he exploded as the top power pitcher in the league.

His strikeout feats were reminiscent of Bob Feller almost four decades earlier. In Nolan's first year in the American League, 329 batters saw the speed of the "Ryan Express" as he led the league in strikeouts. Ryan also topped the league in walks with 157. He also was the league leader in shutouts with 9. This gave him an impressive E.R.A. of 2.28. Out of his nine shutouts, one was a one-hitter on July 9 versus the Boston Red Sox defeating them 3–0. In the first inning, Carl Yastrzemski got the lone hit for the Bosox. After Yaz's hit, eight consecutive Red Sox were struck out. It looked like the change in uniforms started to bring out Ryan's potential.

In 1973, California still struggled with a losing record but Nolan was better than he was the previous year. He broke the 20-win mark for the first time at 21–16. His E.R.A. was 2.87 based on four shutouts. Three of his shutouts were notable. His first on May 15 was the first no-hitter of his career as he blanked the Kansas City Royals 3–0. He struck out 12 batters while walking only three.

On July 15, he tossed his second no-hitter, this time stymieing the Detroit Tigers 6–0 with 17 strikeouts while walking only four. On August 29, he shut out New York on one hit. A single by Thurman Munson in the first inning spoiled Ryan's chance for three no-hitters in one season. The two he did achieve put him in a class with Johnny Vander Meer, Allie Reynolds, and Virgil Trucks as the only men to pitch two no-hitters in one season. Vander Meer is noted for pitching no-hitters in consecutive games. (Some record books give Jim Maloney credit for pitching two no-hitters in one season, but the record keepers discarded the game Maloney pitched against the Mets when he yielded up one hit, a home run in the 11th by Johnny Lewis.)

It also must be mentioned that Ryan set the season strikeout record at 383 topping Koufax's record by one. He also tied Koufax and "Rube" Waddell as the only men to break 300 strikeouts in a season for two years. The only blemish on Nolan's stats was again leading the league in walks with 162 and also leading in losses.

In 1974, the Angels fell into last place. It was no fault of Ryan's, for he posted his winningest season at 22–16. His E.R.A. again was a respectable 2.89 based on three shutouts. His first shutout on June 27 was a one-hitter against the Texas Rangers, defeating them 5–0. Alex Johnson was the spoiler in that game with a single. On September 28 his 4–0 whitewashing of the Minnesota Twins became his third no-hitter. In that game he fanned 15 Twins, but his control was off as he walked eight. This no-hitter placed him in elite company, and he became the fourth man to have that distinction since 1900. He joined Cy Young, Bob Feller, and Sandy Koufax. Koufax held the record with four.

During 1974, Ryan became the first man to have 300 or more strikeouts for a third consecutive year as he led the league with 367. This also was his third consecutive year of reaching 300 or more K's. On the negative side, he again led the league in walks and passed the 200 mark in that category with 202. This made him and Bob Feller the only pitchers to reach that stage of wildness.

As the 1975 season began, Dick Williams, who took over the team in the last half of the 1974 season, tried to revitalize the Angels with the magic he showed in Boston and Oakland. It didn't occur as the Angels finished last for the second consecutive year. Some of their failure could be attributed to an elbow injury that Nolan suffered during the year. His three previous seasons he averaged close to 40 starts, but because of his injury, his number of starts went down to 28. His complete games also diminished as he finished only ten. Usually he completed more than 50 percent of his starts.

His record for the year was 14–12. Five of his wins were shutouts and all of them came before the middle of June. Despite this, he had a high E.R.A. of 3.45, which indicated that he was toiling with physical stress.

One of his shutouts was on June 1 when he no-hit the Baltimore Orioles 1–0. This game tied him for the major league record with Sandy Koufax at four. He now had the American League record topping Bob Feller by one. The no-hitter also gave him his 100th career victory. His injury also curtailed his strikeout total, which was under 300 for the first time since he joined the Angels. Teammate Frank Tanana took his place as strikeout leader.

As 1976 opened, the Angels still struggled. As the season passed the midpoint, Dick Williams was released and Norm Sherry took his place at the helm. The Angels would endure another losing season, finishing in a tie for fourth with the Texas Rangers.

Nolan also saw his first losing season since he joined California and finished the year at 17–18. He led the league in strikeouts, BB's, and shutouts. His strikeout total again passed the 300 mark for the fourth time. His E.R.A. was well above 3.00 at 3.36 despite having seven shutouts. On June 15 he logged his 25th career shutout as he stifled the Milwaukee Brewers 1–0 on two hits. He had two other 1–0 victories, one against Texas as he stopped them on three hits when he hooked up against Bert Blylevyn. His other was against the Oakland A's in which he doled out two hits.

The Angels were only a two-man pitching staff that consisted of Nolan and lefty Frank Tanana. The rest of the staff was marginal as a good many of them showed losing records. This was the major reason for California's fifth-place finish in 1977. Regardless, Nolan regained winning form coming in at 19–16. He again led the league in strikeouts and BB's. This was the fifth time he passed the 300 mark, showing 341 strikeouts. In his 19 victories, four were shutouts with the first two coming in April. His second was a one-hitter against the newly formed expansion team Seattle Mariners. Seattle's catcher, Bob Stinson, produced a hit that deprived Nolan of his fifth no-hitter. Because of his four shutouts, he finished third in the E.R.A. totals at 2.77, behind teammate Frank Tanana.

The Angels again made another managerial change by releasing Norm Sherry and replacing him with Dave Garcia. They performed worse as the season progressed despite the change in leadership.

In 1978 the Angels had their first winning season since 1970. They again made another managerial change when they brought in longtime favorite Jim Fregosi to replace Dave Garcia. Ironically, this was the same Fregosi who was traded for Ryan. The Angels tied for second with the Texas Rangers.

Nolan suffered a leg injury that hampered his performance, and he showed only a 16–13 mark. His E.R.A. was high at 3.71 with three shutouts. His game of May 5 was another one-hitter. In that game he downed Cleveland 5–0 and struck out 12. Duane Kuiper was the spoiler in that game with a single. Nolan again led the league in strikeouts for the sixth time in seven years with 260.

Sadly, near the end of the season outfielder Lyman Bostock was fatally shot by a jealous suitor who mistook him as the "other man." Bostock, who was acquired as a free agent, showed a positive desire to play baseball when he refused to take his salary because he didn't feel he was earning it by his underachieving performance at the time.

The Angels finally captured the American League West title for the first time in their history. They prevented the Kansas City Royals from winning their fourth consecutive division title by edging them out by three games. The Angels improved themselves by obtaining free-agent Rod Carew to bolster their hitting attack. Don Baylor had a career year. He led the league with 139 R.B.I.'s which earned him the MVP award.

Nolan rebounded with a 16–14 record, which tied him for the team lead in victories. He also was the leader in strikeouts (223) for the seventh time in eight years. He also tied for the shutout crown with Baltimore's Mike Flanagan and Kansas City's Dennis Leonard at five. On May 2 he blanked the Yankees 1-0, defeating the previous year's Cy Young winner, Ron Guidry.

In the league championship series, he started the opener versus Baltimore's Jim Palmer. He went seven innings, giving up three runs on only foul hits. He left with the score tied 3–3; therefore, he wasn't charged with the defeat. Baltimore pushed across three runs in the bottom of the tenth on a home run by pinch hitter John Lowenstein to win it 6–3. They eventually defeated the Angels in four games. California lost Ryan at the end of the season due to free agency. He desired to pitch closer to his home in Texas, so he signed with the Houston Astros.

On his arrival back to the National League in 1984, Nolan did not set the league on fire. He sported an 11–10 mark and showed a 3.35 E.R.A. He completed only 4 of 35 starts. Two of his complete games were shutouts. Both of them came in May as he defeated Philly 3-0, giving up four hits and striking out ten. Ten days later he blanked San Diego 1-0, striking out seven. He did reach 200 strikeouts, but a noteworthy sign was that he led the league on BB's with 98. It was the first time since 1970 as a starter that he issued fewer than 100 walks.

Regardless of his low stats, Ryan seemed to bring an aura of good fortune because the Astros finally won a title after 18 years. Winning the Western Division in a playoff versus the Dodgers, they gained the right to meet the Eastern Division winners, the Philadelphia Phillies, in the league championship series. At the time Nolan became the only man to go from a division winner in one league to a division winner in another in consecutive years. In his last year with the Angels, he was also instrumental in their first title.

In the playoffs, he didn't fare that well as he pitched the second game and left with the score tied at two apiece. He also started the fifth and deciding game and was shelled in the eighth inning when the Phils erupted for five runs. He escaped the loss as Houston tied the game in the bottom of the eighth but lost the pennant in the tenth. Nolan gave up 16 hits in 13⅓ innings pitched. His E.R.A. ballooned to 5.54!

The following year in 1981 was the first extended strike in baseball history. The season was divided into halves with each half-winner meeting for the right to play in the league championship series. Despite the strike, Nolan had a good year. He logged in at 11–5 and still led the league in E.R.A. with a marvelous 1.69. He did that on the strength of three shutouts. In his first shutout, he defeated Cincinnati 5–0 giving up 7 hits and striking out 11. Cincinnati had the best overall record in 1981 and failed to make the playoffs! His shutout of the Mets was a five-hitter when ten batters went down swinging. Both of these were prior to the strike. After the strike settlement, he pitched his third shutout which was an all-time classic as he spun his fifth no-hitter on national television, blanking the Dodgers 5–0. This gave him the all-time record for no-hitters as he surpassed Sandy Koufax. He fanned 11 batters in that game and only walked three.

In the division playoff versus the Dodgers, he started the first game and was matched against Fernando Valenzuela, the rookie whiz who captured the headlines throughout the year. Nolan won the game 3–1 as Fernando escaped the loss. In the deciding fifth game, the Dodgers gained revenge and defeated him 4–0 claiming the right to meet the Montreal Expos in the league championship series. Nolan pitched credibly and gave up only three runs in 15 innings. In the deciding game, the Astro defense became porous and gave up two unearned runs in the sixth inning as Nolan pitched shutout ball for the first five innings.

In 1982, the Astros slipped under .500 to finish in fifth place, but Nolan enjoyed a good year at 16–12. His E.R.A. was an acceptable 3.16 based on three shutouts. He defeated the World Champion Dodgers, striking out ten. His next shutout was a one-hitter against the San Diego Padres. The culprit in that game was catcher Terry Kennedy who singled. The third shutout was against the Mets whom he defeated 4–0 on two hits. This game was a milestone because it was the 50th shutout of his career.

In 1983, the Astros gained a winning stride and finished third only six games behind the division-winning Dodgers. Nolan had another good season (14–9) despite being hampered by another leg injury. His E.R.A. was a fine 2.98 with only two shutouts (both being against San Diego). The game on August 3 was a 1–0 squeaker in which he again gave up one hit. Tim Flannery, a .234 hitter, stroked the only safety for the Padres. Nolan was now 36 years old and the question was how long could he continue to power pitch his way to victories.

The next year, 1984, saw Houston again finish third, a distant 12 games behind division winner San Diego. The Astros dropped below .500 (80–82), but Ryan held his own as the ledger showed him at 12–11. His E.R.A. was a splendid 3.04 with two shutouts, both of which were against the Pirates. He defeated them by the scores of 5–0 and 1–0 and allowed five hits in each game.

The Astros tied with the San Diego Padres for third in 1985. Nolan's won-lost record was 10–12 with no shutouts. That was the first time that happened to him since 1971. He managed to strike out 209 batters, which indicated there wasn't anything wrong with the velocity on his fast ball.

The year 1986 saw Houston sprint to the division title by romping over second-place Cincinnati by ten games. This was, by far, the best team in their history. Nolan had a good year at 12–8, but his E.R.A. was 3.34, and for his second straight year he had no shutouts. His starts were down to 30, which could be attributed to an elbow injury that had occurred during the year. He was still an integral part of the pitching staff at the age of 39.

Houston's only problem was at the end of the year when they confronted a Mets team having their best season ever. The Mets turned in one of the best records in baseball history (108–54) against the Astros who won 96 and lost 66. The Astros would go on to lose the league championship series in six games but had nothing to be ashamed of due to the fact that five of the six games were spellbinders.

Nolan started game two and left after five innings, losing 5–0. The Mets captured that game 5–1 behind Bob Ojeda. In the fifth game, Nolan was superb as he dueled Dwight Gooden after nine innings. He was relieved in the 10th and New York broke though in the 11th to go up three games to two. The Mets would go on and win the sixth game in a 16-inning thriller.

The Astros' bubble burst in 1987 as they fell to third with a losing record (76–86), 14 games behind division-winning San Francisco. Nolan had his worst record ever at 8–16. His season was an enigma because he led the league with 270 strikeouts, but at the same time, he led the league in E.R.A. with a 2.76 mark. This made him the second losing pitcher in history to make that claim. Dave Koslo of the Giants did it in 1949. Nolan also went his third consecutive year without pitching a shutout. This was another reason his winning E.R.A. title was remarkable.

Houston finished fifth in 1988 but showed a winning record

(82–80). Nolan also responded on a positive note, as he was 12–11. He pitched his first shutout in over three years as he whitewashed Philly 2–0, yielding three hits. His E.R.A. was above the 3.00 level, settling at 3.52. At age 41, he also led the league in strikeouts with 227.

Little did anyone know, but he decided at the end of the year to sign for more money with the Texas Rangers. They needed someone to draw people in and felt that Nolan would generate more revenue than they would pay him.

In 1989 the Texas Rangers rose to third with a winning record (83–79) mainly due to the addition of Nolan. At 42, he became the ace of the staff with a 16–10 mark. He led the league in strikeouts with an amazing 301 and only 239 innings pitched. Like "O' Man River," he not only "kept rolling" with a flow, but with a torrent. He also pitched two shutouts which made his E.R.A. somewhat respectable at 3.20. Both of these were against the California Angels where he allowed three hits in each game. He struck out 12 men in the first game and 13 in the second. In that second game, his control was impeccable and he didn't allow a walk. The question was, how long could this continue?

The Rangers again finished third in 1990 with Nolan coming in at 13–9 and still leading the league with 232 strikeouts. He pitched two shutouts, both of them gems of brilliance. On April 26, he one-hit the Chicago White Sox 1–0 with 16 strikeouts. Ron Kittle ruined his chance to get his sixth no-hitter.

On June 11, against the Oakland A's, who would go on and win their third consecutive pennant, he did achieve his sixth no-hitter, defeating them 5–0. In that game, he fanned 14 and only walked two. It made everyone wonder when the end was in sight for the durable fireballer.

During the end of the season, he achieved another milestone with his 12th victory, his 300th career win as he defeated the Milwaukee Brewers 11–3.

In 1991, Nolan again was competitive as he showed a record of 12–6. He started 27 games and finished only two, both shutouts. These were both marvelous performances. His first shutout of the year against the Toronto Blue Jays was his seventh and last no-hitter. In that game he struck out 16. At 44, he seemed to be superhuman as he continued to amaze the baseball world. On July 7th he pitched his last shutout, blanking the California Angels on two hits. In that game, 14 Angels went down swinging. Nolan's control was outstanding and he walked only one. His strikeout total was over 200 (203) and his E.R.A. was a commendable 2.91.

Inevitably Ryan slowed down. In 1992 he logged in his first losing season at 5–9 for the Texas Rangers. His E.R.A. was high at 3.72 with no shutouts, but he struck out 138 in 157 innings pitched.

In 1993, his last year, he went 5–5. His career stats showed a strikeout total of 5,714, topping the original record held by Walter Johnson by 2,205! He had 324 victories with 61 shutouts. A remarkable accomplishment in his career would be his seven no-hitters, topping Sandy Koufax by three. It boggles the mind to realize that he also had 12 one-hitters to go along with the no-hitters! In 1999 he was enshrined in Cooperstown in his first year of eligibility.

Nolan Ryan

Date	Team	Score	Hits	S.O.	Walks	Loser
4/18/70(H)	Phi.	7–0	1	15	6	Bunning
8/4/70(H)	Chi.	4–0	3	13	5	Decker
4/18/72(H)	Min.	2–0	4	10	5	Perry
5/5/72(H)	Mil.	4–0	3	14	5	Brett
5/30/72(H)	Chi.	6–0	7	10	4	Bahnsen
7/5/72(H)	Mil.	1–0	4	8	4	Stephenson
7/9/72(H)	Bos.	3–0	1	16	1	Siebert
7/27/72(H)	Tex.	5–0	2	14	6	Paul
8/22/72(A)	Bal.	2–0	1	11	6	McNally
8/27/72(H)	Cle.	1–0	6	10	5	Henningan
8/31/72(H)	Det.	4–0	3	10	2	Fryman
5/15/73(A)	K.C.	3–0	0	12	3	Dalcanton
6/7/73(H)	Det.	3–0	5	7	2	Fryman
7/15/73(A)	Det.	6–0	0	17	4	Perry
8/29/73(H)	N.Y.	5–0	1	10	3	Medich
6/27/74(H)	Tex.	5–0	1	6	1	Brown
7/20/74(A)	Bal.	2–0	5	8	1	Garland
9/28/74(H)	Min.	4–0	0	15	8	Decker
4/11/75(H)	Chi.	3–0	6	10	4	Osteen
5/8/75(H)	Oak.	5–0	4	10	5	Hamilton
5/13/75(H)	N.Y.	5–0	2	7	5	Medich
6/1/75(H)	Bal.	1–0	0	9	4	Grimsley
6/6/75(H)	Mil.	6–0	2	6	6	Slaton
4/20/76(H)	Bal.	5–0	3	11	4	Alexander
6/15/76(H)	Mil.	1–0	2	9	2	Colborn
7/7/76(H)	Cle.	2–0	5	10	5	Waits
7/30/76(H)	Chi.	3–0	3	10	2	Brett
9/20/76(H)	Tex.	1–0	3	4	7	Blyleven
9/29/76(H)	Chi.	3–0	2	11	6	Brett
10/3/76(A)	Oak.	1–0	2	14	5	Torrez

Date	Team	Score	Hits	S.O.	Walks	Loser
4/7/77(A)	Sea.	2–0	3	6	6	Romo
4/15/77(H)	Sea.	7–0	1	8	6	Abbott
6/29/77(H)	K.C.	7–0	5	12	3	Colborn
7/12/77(H)	Min.	3–0	4	8	3	Thormodsgood
4/29/78(H)	Tor.	5–0	2	11	6	Lemanczyk
5/5/78(H)	Cle.	5–0	1	12	5	Wise
7/19/78(H)	Cle.	3–0	6	10	4	Wise
4/17/79(A)	Min.	6–0	4	10	3	Goltz
5/2/79(H)	N.Y.	1–0	6	7	2	Guidry
5/20/79(H)	Chi.	4–0	2	11	1	Baumgarten
6/18/79(H)	Tex.	5–0	2	10	2	Jenkins
7/9/79(H)	Bos.	6–0	6	12	2	Torrez
5/18/80(H)	Phi.	3–0	4	10	4	Lerch
5/28/80(H)	S.D.	1–0	2	7	5	Wise
5/11/81(A)	Cin.	5–0	7	11	3	Lacoss
6/5/81(H)	N.Y.	3–0	5	10	2	Jones
9/26/81(H)	L.A.	5–0	0	11	3	Power
7/4/82(A)	L.A.	3–0	4	10	2	Ruess
8/11/82(A)	S.D.	3–0	1	6	3	Show
8/31/82(A)	N.Y.	4–0	2	9	3	Lynch
6/12/83(H)	S.D.	2–0	5	11	0	Show
8/3/83(A)	S.D.	1–0	1	10	6	Lollar
5/16/84(A)	Pitt.	1–0	5	11	2	Candelaria
5/26/84(H)	Pitt.	2–0	5	9	1	Deleon
7/21/88(H)	Phi.	2–0	3	9	4	Maddux
7/6/89(A)	Cal.	3–0	3	12	2	McCaskill
9/30/89(A)	Cal.	2–0	3	13	0	Finley
4/26/90(H)	Chi.	1–0	1	16	2	Perez
6/11/90(A)	Oak.	5–0	0	14	2	Sanderson
5/1/91(H)	Tor.	3–0	0	16	2	Key
7/7/91(H)	Cal.	7–0	2	14	1	Finley

American League

Year	Home	Away	Total
72	8	1	9
73	2	2	4
74	2	1	3
75	4	1	5
76	6	1	7
77	3	1	4
78	3	0	3
79	4	1	5
89	0	2	2
90	1	1	2
91	2	0	2
	35	11	46

National League

70	2	0	2
80	2	0	2
81	2	1	3
82	0	3	3
83	1	1	2
84	1	1	2
88	1	0	1
	9	6	15

Nolan Ryan's Shutouts by Team

American League

Bal.	Bos.	Cal.	Chi.	Cle.	Det.	K.C.	Mil.	Min.	N.Y.	Oak.	Sea.	Tex.	Tor.	Total
5	1	3	6	4	3	2	4	4	3	3	2	4	2	46

National League

Atl.	Chi.	Cin.	Hou.	L.A.	Mon.	N.Y.	Phi.	Pit.	Stl.	S.D.	S.F.	Total
0	1	1	0	2	0	2	3	2	0	4	0	15

Both Leagues 61

Shutouts by Team Finish

American League

1	2	3	4	5	6	7	Total
6	8	10	6	4	10	2	46

National League

1	2	3	4	5	6	Total
1	3	0	4	2	5	15

Bert Blyleven
A Class Act

Before I go on to discuss the career of Bert Blyleven, I would like to state that of all the players covered in this book, the only one I met in person was Bert Blyleven. The first time I met him was in April of 1976 right after the game played on Patriot's Day between the Boston Red Sox and Minnesota Twins. I was with my two sons, Frank and Gordon, who at the time were 9 and 11. We were standing outside a courtyard separated from the Minnesota Twins' bus by an iron gate. We were hoping to get some autographs from the players as they boarded the bus, but our calls fell on deaf ears. A young man emerged, probably from the clubhouse, dressed in a business suit. He was tall and slender and we asked him if he was a ball player. He said his name was "Bert Blyleven" as he approached my sons and obligingly signed their index cards. He was a pitcher of class as he made a successful and gratifying day for my sons. He was the only one to hear the voices of the two young boys.

The next time we met Mr. Blyleven was in Atlanta's Fulton County Stadium in August of 1978 when he was a member of the visiting Pittsburgh Pirates. We again requested his autograph and without any qualms, he signed. My son Frank mentioned that he was probably going to be a Hall of Famer some day, which somehow caused him some embarrassment as he walked away shaking his head in disbelief.

The truth of the matter is that "out of the mouth of babes" a prophecy was in its infant stages. Bert Blyleven, with the statistics he compiled over his career, is entitled to the Hall of Fame. The trouble with baseball's fans is that they soon forget the stars after they retire, especially those who played in a small media market. I hope with this writing that I shine some light into the minds of those who witnessed his performances and would say, "Bert Who?"

Bert is only one of eight men who can claim the distinction of winning over 250 games, striking out over 3,000 batters, and pitching over 50 shutouts. The list contains Walter Johnson, Tom Seaver, Nolan Ryan, Gaylord Perry, Don Sutton, Bob Gibson, and Steve Carlton. If this sounds like a pitch for Blyleven's enshrinement, then let it be, because he ranks 23rd in the most victories of modern times, ranks 5th in strikeouts, and ninth in shutouts.

The rap against Blyleven is that he never had enough winning years to be a top-notch candidate for immortality. When looking through his record, it can be assumed that he had more winning seasons than losing ones. The teams that he pitched for were not outstanding outfits. Most of them were teams whose best efforts were at the break-even point. Only three times in his career was he afforded the luxury of pitching for a division winner (Minnesota in 1970, Pittsburgh in 1979, and Minnesota in 1987). In post-season play, his record was an outstanding 5–1 with an overall E.R.A. of 2.47. In 47⅓ innings pitched, he allowed only 43 hits. This is indicative of his ability to pitch under pressure. Another gauge to compare his worthiness for enshrinement is during his career, the overall record of the teams that he played for was .502. His lifetime percentage was .534, showing that he rose above the lack of support afforded him. Comparing his record to some of the Hall of Famers, he has a better percentage than Ted Lyons (.531) and Eppa Rixey (.515). To also illustrate this comparison, we can throw in Rollie Fingers whose percentage (.491) didn't even rise above .500! Included in the comparisons, Nolan Ryan was a definite shoe-in to the Hall of Fame based on his strikeouts and no-hitters. Ryan compiled a 324–292 record for a .526 percentage, which is still below Blyleven's. How can anyone cast doubt about Blyleven's career?

Only once did he have a losing season with a winning team not counting the 1976 season when he was 4–5 with Minnesota in an abbreviated stay before being traded. In 1980, he was 8–13 with the Pirates who were defending their world championship. That Pittsburgh team was only 83–79, showing that they were not as proficient as the 1979 team. Combing through the archives, we can find Hall of Famers like "Red" Ruffing who struggled with a 9–14 record in 1933 for the defending world champion New York Yankees. That team finished second with the likes of Gehrig, Ruth, Lazzeri, Combs, and Dickey—all of whom are Hall of Famers.

In 1935, "Lefty" Gomez, the other half of the Yankee lefty-righty tandem of Ruffing and Gomez, posted a 12–15 record for the second-place Yankees who finished only three games behind Detroit, who went on to become world champions. Gomez was only 26 when he witnessed that miserable year, which in all reality probably cost the Yankees the pennant. So, this argument against Blyleven's credentials can be erased!

Born in Zeist, Netherlands, he arrived in the United States at age two. He proceeded through Little League and high-school ball. Drafted and signed by the Minnesota Twins, he was sent to Sarasota of the Rookie Gulf Coast League where he split four decisions. That same year he was moved to Orlando of the Florida State League (class A) where he showed a 5–0 mark in six games. He allowed only six runs in 37 innings for a sparkling 1.46 E.R.A. He struck out 41 batters along the way, doing it with a masterful curve ball as well as his fast ball.

In 1970, the Twins elevated him to Evansville of the American Association (Class AAA). He was only 19, and after only eight games, he sported a 4–2 mark with a respectable 2.50 E.R.A. He also had 63 strikeouts in only 54 innings pitched. This earned him a promotion to the parent club where he made his debut on June 5, 1970, just two months past his 19th birthday. He made it a winning one as he stopped the Washington Senators 2–1. He was on his way to becoming one of the premier right-handers. On August 26, he pitched his first shutout, defeating the Boston Red Sox 7–0 while yielding only four hits. He finished his rookie year at 10–9 as the Twins were in the midst of capturing their second consecutive Western Division title in the American League. Bert was not the top gun on the staff, but he was a major hope for the future on a team that was starting to show its age. Bert impressed many people, especially *The Sporting News*, which awarded him the American League Rookie Pitcher of the Year award.

In 1971, Minnesota collapsed to fifth place 26½ games behind the Oakland A's who would win the first of five division titles. In between the first and the fifth would be three consecutive world championships. This was the first time that occurred since the Yankees of 1949–53 accomplished the feat.

The year would be another winning one for Bert as he posted 16 wins versus 15 losses. This was the first of five consecutive years of 15 or more victories. Bert also showed an E.R.A. of 2.82 based on five shutouts. His last three were by the identical scores of 1–0. During his illustrious career, he pitched fifteen 1–0 games with only Walter Johnson (37) and Grover Alexander (17) surpassing him. With regard to his 15 losses, it must be stated that the Twins only scored 18 runs in those games. Also during the year, he surpassed the 200-strikeout mark for the first time as he totaled 224 K's. This started a run of six consecutive years of 200 or more strikeouts.

In 1972, the first baseball strike reared its ugly head and lasted 13 days. Bert was able to finish with a .500 record at 17–17. The Twins also finished at the break-even mark, rising to third 15½ games out of third place. During that season, Bert threw three shutouts, which helped to lower his E.R.A. to 2.73. His strikeout total reached 228, well behind league leader Nolan Ryan (329).

The year 1973 saw Blyleven become a 20-game winner for the only time in his career as he posted a 20–17 ledger. Minnesota was still a .500 ball club (81–81), as Bert had to extend himself more. This reflected in his innings pitched as he passed the 300-inning mark for the first time with 325.

As for his other statistical accomplishments, his E.R.A. was the lowest of his career (2.52). His strikeouts were also his highest total (258), which again placed him second behind Nolan Ryan for the year. This was the year Ryan set the Major League record at 383. Bert did lead the league with nine shutouts.

His first shutout was on May 24 as he stymied the Kansas City Royals on one hit. The hit was a drag bunt by Ed Kirkpatrick early in the game. His June 29 shutout of California gave him the satisfaction of defeating Nolan Ryan in head-to-head competition.

The Twins were still around the .500 mark in 1974 (82–80) which placed them third, eight games behind Oakland. Bert logged in with a 17–17 mark leading the team in victories. Included in these victories were three shutouts—one of which was against the division-winning Oakland A's, 1–0. His E.R.A. was still a highly commendable 2.66. His strikeouts again were over 200.

Another game he pitched during the year that is worthy of note was on July 4 when he one-hit the Texas Rangers. Toby Harrah spoiled both the no-hitter and the shutout when he homered in the third inning. Bert was on the verge of losing the game until Larry Hisle hit a three-run homer in the ninth to notch the victory for him.

In 1975 Bert's record improved to 15–10 as his team fell below .500 (76–83). In his victory total there were three shutouts which all came late in the year. His best effort was against the Milwaukee Brewers on August 27 when he blanked them 1–0 in 11 innings. He doled out six hits and struck out 13, while walking only one in that game. His E.R.A. edged up to 3.00—the first time since his rookie year that it wasn't below that mark. His strikeout total of 233 placed him second behind league leader, Frank Tanana.

In 1976 Bert departed from the Twins in a trade with the Texas Rangers. He was dealt along with Danny Thompson (who would die of leukemia in December of that year). The Twins received in exchange Bill Singer, Roy Smalley, Mike Cubbage, and Jim Gideon, along with $250,000 in cash. If the trade seemed top heavy in favor of the Twins that was because Bert was a valued commodity at the time.

While with Minnesota, Bert compiled a 4–5 mark with no shutouts. With Texas, he posted a 9–11 ledger; six of those victories were whitewashes, four of them 1–0. His first shutout was a one-hitter in which he defeated Oakland 1–0 in ten innings. Ken McMullen spoiled his gem by getting a single early in the game. His second shutout was again by a 1–0 score also in ten innings. This time it was against the Chicago White Sox. He had two consecutive shutouts, winning both by the score of 1–0 in a total of 20 innings. He had carried his reputation as a workhorse over from the Twins as he totaled over 275 innings pitched for the sixth consecutive year.

Although his combined record was only 13–16, he was not supported offensively in many of his starts. Regardless of his losing record, his E.R.A. was still a splendid 2.87. His strikeout total was over 200 for the sixth consecutive year. His six shutouts placed him one behind league leader Nolan Ryan.

In 1977, he recorded a 14–12 benchmark for Texas, which rose its best record (94–78). Included in his victory total were another five shutouts, highlighted by the best game of his career—his only no hitter fashioned against the California Angels, defeating them 6–0.

That year his strikeout total dwindled to under 200 and innings pitched falling under the 275 level. Regardless, Bert compiled an excellent E.R.A. of 2.72. His hits allowed per inning pitched was a sparkling 0.77, which comes out to a ratio of 6.9 hits per nine-inning game.

The inconsistency of the Texas front office might have had an unsettling effect on the team (especially in the beginning of the season). They employed four managers for the year. They started with Frank Luchessi who was replaced by Ed Stanky who quit after only one game. The team was managed by Connie Ryan for six games. Finally, Billy Hunter showed a stabilizing effect as the team finished the year under him at 60–33.

At the end of the season, Bert was traded to the Pittsburgh Pirates along with John Milner for Al Oliver and Nelson Norman. Oliver was one of the better all-around hitters whose average was always around or over the .300 mark.

Bert's first year (1978) with the Pirates was a winning one. His victory total enabled him to tie for the team league in wins with Don Robinson. He tossed four shutouts with his first National League blanking against the New York Mets 1–0. He went 11 innings in that game, scattering six hits. His E.R.A. was slightly over 3.00 (3.02). His contributions to the team kept the Pirates in the thick of the division-title race until the final weekend of the season as they finished only 1½ games below the Phillies.

In 1979, the Pirates ended the Phillies string of division titles at three. Pittsburgh was able to edge the Montreal Expos by two games. The Pittsburgh staff was not an awesome one as John Candelaria led the team with 14 victories, but Bert was a stabilizing factor with a 12–5 record. The reason why the starters had low victory totals was the frequent use of the bullpen by manager Chuck Tanner. This would be a major complaint of Bert's because he always desired to finish what he started. This possibly was a major reason he did not pitch a shutout during the season, which would make it the first time that this would happen to him during his career. In the League Championship Series versus Cincinnati, he won the third game 7–1 going the distance. That game gave the Pirates the right to meet the Baltimore Orioles in the World Series.

In the Series, he held Baltimore to two runs in six innings during the second game. He didn't get credit for the win because the Pirates scored the winning run in the ninth. In the fifth game, he was called on an infrequent relief appearance. He took over when the Pirates were down 1–0 in the game and the Orioles ahead in the Series 3–1. Historians will look at this as the rallying point for the Pirates as Bert stopped the "Birds" for four innings and gained the win 7–1. The Bucs went on to take the next two games, giving them the championship, but a major contribution was Bert's yeoman relief effort in game five.

The following year, 1980, saw the decline of the Pirates as they yielded the championship to their division rivals, the Philadelphia Phillies. This was Blyleven's last year with the "Steel City Contingent." He was disillusioned with manager Chuck Tanner who was quick to yank a starter when it seemed that he was getting into trouble. Bert's record was a disastrous 8–13 with a 3.82 E.R.A. He did manage two shutouts in his eight wins.

At the end of the season, Bert was traded to the Cleveland Indians along with Manny Sanguillen for four players who were not highly regarded. Cleveland got the best of the deal.

The extended strike of 1981 forced the leagues to break into two halves. Cleveland, which was not a highly rated team, was often ridiculed. They had not been a true contender since the late 1950s. Despite all this, Bert proved that his last year in Pittsburgh was not a true barometer of his abilities. With Cleveland, he won 11 against 7 losses with a commendable E.R.A. of 2.89. His win total was not that bad as the league leader had only 14. He pitched one shutout against the Milwaukee Brewers in April, a four-hitter against a contingent of sluggers considered to be one of the league's best.

In 1982, Bert appeared in only four games with a 2–2 record. He was placed on the disabled list in May due to an elbow injury and did not return to active duty for the rest of the year.

Bert returned to active duty in 1983 with a 7–10 mark. The previous year of inactivity might have been a reason for his poor showing along with the fact that the Indians finished at the bottom of the American League East. He didn't record a shutout during the season and his E.R.A. was at a high 3.91. The injury and poor season seemed to indicate that he might be at the end of the proverbial line at 32 years of age.

The year 1984 dispelled all doubts as Bert rebounded with his best percentage year (19–7) at this point in his career. Cleveland escaped the cellar mainly because of his efforts. In his victory total, there were four shutouts, one of which was a one-hitter versus Texas. Larry Parrish singled to right to spoil his no-hitter. His E.R.A. improved to a respectable 2.87.

In 1985, Cleveland's ineptness was illustrated by the 102 losses they incurred. This was the worst season for the franchise since 1971 when they matched the futility of that team. In fact, the total number of losses matched the highest loss total the franchise had ever achieved. Bert was traded back to his original team, the Minnesota Twins, for three utility players. His record for the Indians was 9–11 with four shutouts. His last shutout for the Indians became the 50th of his career. On June 19, he blanked the California Angels, yielding just three hits for that milestone victory. After he arrived at Minnesota, he compiled an 8–5 mark with one shutout. That shutout, with the four at Cleveland, gave him the league lead in that department. Between the two teams, he was 17–16 with a 3.16 E.R.A. He broke the 200-strikeout mark for the first time since 1976. In fact, his 206 K's led the league, the first time in his career he was able to top that category. He also led in innings pitched (293⅔), complete games, and games started.

The 1986 Twins were a pathetic bunch who finished sixth with a 71–91 mark. This placed them 21 games behind division winner California but only four games ahead of last-place Seattle. Bert had a 17–14 record with a high E.R.A. of 4.01. This could be attributed to the home-run haven, the Metrodome, which he had to pitch in for the Twins. His victories led the team and they included three shutouts. Blyleven again led the league in innings pitched (271⅔) and broke the 200 mark in strikeouts (215). He was still productive after 17 seasons.

In 1987, the Twins rebounded dramatically. They not only won their division but upset the Detroit Tigers who sported the best record in baseball that year. The Twins polished Detroit off in a quick five-game series. Bert, despite another high E.R.A. (4.01), contributed greatly to the Twins' success as he came in at 15–12 with only one shutout. He was an important factor in the playoffs winning two games, including the clincher at Detroit. His E.R.A. for the league championship series was high at 4.05. This could be attributed to the two ballparks which were home-run paradises.

In the World Series, he posted a 1–1 record against the St. Louis Cardinals. Even with the one loss, which is the only time he lost in the post-season, he pitched effectively, indicated by his E.R.A. of 2.77.

The Twins' record improved in 1988 to 91–71, but it was not good enough to compete with the Oakland A's who blazed their way to the division crown and pennant. They left the Twins in their shadow as they won 104 games plus four more in the playoffs versus the Red Sox.

Despite the improvement in the Twins, Bert's season was a

disaster. His 10–17 record attested to that. His 5.43 E.R.A. was astronomical. Many thought that this was an indication that he was coming to the end of the line as a full-time player. He was hampered by a thumb injury, which kept him on the disabled list part of the year.

Bert became a free agent at the end of the season and decided to sign with the California Angels. He was dissatisfied with the wording of the contract that the Twins wanted to give him, so he opted for the sunnier times of southern California right outside his home in Villa Park.

The year 1989 was a resurrection for Bert as he turned in his best won-loss percentage ever (17–5 and .773). He led the league with five shutouts. This enabled him to lower his E.R.A. to under 3.00 at 2.73. It was the first time in five years he'd accomplish that. His stellar performance raised the Angels to third place only eight games behind the Oakland A's. On September 28, his last career shutout was versus the Kansas City Royals, blanking them 2–0 on seven hits.

In 1990, he posted an 8–7 mark but a sore shoulder kept his performance below par. His E.R.A. skyrocketed to over 5.00 (5.24). His age was a factor in the healing process and his shoulder injury kept him out for the entire 1991 season. He tried coming back in 1992 when he won 8 and lost 12. His shoulder miseries continued throughout the year, and the realization that it was over was quite obvious now. His E.R.A. was an uninspiring 4.74, and his strikeout total for the second year in a row was below 100.

The strike-shortened season of 1981 and his injury year of 1982 cost him the chance of breaking into the 300-win category. This would've made a more convincing argument that his name should be included with the immortals of the game. Notwithstanding, his record speaks for itself. These are class figures for a class act.

Bert Blyleven

Date	Team	Score	Hits	S.O.	Walks	Loser
8/26/70(H)	Bos.	7–0	4	8	4	Culp
4/7/71(H)	Mil.	4–0	4	6	2	Krausse
4/12/71(A)	K.C.	2–0	3	3	2	Drago
5/12/71(H)	Bos.	1–0	7	10	0	Culp
9/15/71(A)	Mil.	1–0	6	7	1	Lockwood
9/29/71(H)	Cal.	1–0	10	7	2	Wright
5/3/72(A)	Mil.	7–0	4	10	1	Slaton
5/26/72(H)	Tex.	7–0	5	7	3	Shellenback

Bert Blyleven

Date	Team	Score	Hits	S.O.	Walks	Loser
9/22/72(H)	Cal.	1-0	5	8	0	Messersmith
5/24/73(H)	K.C.	2-0	1	7	2	Drago
5/29/73(A)	Mil.	1-0	6	9	2	Slaton
6/8/73(A)	Bal.	2-0	2	5	3	McNally
6/16/73(A)	Det.	5-0	4	7	0	Coleman
6/21/73(H)	Cal.	1-0	8	7	1	Wright
6/29/73(A)	Cal.	4-0	4	2	1	Ryan
7/11/73(H)	Bos.	3-0	6	5	1	Curtis
9/4/73(A)	K.C.	6-0	4	4	3	Splittorf
9/14/73(A)	Chi.	6-0	4	12	1	Bahnsen
5/4/74(H)	Det.	10-0	4	6	2	Lolich
5/24/74(H)	Tex.	9-0	5	11	0	Clyde
9/25/74(A)	Oak.	1-0	4	5	1	Abbott
7/21/75(H)	N.Y.	3-0	4	5	1	Dobson
8/10/75(A)	Det.	4-0	4	6	1	Bare
8/27/75(A)	Mil.	1-0	6	13	1	Travers
6/21/76(A)	Oak.	1-0	1	8	4	Mitchel
6/26/76(H)	Chi.	1-0	10	5	2	Brett
7/26/76(A)	Minn.	3-0	2	9	1	Goltz
8/5/76(H)	Cal.	1-0	6	4	0	Ross
8/20/76(H)	Cle.	3-0	3	8	2	Bibby
9/25/76(H)	K.C.	1-0	4	11	2	Hassler
4/27/77(A)	K.C.	5-0	7	6	1	Leonard
5/3/77(A)	Det.	13-0	4	12	1	Ruhle
6/13/77(A)	Cle.	3-0	4	6	1	Eckersley
7/26/77(A)	Tor.	14-0	4	6	5	Clancy
9/22/77(A)	Cal.	6-0	0	7	1	Hartzell
4/26/78(A)	N.Y.	1-0	6	8	4	Myrick
5/20/78(A)	Mon.	6-0	3	8	3	Twitchell
6/25/78(A)	N.Y.	4-0	5	5	2	Espinosa
8/29/78(A)	Cin.	5-0	4	8	2	Lacoss
5/31/80(H)	N.Y.	5-0	7	6	1	Swan
8/16/80(H)	Mon.	5-0	2	12	1	Sanderson
4/18/81(A)	Mil.	5-0	4	8	0	Slaton
4/6/84(A)	K.C.	2-0	4	8	2	Gubicza
6/24/84(A)	Sea.	5-0	2	5	1	Stoddard
7/13/84(A)	Tex.	5-0	1	5	5	Mason
9/26/84(H)	Sea.	1-0	7	6	1	Beattie
5/3/85(H)	Tex.	4-0	4	9	3	Mason
5/12/85(A)	Tex.	6-0	6	1	1	Noles
5/27/85(A)	Mil.	8-0	3	10	0	Darwin
6/19/85(H)	Cal.	2-0	3	7	0	Slaton
8/17/85(H)	Sea.	2-0	3	8	4	Wills
7/13/86(H)	N.Y.	5-0	3	8	1	Tewksbury
8/11/86(A)	Cal.	2-0	3	6	2	Sutton
9/2/86(H)	Mil.	4-0	5	8	1	Vuckovich
6/15/87(A)	Mil.	5-0	4	6	2	Wegman

Date	Team	Score	Hits	S.O.	Walks	Loser
4/16/89(A)	Sea.	10–0	4	6	1	Campbell
7/18/89(A)	Tor.	1–0	5	6	1	Key
8/2/89(A)	Sea.	7–0	6	6	3	Reed
8/24/89(A)	K.C.	5–0	4	4	1	Aquino
9/28/89(H)	K.C.	2–0	7	6	1	McWilliams

American League

Year	Home	Away	Total
70	1	0	1
71	3	2	5
72	2	1	3
73	3	6	9
74	3	1	4
75	1	2	3
76	4	2	6
77	0	5	5
81	0	1	1
84	1	3	4
85	3	2	5
86	2	1	3
87	0	1	1
89	1	4	5
	23	31	54

National League

Year	Home	Away	Total
78	0	4	4
80	2	0	2
	2	4	6
	25	35	60

Bert Blyleven's Shutouts by Team

American League

Bal.	Bos.	Cal.	Chi.	Cle.	Det.	K.C.	Mil.	Min.	N.Y.	Oak.	Sea.	Tex.	Tor.	Total
1	3	8	2	2	4	8	9	1	2	2	5	5	2	54

National League

Cin.	Mon.	N.Y.	Total
1	2	3	6

Both Leagues
60

Shutouts by Team Finish

American League

1	2	3	4	5	6	7	Total
7	10	7	6	9	11	4	54

National League

1	2	3	4	5	6	Total
0	1	1	1	1	2	6

Don Sutton

A Quiet and Consistent Performer

Don Sutton's career can be compared to an artist's whose work cannot be appreciated until the final stroke of paint has been applied. He, like only seven others, can boast the final stats of at least 250 victories, 50 or more shutouts, and over 3,000 strikeouts. In fact, Sutton had 324 victories, which in the 20th century places him sixth on the all-time list, tied with Nolan Ryan. His 3,574 K's ranks him seventh in that category. The 58 shutouts he carded leaves him tied for tenth place with Ed Walsh. These accomplishments are quite impressive and finally granted him admission into the Hall of Fame. It makes one wonder why the baseball writers who vote for the candidates did not do their homework properly and grant Sutton his just position among the game's elite. They would then have granted Sutton his just position among the game's elite sooner.

When Sutton came up in his first year, the legendary Sandy Koufax noticed him as someone who couldn't miss. Koufax's prediction was never more accurate and Don continued to compile impressive numbers.

The Dodgers signed Sutton as a free agent back in September 1964. They assigned him to Santa Barbara (Class A California League). He pitched ten games with an 8–1 record with a sparkling 1.50 E.R.A. This prompted a move up to Albuquerque of the Texas League. The quick rise did not hamper his performance and he adapted to the more challenging competition. He sported a 15–6 record in 21 games showing a 2.78 E.R.A. His outstanding achievement won him the Texas League Player of the Year Award.

The following year, 1966, he was promoted to the Dodgers where he was thrust into the company of Koufax, Drysdale, and Osteen. The Dodgers the previous year had won the World Championship and with that array of pitching talent were going to be in the thick of things.

Don impressed manager Walter Alston enough that he started him in the team's fourth game on April 14. The results were disheartening as he bowed to Houston and Bob Bruce 4–2. Four days later, he was rewarded with another start versus Houston. The outcome was more gratifying and Don reaped his first major league victory, winning 6–3. He defeated the future Hall of Famer Robin Roberts in that encounter. Don's final figures for the year were a 12–12 record with a 2.99 E.R.A. He also fanned 209 batters for the year, which placed him seventh in that category. This was the era of strong pitching in the National League, which could flaunt the names of Sandy Koufax, Juan Marichal, Bob Gibson, Jim Maloney, and Jim Bunning. In fact, Sutton's first-year performance surpassed that of the Dodgers' number-two man, Don Drysdale, whose 13–16 record (3.42 E.R.A.) and 177 K's were an underachievement compared to Sutton's. Included in Don's victories were two shutouts. His first career one came on May 11 versus the Philadelphia Phillies, defeating them 5–0 on six hits. His other shutout was a splendid two-hitter versus the Cincinnati Reds. His performance impressed *The Sporting News*, and they selected him National League rookie pitcher of the year.

The year 1967 saw the Dodgers without their stellar performer, Sandy Koufax, who retired prematurely with an arthritic condition in his elbow after the season. This left the Dodgers without the soul of their team, which showed in the standings as they collapsed to eighth place, 16 games below .500. The remaining nucleus of the once-dominant pitching staff wasn't enough to keep Los Angeles afloat. Drysdale was again at 13–16, Osteen made .500 at 17–17, and Sutton logged in at 11–15 with an unimpressive E.R.A. of 3.94. He did chalk up three shutouts during the year. His best efforts were a two-hitter versus Cincinnati and a 1–0 victory over Philadelphia. With his impressive rookie year behind him, it seemed that he was now bitten by the sophomore jinx.

In 1968, Don made a trip back to the minors to Spokane during

April to work on his mechanics. He was back quickly after splitting two decisions. He made his first start on April 29, a winning one versus St. Louis. The Dodgers again struggled, falling into a seventh-place tie with the Phillies. Don duplicated his record in 1967, but his E.R.A. was more than one run lower at 2.60. His 15 losses were not a true indication of his worth and potential. This was the year of the pitcher, with teammate Don Drysdale reeling off six consecutive shutouts and topping Walter Johnson's string of 56 scoreless innings. Bob Gibson posted 13 shutouts, the highest single-season total since Grover Cleveland Alexander's 16 in 1916.

Don had only two shutouts himself. Because of Los Angeles' weak offense, Don struggled to gain victories. Ironically, his two blankings occurred in September, when the toll of the season wears down hurlers.

Regarding Sutton's 15 losses, the statistics do not lie. The Dodgers only scored five runs in 11 of his losses (seven of those were shutouts). Many of his mound opponents were the aces of the opposition (Seaver, Marichal, and Gaylord Perry).

Division play began in 1969 when the two leagues expanded to 12 teams each. The divisions were set up so that each division winner would play for the right to meet the other league's representative in the World Series. Because of the low batting averages of 1968, the powers of baseball decided on a shorter strike zone and lowering the pitching mound. They felt that this was critical to install more potency into the offensive phase of the game. Regardless of these changes, 15 pitchers, representing both leagues, broke the magic barrier of 20 or more victories. This could be attributed to the watering down of the competition due to the expansion. The Dodgers had two of these 20-game winners in Bill Singer and Claude Osteen, with Sutton contributing a 17–18 mark. Among his victories were four shutouts which didn't do that much for his E.R.A. of 3.47. The shutout of the San Francisco Giants on May 1 was the best of his career so far. He doled out only one hit, beating them 5–0. Jim Davenport singled to spoil his gem. This strong Giant team was a serious contender until the end of the season. They were loaded with good hitters, including the "Frisco Willies" (Mays and McCovey).

After the 1969 season, Don's record stood at 51–60 lifetime. It didn't look as if Koufax's appraisal was going to be an accurate one. As soon as the 1970s began, Sutton emerged as one of the quality pitchers of the decade.

In 1970, the Dodgers got off the skids and posted a winning

record (87–44) for the first time since 1966. It was also Sutton's first winning season in the majors. He finished the year at 15–13, but his E.R.A. was a high 4.08 despite having four shutouts. His victory total enabled the Dodgers to finish in second place, a distant 14½ games behind the Reds who were witnessing the birth of the "Big Red Machine." This was Sparky Anderson's first pennant winner.

As for Don, his best games were a two-hit shutout of Houston in April and two 1–0 victories, one versus the Pirates in June and another against the defending world champion New York Mets. In that game he went ten innings, scattering only five hits.

In 1971, the Big Red Machine bogged down, settling for a fourth-place tie (four games under .500). The Dodgers battled down to the wire but were unable to overcome a once-large lead by their arch rivals, the Giants. The Giants secured the division title by winning on the last day of the season and edging the Dodgers by one game. Don had his best year to date and came in at 17–12. His E.R.A. was an impressive 2.55 aided by four shutouts. The game he pitched against Houston on June 19 was a classic performance in which he gave up one hit. Jimmy Wynn spoiled Don's bid for fame by singling in the sixth inning.

The year 1972 saw the first modern-day baseball strike, which lasted 13 days; it was harbinger of future labor strikes to come. The Big Red Machine was reassembled through a trade with Houston, who got future Hall of Famer Joe Morgan. The Dodgers came in third, 10½ games back, but no one could have blamed Sutton for their failure to move up. He logged in with 19 wins versus 9 losses and probably would have broken the 20-game mark if he hadn't missed two starts due to the strike. He had a league-leading nine shutouts and tied Nolan Ryan of California for the major league lead. Two of his victories were by the score of 1–0. In one of these games he defeated the Giants by yielding only three hits in a game that went 11 innings. His E.R.A. was an outstanding 2.08 as he completed his 33 starts. He showed great stamina as he compiled 273 innings pitched. His E.R.A. and innings pitched placed him second in both categories. This year, Steve Carlton (Cy Young winner) dominated the majority of the league's pitching stats.

Don also notched his 25th career shutout on August 6 as he polished off San Francisco 6–0. His career record was now on the positive side and he now had a winning mark with over 100 victories. He was now a pitcher to be held in high regard.

The next year, 1973, the Dodgers geared themselves for the

pennant with the addition of Andy Messerschmidt, whom they acquired from the neighboring California Angels for Frank Robinson. In 1972 they had acquired Tommy John for Dick Allen. With these additions, the pitching staff was highly formidable along with an infield that would be together for a decade. Steve Garvey, who split the duties at first base in 1973 with Bill Buckner, anchored the infield, as would Davey Lopes at second, Bill Russell at shortstop, and Ron Cey at third.

The Dodgers made a strong run at the Reds but fell short by 3½ games. Sutton emerged as the ace of the staff with 18 wins versus 10 losses. His E.R.A. was a strong 2.43, bolstered by three shutouts, two by the score of 1–0. In each of these games he showed flawless control by not walking a batter.

In 1974, Los Angeles broke through and won the Western Division by four games over the Reds. Don had another fine season as he logged in at 19–9. His E.R.A. was slightly high at 3.23, but with the addition of a steady infield and improved offensive support, he could pitch more relaxed. He netted five shutouts, two of those once again by 1–0 scores. His shutout on May 9 versus San Diego was another disappointment for a bid at no-hit fame. Johnny Grubb deprived him of his moment of glory.

In the league championship series, Sutton was given the assignment of opening the series in Pittsburgh. He was brilliant as he went the distance for a 3–0 win, spreading out only four hits. The game wasn't clinched until the ninth inning when Los Angeles pushed across two insurance runs. This was the first league championship victory in Dodgers history. The Dodgers made short work of the Pirates and defeated them in four games.

The World Series opened versus Oakland, with Don starting the second game. He had the A's stymied until the ninth inning, leading them 3–0. He faltered and had to be relieved by Mike Marshall in the ninth, saving the win for him. In game five, he gave up two runs early and was not charged with the loss when Los Angeles tied the game in the sixth. Oakland rallied to capture the Series in that game. Sutton's performance was a worthy one as he gave up nine hits in 13 innings and posted an E.R.A. of 2.77. His outings in post-season play were admirable. His victory in game two of the World Series was the first Dodgers World Series win since 1965, when Koufax won the seventh game.

In 1975, the Dodgers failed to defend their championship. The Big Red Machine roared to the pennant, leaving Los Angeles 20 games behind. Don's record was 16–13, as he won 15 games or more for the eighth year in a row. His E.R.A. was again under 3.00 (2.87). He pitched four shutouts, with the first coming on April 11. Possibly his best-pitched game was his next start against Cincinnati on April 15 at Los Angeles.

In that game he walked Joe Morgan on a 3–2 pitch. He then enticed Johnny Bench to hit into a double play. The next 17 batters were retired effortlessly. He faced Bench in the seventh inning with two outs. It looked like he was going to succeed in getting that elusive no-hitter which escaped him on three previous occasions. With two outs in the seventh inning, the first pitch to Bench was quickly deposited into the left field seats, breaking up his chance again for fame. He proceeded to retire the next seven hitters for a 3–1 victory. The home run, Bench's first of the year, also stopped a string of 17 scoreless innings.

In 1976, the Dodgers improved as they cut the deficit between the Reds and themselves to ten games. Sutton had his greatest winning season by finally breaking the 20-win mark (21–10). His E.R.A. was 3.06 with four shutouts. His victory total was two behind Steve Carlton and tied with Randy Jones, who won the Cy Young Award. Don's efforts earned him a distant third in the balloting. Still, he was the main cog on the Dodgers pitching staff.

Finally, in 1977 the Dodgers succeeded in halting the Reds' dominance in the National League as they would cakewalk to the pennant by ten games. Sutton's victory total fell below 15 for the first time since 1969. His 14–8 record gave him a percentage greater than the team's. Out of Don's 14 wins, there were three shutouts, all happening after July 1. He pitched another heartbreaking one-hitter versus the Giants on August 18 with Marc Hill getting a single to thwart the masterpiece. This gave him a career total of five one-hitters. Never again would he come close to achieving a pitcher's dream. Even with his three shutouts, his E.R.A. went up to 3.19. This Dodgers team was a high-powered offense and they led the league with 191 homers. This was the first time a team had four men hitting 30 or more homers in a single season (Steve Garvey with 33, Reggie Smith with 32, Ron Cey with 30, and Dusty Baker with 30).

In the league championship series, Sutton started the second game versus the Phillies, who were ahead 1–0. Sutton scattered nine hits as he went the distance, winning 7–1. This seemed to instill a confidence within the Dodgers, as they turned around and won the next two games to capture the pennant. The Series pitted them against the Yankees.

In the world championship, Sutton was given the honor of starting the opener. He left the game tied at 3–3, and the Yankees would win in the 12th inning. Sutton was again called to stem the Yankee tide in the fifth game as the New Yorkers held a commanding 3–1 lead in the games. Sutton was given more than ample support to breeze by the "Bronxites" 12–4. The Series was won by the Yankees on the might of Reggie Jackson's three homers in game six.

The following year the Dodgers and the Reds staged a dogfight for the pennant, but Los Angeles prevailed by 2½ games over their persistent rivals. The Dodgers strength was prominent in their pitching with four hurlers winning 15 or more games. Don broke that barrier, as his final mark was 15–11. His E.R.A. was quite high at 3.55, with two shutouts.

In the league championship series the Dodgers met the Phillies, again with the same results. The only game Los Angeles lost out of the four played was the third and Sutton took that loss. He was hit hard as the Phils, behind Steve Carlton, gained some respectability in winning 9–4.

Don's performance in the World Series was more disastrous as he took a defeat in the third game and again in the sixth game. It didn't help him to be pitted versus Ron Guidry and Jim "Catfish" Hunter. Regardless of that, he was hit rather severely as he gave up 17 hits in 12 innings.

The year 1979 saw the Dodgers crash to third, four games under .500. This was the first time that they had finished in the red since 1969. Sutton also came in with a deficit at 12–15. It seemed that the team's success was contingent upon Don's performance. Don's E.R.A. was an unimpressive 3.82 with only one shutout to his credit, but it was a memorable one. On August 10th he blanked the San Francisco Giants 9–0 on five hits, making it his 50th career shutout.

The Dodgers rebounded in 1980 from their disastrous season by battling to a first-place tie in the West with the Houston Astros. A one-game playoff for the division title was scheduled in Los Angeles, with Houston taking the title by a 7–1 score behind knuckleballer Joe Niekro.

The improvement in the Dodgers was due to the revitalization of their pitching staff. Sutton's record of 13–5 was a major contribution in keeping the team close to the top. He led the league in E.R.A. at 2.21. He pitched two shutouts, both against the Giants, giving up four hits in each game.

As 1981 approached, the year of the free agent was in full effect.

Dave Winfield signed a fantastic contract with the New York Yankees and became a two-million-dollar-a-year man for almost a decade. Sutton also opted for the free-agent route and cast his lot with Houston. The strike of 1981 brought the sport to a standstill for almost two months. The season would be rearranged into two halves with the two winners of the National League West facing off—the Dodgers from the first half versus the Astros from the second half. Don contributed greatly to Houston's success and at 11-9 tied for the team lead in victories with Nolan Ryan. He had another good year in the E.R.A. department at 2.60 with two shutouts—in an abbreviated season! For some untold reason, the Astros refused to use Don in the playoffs versus the Dodgers as they succumbed in five games after having a 2-0 lead. The Dodgers would go on to not only to capture the pennant but also the World Series.

In 1982, with the labor strike settled for the time being, Houston descended to a fifth-place finish, going eight games under .500. Sutton had a healthy 13-8 record and led the team in winning percentage. His E.R.A. was a strong 3.00, but he failed to pitch a shutout for Houston.

Near the end of 1982, Houston saw the chance to dispose of his high salary, which was a high risk for his age (37). The Milwaukee Brewers were in a fight for the American League East title and were looking for help down the stretch. Sutton was available and Houston waived him to the "Beer City."

His acquisition was a stroke of genius by their manager because Sutton secured the Eastern Division title for the "Brew team." He won four of five decisions and shut out Detroit (7-0) on September 7. He meted out seven hits in that game, walked none, and struck out nine.

The final game of the season saw the Brewers and Orioles deadlocked for first place on the strength of three consecutive wins by the Orioles over the Brewers. The final game of the season was played at Baltimore with Sutton matched against Jim Palmer. Don clinched the division title by edging the O's 10-2.

In the league championship series, the Brewers fell behind the Angels and came limping home for the final three games. Manager Harvey Kuenn handed the ball to Sutton in the third game and he had the Californians shut out going into the eighth inning. He weakened and gave up three runs, but Pete Ladd quelled the uprising and saved the win for him. This effort by Don rallied the Brewers and they captured the remaining two games for the pennant.

In the World Series he was the starter in the second game for Milwaukee. They were already one game up on the St. Louis Cardinals. Sutton was leading the Cards 4–2 as the game entered the sixth inning. St. Louis rallied to tie the score; Don was lifted for a pinch hitter in the seventh and escaped the loss. The Cards pushed the winning run across in the eighth to secure the win. In the sixth game, with Milwaukee ahead three games to two, he was soundly beaten 13–1. The Cardinals went on to annex the world championship. Don did have a commendable year and finished with a respectable 17–9 record between Houston and Milwaukee.

In 1983, the Brewers failed to defend their title and slid all the way to fifth place. They were still a winning ball club but Sutton had a poor year. He was 8–13 with a high E.R.A. of 4.08. It was the first time in his career that he didn't pitch at least one shutout during a season.

In 1984, Don improved as he went 14–12 while the Brewers fell into last place, 27 games under .500. Don led the team in victories and had the best E.R.A. of any starter (3.77). Again he failed to pitch a shutout.

In 1985, he was traded by Milwaukee to Oakland for Ray Burris. The Brewers felt that the 40-year-old Sutton didn't figure in their plans for the future. He pitched superbly for Oakland, winning 13 and losing 8 with one shutout against the Chicago White Sox. During the latter part of the year, the California Angels needed pitching help in their quest for the division title. They secured Don's contract but he was only able to split four decisions. The Angels fell one game short of the Royals, who went on to win the World Series. Don's final figures for the year were 15–10, which were not bad for a 40-year-old.

Don was a major contributor to the Angels' success in 1986 when he helped them to win the American League's western title. His 15–11 record gave him a winning percentage higher than the team's, but his 3.74 E.R.A. was nothing to rave about. The year also saw some milestones for Don that would add luster to an already impressive career. On June 9, Sutton hooked up in a duel with Tom Seaver of the White Sox. He emerged as the victor, shutting out the Chisox on two hits. This was his last career shutout, which put him ahead of Ed Walsh.

On June 19, he defeated the Texas Rangers 5–1 for his 300th career victory, putting him in the same class as his contemporaries Carlton, Seaver, Niekro, and Perry. In his book, *The Ballplayers*, Mike Shatzkin noted that in a game on June 28, Sutton was matched against Phil Niekro of the Cleveland Indians. This was the first time that 300-game winners faced each other since Tim Keefe and "Pud" Galvin were mound opponents in 1892. Neither Sutton nor Niekro were involved in the final decision.

In the league championship series versus Boston, he started the third game and dueled a young Roger Clemens (MVP and Cy Young winner that year) for six innings, losing 1–0. He held the Red Sox at bay until the Angels rallied and defeated Boston in the 11th. He relieved in the deciding seventh game as the Red Sox coasted to clinch the pennant, winning 8–1. This was after they were down three games to one.

The Angels fell heavily to a sixth-place tie 12 games under .500. Don held on to finish the year at 11–11 with an extremely high E.R.A. of 4.70.

The following year was his last. He finished up with his original team (the Dodgers) where he posted a 3–6 mark. An elbow injury finished his season and ultimately his career.

This was the only time he missed part of a season due to an injury. His ability to avoid injuries was due to his zeal for being physically fit.

In looking through his career, many will say he was able to reach the numbers he did because of his longevity. That, in reality, is to his credit. Others have put up equal or superior statistics due to longevity such as Nolan Ryan, but that wasn't a deterrent towards Sutton's admission to the Hall of Fame. So why should Sutton's career be tarnished by such palaver? The door to Cooperstown did swing widely open to allow such a consistent performer to enter.

Don Sutton

Date	Team	Score	Hits	S.O.	Walks	Loser
5/11/66(A)	Phi.	5–0	6	8	1	Jackson
8/16/66(H)	Cin.	2–0	2	8	1	Nuxhall
5/17/67(H)	Hou.	7–0	7	2	0	Ceullar
6/27/67(A)	Cin.	9–0	2	11	0	Ellis
7/30/67(H)	Phi.	1–0	8	7	2	Short
9/4/68(A)	Phi.	3–0	3	12	4	L. Jackson
9/14/68(H)	Atl.	3–0	6	6	1	Pappas
4/27/69(H)	Atl.	10–0	4	7	2	Jarvis
5/1/69(A)	S.F.	5–0	1	8	2	Sadecki
5/24/69(H)	Stl.	5–0	9	2	1	Torres
5/28/69(A)	Mon.	6–0	5	6	1	Robertson

Date	Team	Score	Hits	S.O.	Walks	Loser
4/13/70(A)	Hou.	2–0	2	4	4	Lamaster
5/10/70(A)	Phi.	7–0	4	4	2	G. Jackson
6/16/70(H)	Pit.	1–0	4	5	3	Veale
7/17/70(H)	N.Y.	1–0	5	12	3	McGraw
5/12/71(H)	Atl.	5–0	5	5	1	Stone
6/19/71(H)	Hou.	4–0	1	3	4	Billingham
8/13/71(H)	Mon.	2–0	6	6	2	Morton
9/19/71(A)	Atl.	4–0	6	5	1	Reed
4/19/72(A)	Atl.	4–0	2	2	1	Niekro
4/30/72(H)	N.Y.	7–0	7	6	1	Capra
6/3/72(H)	Stl.	1–0	7	6	0	Spinks
6/28/72(H)	Hou.	5–0	2	9	2	Reuss
7/21/72(H)	Phi.	3–0	5	5	1	Reynolds
8/6/72(H)	S.D.	6–0	6	2	1	Norman
9/16/72(A)	Hou.	10–0	7	6	3	Forsch
9/22/72(H)	S.F.	1–0	3	11	4	Willoughby
9/27/77(H)	S.D.	2–0	3	8	2	Arlin
4/21/73(H)	S.F.	1–0	9	7	0	Bryant
6/26/73(H)	S.D.	7–0	2	5	1	Jones
7/16/73(A)	Pit.	1–0	6	9	0	Briles
4/5/74(H)	S.D.	8–0	6	8	2	Grief
5/9/74(A)	S.D.	6–0	1	5	2	Grief
5/14/74(H)	Hou.	1–0	4	9	3	Dierker
8/24/74(H)	Stl.	3–0	7	8	1	Curtis
9/10/74(A)	Atl.	1–0	4	6	1	Morton
4/11/75(A)	Hou.	7–0	4	9	1	Griffin
5/2/75(H)	S.D.	3–0	5	9	2	Spillner
5/11/75(A)	Pit.	7–0	8	2	0	Brett
8/5/75(H)	Atl.	5–0	5	3	3	Niekro
4/29/76(H)	Stl.	4–0	5	4	1	Falcone
5/11/76(A)	Stl.	4–0	5	3	0	Curtis
9/12/76(H)	Atl.	2–0	4	5	0	Moret
9/27/76(H)	Hou.	2–0	4	3	2	Larson
7/4/77(A)	S.F.	4–0	3	6	4	Halicki
8/18/77(H)	S.F.	7–0	1	5	4	Barr
8/28/77(H)	Stl.	11–0	6	5	0	Forsch
6/18/78(H)	Mon.	5–0	6	6	1	Twitchell
9/15/78(H)	Atl.	5–0	6	6	1	Solomon
8/10/79(A)	S.F.	9–0	5	6	3	Knepper
4/22/80(H)	S.F.	6–0	4	8	1	Knepper
7/4/80(H)	S.F.	4–0	4	3	0	Ripley
5/13/81(H)	Stl.	3–0	5	4	1	Shirley
9/11/81(H)	S.F.	6–0	5	6	1	Blue
9/22/81(H)	Atl.	3–0	3	3	0	Perry
9/7/82(H)	Det.	4–0	7	9	0	Peatry
6/26/85(H)	Chi.	10–0	4	3	2	Bannister
6/9/86(A)	Chi.	3–0	2	8	2	Seaver

Don Sutton

National League

Year	Home	Away	Total
66	1	1	2
67	2	1	3
68	1	1	2
69	3	1	4
70	2	2	4
71	4	0	4
72	7	2	9
73	2	1	3
74	3	2	5
75	2	2	4
76	3	1	4
77	2	1	3
78	2	0	2
79	0	1	1
80	2	0	2
81	3	0	3
	39	16	55

American League

Year	Home	Away	Total
82	1	0	1
85	1	0	1
86	0	1	1
	2	1	3
	41	17	58

Don Sutton's Shutouts by Team

National League

Atl.	Chi.	Cin.	Hou.	L.A.	Mon.	N.Y.	Phi.	Pit.	Stl.	S.D.	S.F.	Total
10	0	2	8	0	3	2	5	3	7	6	9	55

American League

Chi.	Det.	Total
2	1	3

Both Leagues
58

Don Sutton's Shutouts by Team Finish

National League

1	2	3	4	5	6	7	8	9	10	Total
3	5	10	13	11	10	2	0	1	0	55

American League

4	5	Total
2	1	3

Ed Walsh
King of the Spitballers

During the first two decades of the 20th century, stars like Jack Chesbro, Ed Cicotte, Burleigh Grimes and Carl Mays made the spitball an integral part of their repertoire. Ed Walsh was probably the most consistent user of the pitch, but in 1920 it would be banned because of the only fatality that ever occurred in a major league baseball game. Carl Mays of the Yankees unleashed an errant pitch that found its way to Ray Chapman's skull, felling him instantly. The thud of the ball making contact with Chapman's cranium was heard, so it was said, throughout the stadium. Many felt that the act was intentional, which created a lot of animosity toward Mays and possibly is the reason he never made the Hall of Fame. The following day Chapman died from the infamous beaning. His death created a ban on the pitch and it would only be allowed by those who already used it. Anyone new coming into the majors could not use the pitch.

Prior to that, the spit ball had its moments of glory as well as days of infamy. Ed Walsh learned it in the majors and rode it successfully into the Hall of Fame. Jack Chesbro lost the pennant in 19-04 for the N.Y. Highlanders when he uncorked a spit ball that sailed over his catcher's head, giving the Boston Pilgrims the pennant on the last day of the season. Ed Walsh, once he perfected it, used it 90 percent of the time, making him one of the most feared pitchers from 1906 to 1912.

Walsh was born in a small town (Plains) a little northeast of Wilkes-Barre, Pennsylvania, which was in the heart of coal mining country. He followed the long list of ball players who migrated from the Keystone State, which included Christy Mathewson, Eddie Plank, Rube Waddell, and Honus Wagner. It seemed that the threat of living one's life in the dark shadows of the coal mines created a strong incentive to succeed in the major leagues, since all of the above mentioned reached the Hall of Fame.

Walsh started his professional career with Wilkes-Barre in the Pennsylvania League in 1902 with an unimpressive 1–2 record. The following year (1903) he moved to Meridian of the Connecticut League where he showed a vast improvement with a 15–5 mark. Pitching the following year for Newark of the Eastern League, he came in with nine wins and five losses. The statistical records in the earlier part of the century were not revered in the minors, so many of the pitching categories were neglected and no reference for them can be validated. Walsh was promoted to the Chicago White Sox in 1904 with an unimpressive minor league record. The White Sox won the initial pennant in 1901 for the American League, which opted for major league status. They were solid in the pitching department. Their rotation included Nick Altrock and Frank Owens who both won 21 games. Frank Smith and Guy "Doc" White chipped in with 16 victories. Roy Patterson was the fifth starter with a 9–9 record. All five hurlers were 27 years old or younger, so when Walsh joined the club it seemed inconceivable that he would be able to break into the rotation. This team finished only six games behind the pennant-winning Boston Pilgrims and 4½ shy of the New York Highlanders.

When he came to the White Sox, Ed had only the regular assortment of pitches (fastball and curve). Something happened after the team's first 40 games that would be a blessing to Ed Walsh. Manager "Nixey" Callahan was replaced at the helm by center fielder Fielder Jones. Jones made Walsh and an undistinguished 27-year-old rookie pitcher roommates. Elmer Stricklet, who only posted a 0–1 mark with Chicago and was let go at the end of the season, had a paramount impact on Ed. Stricklet pitched the next three years for Brooklyn in the National League, sporting a 35–51 record. His best year was a 14–18 record in 1905. Stricklet taught Walsh how to throw the spit ball, and the pitch help skyrocket Ed's career.

During Ed's rookie year, he won six and lost three. He still hadn't mastered the "saliva sphere." He made his debut on May 7, and on

May 19 he pitched the first of his career shutouts, whitewashing the hapless Washington Senators 5–0 on two hits.

One of the starters, Doc White, during the latter part of the season pitched five consecutive shutouts in September. This was a record that stood 64 years until Don Drysdale pitched six in a row in 1968. White's September heroics were even more fantastic as he added another one later, giving him six in one month. This record still stands, but Walsh tied it twice. Amazingly, White started the month with only one shutout to his credit.

In 1905, the Sox made a strong run against the Philadelphia A's, finishing second, only two games in arrears. The oddity of the race was that they tied the A's in victories (92). The White Sox had only six pitchers during the whole season. Frank Owen and Nick Altrock again won over 20 games each. Frank Smith and Doc White each contributed 19. Walsh improved his status on the staff by winning eight and losing three. He replaced Roy Patterson as the fifth starter. Ed again pitched one shutout against the Washington Senators. This time the game was close, and they lost 2–0 with six hits to their credit. Ed posted an E.R.A. of 2.17, which was higher than the team's 1.99. This was the first time in modern baseball that a team had a combined E.R.A. of under 2.00!

Ed started 13 games and completed 9. He had a dual role as a spot starter and reliever. In the nine games as a reliever he had only one save. This was an era where most pitchers finished what they started. It seems that Ed's chances of cracking the top four starters were remote.

The Chicago team was strong on pitching and fielding, but not hitting; the name "Hitless Wonders" would be forever imprinted in their history. In 1906, when the moniker was attached to the team, they had a team .230 batting average and a paltry six home runs as a team! With that meager offensive support, the pitching had to be superior, and it was during this period.

In 1906, the American League pennant was another hotly contested, down-to-the-wire spectacle. It was between the White Sox and the Highlanders, and the Chisox prevailed at the end by three games. This was the year Walsh perfected the spit ball and it propelled him to the fourth starter in the rotation. Owens was again a 20-game winner for the third consecutive year. Walsh came in at a 17–13 mark with his win total topping his two previous years combined. His contribution down the stretch was phenomenal. His 1.88 E.R.A. was well under 2.00, but it didn't place him in the top five. Teammate

Doc White led the league with a 1.52. The White Sox set an American League record of 19 consecutive wins, which was tied by the 1947 Yankees; seven of those wins were recorded by Walsh.

Ed had a remarkable ten shutouts in his 17 victories, which was more than half of his victory total. Ed's first shutout of the year was a splendid one-hitter on May 6 versus Cleveland and their ace, Addie Joss. Walsh and Joss hooked up in another game two years later which would go down in baseball annals as one of the classic pitching duels of all time. In the game of May 6, Cleveland catcher Harry Bemis spoiled the masterpiece by getting a hit with no outs in the ninth inning. Shortstop George Davis missed snaring the ball by less than a foot as it went into left field. Walsh gave up one walk in the first inning to Bill Bradley.

His next shutout was on June 14, beating Washington 2–0. As the race entered into August, Ed's spit ball must have picked up added moisture and he saturated the hitters' bats. He pitched six shutouts during that month, tying Doc White's record set in 1904. On August 3, he defeated the Boston Pilgrims 1–0. In that game, he was aided by two outstanding plays to keep his no-hitter intact. Shortstop George Davis speared a line drive while player/manager Fielder Jones flagged down another line drive in center field. In the ninth inning, Jack Hayden dumped a looping fly in the outfield, marring Ed's quest for fame. His game of August 27 was another one-hitter. This was an abbreviated contest that went only six innings versus the Philadelphia A's. Topsy Hartsel got the hit in that game to erase any hope of a no-hitter. Ed's two shutouts gave him ten for the season. He pitched eight during the last two months of the year. The ten also gave him a share of the modern major league record and he tied Cy Young's total, which was registered in 1904.

The closeness of the American League pennant race was contrary to the results in the National League. The White Sox's crosstown rivals, the Chicago Cubs, won their title by leapfrogging away from the rest of their competitors. They won by 20 games over the defending world champions, the New York Giants, as they set a victory record and percentage that still stands (116–36). This was the Tinkers, Evers, and Chance combination that won four pennants in a five-year span. They were led by player/manager Fred Chance, who had the luxury of an extremely deep pitching staff. All six starters had at least 12 victories. The staff was headed by Mordecai "Three Finger" Brown, who led the team with a 26–6 record. Jack Pfiester was 20–8, and Ed Ruelach led the league in percentage with a 19–4 mark. They added Orville Overall and Jack Taylor through trades. This staff was any manager's dream.

When it was realized that the two Chicago entrants would meet in the World Series, it was assumed the Cubs would blow away the weak-hitting Sox. The "Windy City Series" would raise some eyebrows with the final results.

When the Series started, the games were played alternately at each team's park. The opener was at the Cub's arena, where Nick Altock bested Brown 2–1. The second game saw the Cubs rebound on the strength of Ed Ruelbach's one-hitter (the very first in World Series play) and they won 7–1. Game three was played again at the Cub's ballpark, and Ed Walsh distinguished himself by blanking the Bruins 3–0 on only two hits. In that game he fanned 12 batters, a record that stood until 1929 when Howard Ehmke of the Philadelphia A's surpassed the mark by one.

With the Series tied at two games apiece, Walsh was called on to put the Sox back into the lead. He did this, winning 8–6. His defense became porous and they committed six errors in the game. The "hitless ones" showed an amazing display of hitting in this game and in the next day's clincher when they combined for 26 hits and 16 runs! Walsh came out the most impressive in the summary of the Series, with two victories and a sparkling 1.20 E.R.A. The Sox victory was considered by many through the years to be the biggest World Series upset until 1969, when the New York Mets shocked the baseball world.

In 1907 the Detroit Tigers edged out the Philadelphia A's by 1½ games. The oddity of this pennant race was that the Bengals lost one game more than the "Mackmen." The White Sox made a valiant try, finishing third (5½ games from the top).

Walsh broke into the 20-game circle for the first time as he came in at 24–18. He led the league in several pitching categories (games, 56; games started, 46; complete games, 37; innings pitched, 422). He also led the league in E.R.A. at 1.60, which was backed by six shutouts. This yeoman duty was a characteristic of his during the height of his career. His total innings pitched was an American League record at the time. Joe McGinnity held the major-league record at 434. Ed's spit ball proved effective, as he struck out over 200 batters (206) for the first time in his career. He always stated that once he would learn how to control the pitch, he would get it to break four different ways.

The following year (1908) was a season in which both leagues witnessed pennant races that are permanently etched in history. The National League pennant was a three-way donnybrook between the Giants, Pirates, and the Cubs. The Cubs won out over the other two by one game. The Cubs were victorious over the Giants in a replay of the famous Fred Merkle boner.

In the American League, it was a four-way fight between the Detroit Tigers, Cleveland Naps, St. Louis Browns, and the White Sox. The results of the race wouldn't be decided until the very last day. St. Louis fell by the wayside in early September, but the last three were so close they could be sheltered by a napkin.

The year would not only be known as the year of the closest dual pennant race in history but also the year of two dominant pitchers. Every so often two pitchers have career years simultaneously that stand out prominently. Christy Mathewson towered in the National League with 37 victories and 11 shutouts. Walsh matched "Matty's" shutout total, but his number of victories overshadowed "Big Six's" by three. Walsh became the second pitcher in modern-day baseball to reach the 40-win plateau and also the last to achieve it.

Ed led in every positive major category except E.R.A. He also led in hits allowed, but that negative stat could be excused because of the number of innings he pitched. He broke Joe McGinnity's major-league record of innings pitched (set in 1903) by 30 when he tallied 464. This marked the second consecutive year that he surpassed the 400-inning mark, matching the "Ironman's" feat in 1903 and 1904. Walsh played a dual role during the year, doubling as a reliever. He was called on to relieve 17 times and saved 7 games. He was responsible for 47 of the White Sox's 88 successes. His seven saves gave him the league lead in that department. As far as E.R.A., his 1.42 could've been tops in most years, but Addie Joss and Cy Young edged him out in that category. Ed pitched 11 shutouts during the season. Along with Mathewson's totals, this was at the time a major league record. This was the first time that any pitcher posted double figures in shutouts more than once. It was one more than he had in 1906. Ironically, all his shutouts were pitched at home, which must also be a season's record. He also tied the record for the most shutouts in a month when he recorded six during September, tying his and Doc White's record.

On September 18, he pitched his 25th career shutout to defeat the Senators 1–0. He spread out eight hits, edging Walter Johnson, who was the new phenom of the league. On August 24 he won his 30th game, defeating the Red Sox 2–1 on six hits.

As the pennant race dwindled down to the final weeks, Walsh's right arm helped keep the Sox in the fight. He was called on frequently, especially when Frank Smith jumped the team. This placed a burden on him and Doc White. Owen and Altrock, the two former 20-game winners, were not as reliable as in the past. They had faltered badly in 1907 and this season was no different. Walsh started every second day while relieving between starts. In the last nine games of the season, Walsh was called upon seven times.

On September 26, Ed Ruelbach of the Chicago Cubs pitched a doubleheader versus the Brooklyn Superbas, shutting them out in both games. This was the only time a performance of that magnitude occurred. On September 29 Walsh almost duplicated Ruelbach's performance. In a doubleheader versus the Red Sox, he defeated them 5–1 in the first game. Chicago took a quick 1–0 lead, but the Bosox tied it in the third when Pat Donoghue scored on Amby McConnell's double. The Chisox scored in the fourth, fifth, and seventh innings to ice the victory behind Walsh's three hits. In the nightcap, Ed was even better and he blanked the Red Sox 2–0, giving up four hits in that contest. He pitched 18 innings and the last 15 were scoreless, yielding only seven hits in the two games.

As the last days of the season approached, the Cleveland "Naps" faced off with Chicago on October 2. Each game was now a life-or-death situation. Out of this matchup emerged one of the most classic confrontations in the history of the American pastime. Addie Joss and Ed Walsh pitched as if they were two titans fighting for supremacy over one another. In the end, Joss recorded the second perfect game of modern baseball and only the fourth of all time. In that game, Sox went to the plate and returned to the bench frustrated. Walsh's performance was noteworthy also as he gave up only one unearned run on four hits. Cleveland dented the plate in the third when center fielder Joe Birmingham led off with a single to right. Walsh picked him off first and first baseman Frank Isbell's throw to second was high, hitting Birmingham in the back of the head. As the ball went into left field, Birmingham went to third. George Perring hit to short and was thrown out as the Nap base runner was held at third. Walsh then fanned his mound opponent, Joss, for the second out. It looked like Ed was out of the jam. Wilbur Goode was up and catcher Ossie Schreck, who they picked up from the Philadelphia A's and who was playing only his sixth game for Chicago, let one of Walsh's pitches get by him for a passed ball, bringing in Birmingham for the only run of the game. Goode was then struck out to end the inning. It's only speculation that this game could've continued indefinitely the way both men exerted themselves. Every pitch had special meaning. An interesting event also occurred in the eighth inning, when Walsh broke the finger of his catcher (Schreck) with a spitball.

Still the heart-wrenching defeat did not seal Chicago's fate because they still had a head-to-head three-game series with first-place Detroit while Cleveland was pitted against the pesky Browns. If Chicago could sweep Detroit and St. Louis upend Cleveland, then the White Sox could claim the pennant.

The White Sox went into Detroit and captured the first two games of the Series. Walsh won the second game on October 5th defeating their ace, Ed Summers, 6–1. This was his 40th win of the year!

Cleveland ran aground in St. Louis and lost their chance to win the flag. In the final game of the Series with Detroit, Fielder Jones selected Doc White to start the crucial game. Ed Walsh, in an autobiographical sketch told to Francis J. Powers that appeared in the *Second Fireside Book of Baseball*, edited by Charles Einstein, reveals his feeling on Jones' choice of starters. Walsh claims he went to Jones and insisted that a better choice for the assignment would be Frank Smith, who returned to the team and contributed to the Sox success. Jones, who still had hard feelings toward Smith, stuck with his original choice. White was hit hard and knocked out early and Walsh had to come in when the game was a foregone conclusion. This gave Detroit the pennant and Chicago tumbled into third place.

To show how weak offensively the team was, they hit only three homers. Walsh hit one of the three. Manager Fielder Jones and Frank Isbell hit the others. Ed can claim the fact that he's the only modern-day pitcher to lead the team in homers!

After the close 1908 race, the White Sox replaced Fielder Jones with Walsh's former catcher, Billy Sullivan, as manager. It was obvious that Walsh couldn't duplicate his efforts of 1908, as he fell way short statistically. This showed up as the White Sox fell to fourth place (20 games off the pace). Ed posted a 15–11 record and had less than half of the innings pitched in 1908 (230 innings). His E.R.A. was an outstanding 1.42, leaving him just behind Harry Krause (1.39) of the A's. Ed's low E.R.A. could be attributed to the eight shutouts he threw, which gave him the league lead in that category. Included in his blankings was a one-hitter versus Cleveland. He defeated them 4–0 with an aging Cy Young as his opponent in the first game of a doubleheader. Terry Turner hit a line-drive single to center, spoiling another chance by Walsh to immortalize his name. Also, on August 29 he had another heroic struggle and blanked the Washington Senators 1-0. In that game he gave up three hits as he bested Waiter Johnson.

In 1910, Ed witnessed his first losing season with an 18–20 mark. His 20 losses led the league. Regardless of this, he still led the league in E.R.A. (1.27). He recorded seven shutouts, far off the record-setting pace of Jack Coombs (13). Chicago had replaced Sullivan as manager with Hugh Duffy, who will always be known for having the highest batting average in a season (.438). Duffy's leadership couldn't prevent the White Sox from sinking into the second division at 68–85. It seemed that Ed had moments of glory during this year, because on June 6 he fashioned a one-hitter versus the Red Sox. Duffy Lewis hit a hard liner to right to ruin that masterpiece. An irony of the game was that Chicago scored the only run, in the fifth inning, without the aid of a hit. Ed seemed to gain stamina in the latter part of the year, as he logged five shutouts in August. The first game that month, on August 4, was a grueling 11 inning tie versus Philadelphia's Jack Coombs, who would dominate the league with 31 victories.

In 1911, Ed rebounded with a 27–18 ledger, helping the Chisox back into the first division. His E.R.A. rose above 2.00 for the first time since 1905. He pitched five shutouts, with three coming in August and one in September. Two of them were outstanding performances, with another one-hitter versus Detroit on August 14. The Tiger backstop, Oscar Stanage, opened the sixth with the only hit. Walsh almost made the play on the ball that was lined back to him. As it squirted by him, shortstop Ray Corhan just missed nipping Stanage at first base. On August 27, he achieved the pitcher's dream when he no-hit the Red Sox. He was in complete control from the start as he struck out eight and walked only one.

In 1912, Ed matched his victory total of the previous year. He also was continuing to perform as a reliever. The ten games he saved, coupled with his wins, was a shade under 50% of the team's total victories. The ten saves was the first time any pitcher got into double figures in that stat. He now had led the league in saves for three consecutive years. His shutout total was six, with the second of the year coming on June 30. This was the 50th shutout of his career. He defeated Detroit 2–0 giving up six hits.

Hugh Duffy was replaced as the year started by former manager Nixey Callahan. Walsh's strong performance made his new manager look good and his right arm kept the Sox in the first division once again.

Usually after the season teams from the same city met in a series of games for the bragging rights of their town. Callahan overutilized Walsh in the city series, therefore creating problems for "Big Ed." Many felt this was the downfall of his career. He wound up with a dead arm. This showed up in 1913 when he went out with a sore arm, and he would never match his glory days. He had only an 8–3 record with one shutout.

In 1914, he sported a 2–3 mark with one shutout. In 1915, he pitched only three games but won all three in complete-game outings. One of these would be his last shutout, topping the St. Louis Browns 8–0 on seven hits. Prior to the year, the Federal League flirted with him to come over to their circuit for the fantastic sum of $75,000. He turned it down, knowing that the proverbial end was near.

In 1916, he appeared in two games, losing one. The following year, 1917, he was released, and journeyed to the National League with the Boston Braves. There he pitched four games and lost his only decision. This was the end of the line for Ed and he bid the majors good-bye as a player. In 1924 he came back to the majors as a coach and managed three games. He donned the blue uniform of an umpire for awhile. He will always be known as a great pitcher that loved the game and whose record could've been more spectacular if he wasn't constantly used in relief. His achievements were honored in 1946 as he was voted into the Hall of Fame by the Veteran's Committee for Old-Timers.

Ed Walsh

Date	Team	Score	Hits	S.O.	Walks	Loser
5/19/04(A)	Wash.	5–0	2	3	0	Jacobson
7/14/05(H)	Wash.	2–0	7	3	0	Wolfe
5/6/06(H)	Cle.	6–0	1	5	1	Joss
6/14/06(H)	Wash.	2–0	5	5	0	Pattern
8/3/06(H)	Bos.	4–0	1	5	3	Harris
8/7/06(H)	Phi.	4–0	3	4	2	Waddell
8/12/06(H)	N.Y.	3–0	9	7	1	Orth
8/15/06(A)	Bos.	6–0	4	6	1	Tannehill
8/18/06(A)	N.Y.	10–0	5	3	0	Chesbro
8/27/06(A)	Phi.	1–0	1	9	1	Coombs
9/14/06(H)	Stl.	3–0	3	11	1	Jacobson
9/26/06(H)	Bos.	2–0	6	8	3	Overlin
4/19/07(H)	Stl.	1–0	3	2	0	Jacobson
5/31/07(H)	Stl.	6–0	6	3	2	Piety

Ed Walsh

Date	Team	Score	Hits	S.O.	Walks	Loser
6/29/07(A)	Stl.	9-0	6	3	2	Blade
7/7/07(H)	Phi.	6-0	3	4	0	Dygert
7/31/07(A)	Wash.	3-0	4	3	3	Gehring
4/18/08(H)	Stl.	3-0	3	4	0	Graham
5/3/08(H)	Cle.	3-0	6	9	0	Chech
5/31/08(H)	Det.	1-0	4	1	1	Willett
6/20/08(H)	Bos.	1-0	5	6	1	Young
8/7/08(H)	Bos.	7-0	4	4	0	Burchell
9/5/08(H)	Cle.	7-0	5	8	1	Joss
9/13/08(H)	Cle.	1-0	5	6	0	Benger
9/18/08(H)	Wash.	1-0	8	7	3	Johnson
9/21/08(H)	Phi.	2-0	3	5	0	Schitzer
9/27/08(H)	Bos.	3-0	6	8	0	Cicotte
9/29/08(H)	Bos.	2-0	4	5	0	Steele
6/7/09(A)	Wash.	8-0	5	4	1	Gray
6/11/09(A)	N.Y.	1-0	3	4	2	Lake
6/20/09(H)	Cle.	4-0	1	5	2	Young
6/26/09(A)	Cle.	2-0	5	7	1	Joss
8/18/09(A)	Det.	2-0	5	7	3	Mullin
8/29/09(H)	Wash.	1-0	2	6	6	Johnson
9/13/09(H)	Cle.	2-0	3	2	2	Joss
9/18/09(A)	Bos.	7-0	6	5	3	Wood
6/6/10(H)	Bos.	1-0	1	5	0	Hall
8/4/10(H)	Phi.	0-0	6	10	3	Coombs
8/7/10(H)	Wash.	4-0	2	10	0	Groom
8/11/10(H)	Bos.	1-0	3	15	2	Smith
8/23/10(A)	Wash.	1-0	5	6	1	Johnson
8/31/10(A)	Bos.	8-0	5	10	3	Smith
9/18/10(H)	Bos.	6-0	6	6	1	Hunt
6/27/11(H)	Det.	3-0	4	8	1	Donovan
8/14/11(H)	Det.	2-0	1	2	1	Willett
8/20/11(H)	Wash.	11-0	7	3	0	Becker
8/27/11(H)	Bos.	5-0	0	8	1	Collins
9/27/11(A)	Bos.	3-0	5	6	0	Collins
4/27/12(H)	Det.	2-0	5	5	4	Covington
6/30/12(A)	Det.	2-0	6	5	4	Covington
7/17/12(A)	Bos.	1-0	2	4	1	O'Brien
9/13/12(H)	N.Y.	2-0	5	11	2	Ford
9/19/12(H)	Phi.	1-0	3	11	1	Houck
9/29/12(H)	Stl.	4-0	4	11	1	Baumgardner
6/22/13(H)	Stl.	2-0	9	5	1	Weilman
7/13/14(A)	N.Y.	2-0	6	3	5	Keating
10/1/15(H)	Stl.	8-0	6	3	2	Koob

Year	Home	Away	Total
04	0	1	1

Year	Home	Away	Total
05	1	0	1
06	7	3	10
07	3	2	5
08	11	0	11
09	3	5	8
10	5	2	7
11	4	1	5
12	4	2	6
13	1	0	1
14	0	1	1
15	1	0	1
	40	17	57

Ed Walsh's Shutouts by Team

Bos.	Cle.	Det.	N.Y.	Phi.	Stl.	Wash.	Total
15	7	6	5	6	8	10	57

Shutouts by Team Finish

1	2	3	4	5	6	7	8	Total
4	8	3	7	8	10	7	10	57

Bob Gibson
The Intimidator

It is often said in baseball that the inside of the plate belongs to the pitcher. If any hurler refuses to believe that, he won't be around very long regardless of the level of competition in which he is involved. Bob Gibson adhered to that philosophy when he established himself as one of the premier pitchers of his day. His desire and competitiveness were trademarks of his demeanor, and he solidified his reputation as someone to hold in awe. Batters feared this man. He deeply resented any hitter digging in on him. If that were to occur, the vulnerable batsman would be sent flying to avoid being plunked by Gibson's fast ball. This was his way of emphatically letting the batter know that he was infringing on Bob's sacred territory.

Ball players through the years felt Gibson's wrath when they tried to inch closer to the plate. In 1961 Hall of Famer Duke Snider suffered a broken elbow when he ventured too close to Gibson's forbidden zone. As a rookie Jim Ray Hart incurred a broken bone in his shoulder because he was unaware of the parameters that Gibson allowed a batter to have. Even a former teammate, Bill White, who played with Gibson from 1955–1965, felt Gibson's wrath when, as a Philadelphia Phillies in 1966, he made first base the hard way. Bygones of the past were just exactly that! Even the legendary Willie Mays feared digging in on the imposing figure glaring in from the mound.

His intense desire can be credited to an older brother who instilled in him a competitiveness on the ball field. Despite a history of asthma and a heart murmur, Bob was a gifted athlete whose first love was basketball. He hoped for a scholarship to Indiana but was denied due to a quota system for black athletes. This was during the 1950s just prior to the civil rights explosion that emerged in the 1960s. As a young Negro man he witnessed bigotry as he grew from a child to an adult. The scar of the intolerance he witnessed and experienced would manifest itself on the basketball court and later on the ball field. He was given a scholarship to Creighton University in his home town of Omaha, Nebraska. There he excelled as their greatest athlete of all time on the basketball court. He also became a member of the university's baseball team. At Creighton University he was spotted by the St. Louis Cardinal organization. They were the only team that showed any interest in him, and they offered him a nominal signing bonus of $4,000. Omaha was a minor-league affiliate of the St. Louis club, which gave them an advantage in scouting any local talent.

In 1957, the first year of his professional baseball career, Bob started out with Omaha with the American Association. He posted a 2–1 record, but an inflated E.R.A. of 4.29 didn't dignify him as a major league prospect. His wildness was another problem that needed work. He walked 27 and struck out 25. This prompted a demotion to Columbus of the Class A Sally League. There he was 4–3 with a 3.77 E.R.A. Again his walks surpassed his strikeouts (34–24). The following year he split time between Omaha and Rochester of the International League, recording a combined record of 8–9. His E.R.A. improved (3.31) at Omaha and 2.45 at Rochester along with his walk/strikeout ratio. However, he still showed a tendency to be wild, but his K's were finally higher than his walks (47–39 at Omaha and 75–54 at Rochester). He still seemed to be a long way from the major leagues with those stats.

In 1959, he started the season with Omaha, posting a 9–9 mark and a respectable 3.07 E.R.A. His strikeout-to-walk ratio was 98–70. He was promoted to the parent club and debuted on April 15. His first victory was on July 30. It was also his first career shutout as he defeated Cincinnati 1–0 on eight hits. He walked three while striking out only two.

In Gibson's autobiography, *Stranger to the Game*, he states that his first years with the Cardinals were somewhat torturous due to the Cardinal manager, Solly Hemus. He was never given the opportunity to develop under Hemus. Hemus always put him in an uncomfortable position and never felt that Bob had the makings of a major-league pitcher.

During the 1960 season, Bob spent some time at Rochester, sporting a 2–3 record. His E.R.A. was a sparkling 2.85, but most importantly, his strikeout-to-walk ratio was better than 2–1 (36–17). With the Cardinals, he struggled at 3–6. The team improved and finished third, nine games back of the pennant-bound Pirates. Bob's E.R.A. ballooned to 5.59 with no shutouts. He was still feeling the sting of Hemus' barbs but would not cave in under the barrage of belittlement. He felt there would be better days ahead in his career.

Expansion of baseball was on the horizon and 1961 saw the American League add two new teams one in Washington, D.C., and another in California. The National League joined the growth movement the following year. The headlines in 1961 were filled with a home-run assault by Mantle and Maris on the sacred 60-home-run pinnacle of the Babe. Maris won on the last day of the season and immortalized his name by taking one of Boston's Tracy Stallard serves for the cherished 61.

In the National League, followers of the Reds finally hailed the toast of their town's first pennant in 21 years. The Reds succumbed to the Yankees, four games to one. Bob Gibson found a new life in the majors as the Cardinals, who were floundering under Hemus, replaced him with Johnny Keane. Keane convinced Bob to continue in his career because he felt he couldn't miss making it big. Keane placed Gibson in the starting rotation to stay, and he responded with a 13–12 record, missing leading the team in victories by one game. His E.R.A. was a much-improved 3.24 with two shutouts. His biggest problem was his control as he led the league in walks. With Keane at the helm, his confidence began to sprout.

Two new pair of teams were added to the National League in 1962. New roots were planted in Texas by adding a team in Houston. The league felt the need to place in New York City a National League team to ease the loss of the Dodgers and the Giants; therefore, the Mets were born. The pennant came down to a flat-footed race between the Los Angeles Dodgers and San Francisco Giants with the Giants emerging as the victors in a three-game playoff (the fourth in National League history—all involving the Dodgers). Gibson had another good year and finished with a 15–13 mark. He threw five shutouts, which lowered his E.R.A under 3.00 (2.85). Better still, he struck out 208 batters while keeping his walk total under 100.

He was emerging as one of the premier right-handers in the league. When he shut out the Milwaukee Braves 6–0 on July 13, he defeated their old warhorse, Warren Spahn. In his shutout of the Mets on August 18, he gave up only three hits while walking eight. Up to this point in his career, all of his whitewashes were on the road. He had yet to pitch one on his home turf.

In 1963, the Cardinals secured the highly regarded Dick Groat from Pittsburgh to play shortstop, which solidified their infield. They could boast the best infield in the league, if not the majors, with Bill White at first, Julian Javier at second, Groat at short, and Ken Boyer at third. This gave them the chance to make a strong challenge, which they did by making a late-season run at the Dodgers. The loss of a three-game series at St. Louis to the Dodgers sealed the fate of the surging Cardinals, who finished second, six games back. This also was the year the great Stan Musial bid adieu to baseball, ending an illustrious career that would earn him a place in Cooperstown.

Gibson was an integral part in St. Louis' fortune in baseball, as his record of 18–9 indicated. This enabled him to tie for the team league in victories with Ernie Broglio. Bob's E.R.A. was high at 3.39, but he was starting to create the image of a pitcher and not just a hurler. His strikeout total was over 200 (204) for the second consecutive year. His walk total was one higher than the previous year, but he pitched more innings. In his two shutouts, he defeated San Francisco 5–0, defeating Juan Marichal. Marichal showed tenacity by going seven innings in the encounter. He had gone 16 innings in his previous start against Warren Spahn. In September, Gibson shut out the Cubs 8–0 in a game in which he and Stan Musial hit home runs. Throughout his career, Bob was not a one-dimensional talent. His often-used role as a pinch hitter and six Golden Glove awards attest to this. As the Cardinal's drive faded near the end of the season, the nucleus of the contending team was now assembled. Better days lay ahead.

In 1964 the Cardinals achieved their goal of winning a pennant for the first time since 1946. Acquiring Lou Brock on a trade was a major factor. This was one of the greatest steals in baseball history as St. Louis swapped the struggling Ernie Broglio for someone who put up Hall of Fame stats. Brock was the catalyst for much of the Cardinals' success during the year.

Also in 1964, one of the greatest "folderoos" occurred in baseball history as the Philadelphia Phillies, with 12 games remaining, blew a six-game lead by losing ten straight games. This swan song was orchestrated by Gene Mauch, who overworked his two most reliable starters, Jim Bunning and Chris Short. Mauch's anxiety forced him to pitch his two aces every second day in order to clinch the pennant. By doing this, he enabled Cincinnati and St. Louis to get back into the race. It would not be the last time that Mauch would blow a pennant.

The last weekend of the season saw St. Louis with a slim ½ game lead over the Reds with the Phillies in third. If the Phillies could sweep the Reds the last two games and the Mets could sweep the Cardinals in their final three games, baseball would witness the first three-way tie for the pennant with a possible round-robin tournament. It didn't materialize because the Cardinals were able to prevent the Mets from sweeping them. This they did on a masterful relief job by Gibson on the last day of the season. The victory gave the mound-city contingent the pennant by one game over the Reds and Phils.

In the World Series the Cardinals would face off versus the Yankees, who won their fifth consecutive pennant. Little did anyone realize that the Yankee dynasty would be over after this Series. Many of their veteran players, such as Mantle and Ford, were on the downside of their fabled careers. In this Series Gibson emerged as one of the game's greatest money pitchers.

Bob started game two and he kept the Cardinals in contention until he was pinched hit for in the eighth inning. He was trailing only 4–2 when the Yanks exploded for four runs in the ninth, sealing the victory and giving Gibson the loss. With the Series tied at 2–2, Bob started the crucial fifth game and had the Yankees groveling at his serves. In the bottom of the ninth he was leading 2–0 with two outs when Tom Tresh homered with a man on, tying the score. In the top of the tenth, Tim McCarver hit a three-run homer to give Bob and the Cardinals a 5–2 victory.

The Cards went back to St. Louis with a one-game lead, which put the Yankees in the unenviable position of needing to win the remaining two games on the road. The New Yorkers rallied to tie the Series, and it came down to the deciding seventh game. Manager Johnny Keane selected Gibson to pitch the "rubber game" with only two days rest. The Yanks and Mel Stottlemyre battled to the fourth inning in a scoreless tie. The Cardinals scored three runs in each of the fourth and fifth innings giving Gibson a commanding six-run lead. The Yanks battled to the end but lost 7–5. Bob was voted the Series MVP. He pitched 27 innings, winning and completing two games. He also struck out a record 31 batters in the Series which surpassed the total of 28 set by Bill Dineen in the 1903 encounter. Dineen set his mark in four games while Bob needed only three. At the end of the Series, the baseball world was shocked when they realized that Yogi Berra would be fired and the Cardinal skipper would quit and take the vacancy with the Yankees.

It didn't matter who piloted the team in 1965 because destiny would have the final say in the outcome of the Yankees and the Cardinals. The Yanks fell below .500 for the first time since 1925 and finished in the second division a dismal sixth, 25 games from the top! This ended a string of 39 consecutive winning seasons and finishing out of the first division. (With only eight teams for the majority of those years, the first four teams were considered the first division and the last four the second division. Further expansion to ten teams increased the number of teams in each level to five.) The Cardinals collapsed and wound up seventh with an 80–81 mark under new manager Red Schoendienst. This was Bob's biggest season at the time and he broke the 20-win mark with a 20–12 record. His E.R.A. (3.07) was aided immensely with six shutouts. His shutout on May 7 was a nifty 2–0 one-hitter versus the Phillies. Johnny Callison singled in the fourth inning to deprive Bob of glory. His strikeout total of 270 placed him third, well behind Sandy Koufax's record of 382.

In 1966 the Cardinals improved slightly with an 83–79 mark and a move up to sixth place, 12 games behind the first-place Dodgers. This could be attributed to the acquisition of Orlando Cepeda, who gave the Cardinals the power hitter they were lacking. Cepeda also provided the leadership that was vital to the team.

With Cepeda in the team's lineup, Gibson could pitch with more ease now knowing that every game wouldn't have to be a hard-fought endeavor. He again joined the 20-win club as he won 21 versus 12 losses. His E.R.A. was his best ever at 2.44. His five shutouts tied him with Koufax of Los Angeles and Jim Maloney for the league lead. On June 15 he shut out Pittsburgh on three hits. It was also his 100th career victory.

The next year (1967) was a bittersweet season as Gibson suffered a broken leg in a game versus the Pirates. Roberto Clemente rifled a shot off Gibson's leg and felled him momentarily. He continued to pitch to the next three batters, but he collapsed in pain as he was following through. This showed a grittiness that few athletes could display. Prior to his mishap, he accrued 11 wins with 2 shutouts. One of these was on opening day when he blanked the San Francisco Giants and Juan Marichal 6–0. His other shutout came on May 2nd when he recorded his 25th career whitewashing. This was a 5–0 two-hitter versus the Reds. To ease the anguish of being on the sidelines, Bob savored the end-of-the-year pennant celebration and the eventual world championship.

Gibson outshined everyone during the Series, as the Bosox shocked the baseball world by capturing the American League pennant. They did this by defeating the Minnesota Twins on the last day of the season. The Sox had finished ninth the previous year, and with triple crown winner Carl Yastrzemski leading the charge, they were made the favorites to win the World Series. Gibson rose to the task and stemmed the Boston tide.

In the first game he doled out six hits as he stymied the Red Sox bats 2–1. The only run off of him was by opposing pitcher Jose Santiago who hit a short fly into the infamous screen atop the Green Monster. In game four, he breezed to a 6–0, giving up only five hits.

The Red Sox rallied to tie the Series at three games apiece with the deciding game to be played at Fenway Park. They brought their ace, Jim Lonborg, back with only two days rest. Bob was masterful as he scattered three hits while waltzing to a 7–2 win. He became the 11th pitcher to win three games in a World Series, and because of this, he was voted the Series MVP for the second time. This made him only the third person to win the award twice, joining Sandy Koufax and later Reggie Jackson. The broken leg that disabled him for eight weeks probably cost him the Cy Young Award.

The next year, 1968, would be known as the year of the pitcher. Many outstanding achievements occurred. Denny McLain won 31 games and Don Drysdale pitched six consecutive shutouts. Drysdale also broke Walter Johnson's record of 55⅔ consecutive shutout innings pitched. Gibson also contributed fantastic statistical accomplishments as the year progressed.

As the season entered into June, Bob was struggling with a 3–5 mark. He had performed credibly with some outstanding pitching, however, being relieved in a couple of extra-inning games deprived him of some potentially well-deserved victories. Gibson would sound the chorus for the song that states "June is busting out all over." From that point on, he was practically untouchable.

The first shutout was on June 6 versus the Astros, who bowed 4–0 with only three hits. As stated before, Drysdale had pitched six consecutive shutouts with a string of 58⅔ consecutive innings of shutout ball. Gibson challenged those marks immediately after Drysdale set the record.

After his shutout of Houston, four more blankings were attained in his next four starts. He now had a streak of five shutouts in a row that encompassed 47 scoreless innings. On July 1 he tried to equal Drysdale's record of six consecutive shutouts in Dodgers Stadium.

In the first inning, he retired the first two hitters but walked their number three man, Len Gabrielson. Tom Haller hit a bad-hop single that found its way into right field, sending Gabrielson to third base. With Ron Fairley up, Bob threw an inside pitch which bounced off Johnny Edwards' glove, enabling Gabrielson to score and ending abruptly any chance for Gibson to surpass the record. The official scorer ruled that it was a wild pitch. Another irony of the game was that the starting and losing pitcher for the Dodgers was Don Drysdale. Gibson was victorious as he defeated Los Angeles 5–1. His next start he blanked the Giants and Juan Marichal 3–0. That one wild pitch possibly prevented him from pitching seven consecutive shutouts and a string of 65 scoreless innings.

Gibson wasn't finished with his whitewashings, as he still had plenty of shutouts remaining. On July 25 he defeated Philadelphia 5–0, giving him a share of the Cardinal shutouts record held by Bill Doke, at 33.

On August 9, he blanked the Atlanta Braves 1–0 to set the club record at 34. On August 19, Philadelphia bit the dust again by a 2–0 score. This was his 15th consecutive win and a tie for the club's single-season record of ten shutouts held by the legendary "Dizzy" Dean. On August 28 he set the club record at 11 when Pittsburgh felt the sting by an 8–0 score. His 20th victory of the season was a 1–0 blanking of the Cincinnati Reds. By the end of the season, he compiled an outstanding total of 13 shutouts. This was the highest total since Grover Cleveland Alexander spun 16 in 1916. Gibson's total for the year equaled the American League record set by Jack Coombs in 1910. Bob's E.R.A. was an unbelievable 1.12 which was second only to Mordecai "Three Finger" Brown's National League record of 1.04 in 1906! His efforts were so outstanding that he was unanimously voted the Cy Young Award and became only the second pitcher to do so in the National League history (Koufax accomplished this feat three times). Not only did Bob win the Cy Young Award, but he captured the MVP Award also. At that point in time, only Don Newcombe and Sandy Koufax could claim that distinction. McLain also took the MVP in his league along with the Cy Young Award. Both of those were unanimous decisions.

The World Series pit the Cardinals versus the Detroit Tigers, who breezed to the pennant by 12 games over the Orioles. The Bengals had captured 103 victories, mainly on the right arm of Denny McLain, who chalked up 31 wins against six losses. This was the first time since Dizzy Dean in 1934 that a pitcher broke into the 30-win column for a season. Ironically, the same year St. Louis and Detroit met for the first time as opponents.

The first game matched Gibson against McLain and was the first contest in baseball annals between winners of the Cy Young Awards in their respective leagues. Gibson was not just outstanding, but awesome! He shut out Detroit 4–0 allowing only five hits, but the major achievement was his 17 strikeouts, which would be a new Series record for one game.

In game four, with the Cardinals ahead two games to one, Bob went up against McLain again, which resulted in a 10–1 victory for St. Louis. He scattered five hits and it looked like St. Louis was going to annex its second consecutive title. Detroit wouldn't be denied as they captured the next two games to tie the Series. The rubber match was set up in St. Louis, and Gibson's mound opponent was the portly Mickey Lolich. Both had won two games each and they had matched goose eggs for six innings. In the top of the seventh, Detroit had two men on when Jim Northrup lined a ball to center field. The usually reliable Curt Flood misplayed the ball into a triple. This was all the impetus Detroit needed as they clinched the Series with a 4–1 win. Gibson had completed the game, making it his eighth complete-game start in World Series competition. The loss stopped his seven complete-game winning streak in Series play.

The following year, 1969, saw the second expansion in both leagues with divisional setups to decide the league championships. The New York Mets shocked the baseball world by becoming world champions. St. Louis finished fourth, 13 games in back of the New Yorkers. Gibson could not be faulted as he again climbed the pinnacle of 20 victories against 13 losses. He notched four shutouts with a 2.18 E.R.A.

The Cardinals fell on hard times in 1970 as they again finished fourth with a 76–86 mark, 13 games behind division-winner Pittsburgh. Bob had another outstanding year as he led the league in victories (23) and winning percentage (.767). His efforts gave him his second Cy Young Award. Included in his victories were three shutouts that kept his E.R.A. a respectable 3.12. His shutout of San Diego on June 17 was a brilliant one-hitter with Ivan Murrell spoiling Bob's chances for no-hit fame.

In 1971, St. Louis finished with a 90–72 record, seven games behind Pittsburgh. Gibson was now 35 years of age and still pitching with the same intensity that he displayed in his youth. His record fell to 16–13 but his E.R.A. was better at 3.07, which was aided by five shutouts. He tied for the league lead with three other pitchers (Milt Pappas of the Chicago Cubs, Al Downing of the L.A. Dodgers, and Steve Blass of the Pittsburgh Pirates). This marked the third time he led the league in that category. On August 14th he defeated Pittsburgh 11–0, spinning his first and only no-hitter. In that game he walked only three and struck out ten.

Bob in 1972 logged in with a 19–11 ledger highlighted by a 2.46 E.R.A. This included four shutouts. One was a sparkling 1–0 three-hitter versus the Cubs and their ace, "Fergy" Jenkins. Gibson's record was more impressive since St. Louis was a losing ball club, finishing 21½ games behind division-winner Pittsburgh.

The next year the New York Mets won the Eastern Division title and pennant with a .509 winning percentage. This was the lowest number for any team going into the World Series. St. Louis finished behind New York by a mere 1½ games at an even .500 (81–81). They probably would've won their division if they had a healthy Gibson. Bob was sidelined the latter part of the year with a knee injury. He still had a 12–10 record, coupled with a 2.17 E.R.A., which indicates that he still had something left to contribute to a stretch drive.

In 1974, St. Louis again finished second by the same 1½ game deficit. This time it was the Pirates who won the division, their fourth in five years. Bob witnessed his first losing season since 1960 with an 11–13 mark. His E.R.A. was at 3.83 with only one shutout. This was his last career blanking as he stymied the Pirates on four hits. In that game he struck out 11 and walked only 3. Even at the age of 38, he was instilled with that competitive spirit to gear up for the best teams.

It was finally over for Gibson in 1975 as he showed only a 3–10 record. In his second win of the season, he defeated the Montreal Expos for his 250th career victory. This, along with the 56 shutouts and 3,117 strikeouts, gave him the distinction of being only the second pitcher in history to attain those figures. Walter Johnson was the other. Bob was the only national leaguer to reach that plateau of distinction.

When he decided to retire, enemy batters who stood intimidated by Gibson's warning pitches gave a sigh of relief. In 1981, the Baseball

Writers of America enshrined Bob on the first ballot with over 84 percent of the vote. This was a deserving recognition for one of the great money pitchers of all time.

Bob Gibson

Date	Team	Score	Hits	S.O.	Walks	Loser
7/30/59(A)	Cin.	1–0	8	2	3	O'Toole
5/21/61(A)	Chi.	3–0	4	11	4	Schaffernoth
10/1/61(A)	Phi.	2–0	6	7	5	Ferrarese
5/6/62(A)	Cin.	3–0	5	8	1	Drabowsky
5/17/62(A)	S.F.	1–0	6	10	2	O'Dell
7/13/62(A)	Mil.	6–0	3	5	4	Spahn
8/8/62(A)	Pit.	2–0	3	10	2	McBean
8/18/62(A)	N.Y.	10–0	3	9	8	McKenzie
7/7/63(A)	S.F.	5–0	6	8	2	Marichal
9/10/63(H)	Chi.	8–0	6	5	2	Hobbie
5/20/64(H)	Chi.	1–0	4	12	0	Jackson
9/11/64(A)	Chi.	5–0	2	5	1	Broglio
4/17/65(H)	Cin.	8–0	8	11	4	O'Toole
4/28/65(A)	Mil.	5–0	3	6	4	Blasingame
5/7/65(A)	Phi.	2–0	1	8	3	Short
6/27/65(H)	Chi.	8–0	5	12	2	Broglio
8/31/65(A)	Chi.	3–0	2	6	2	Ellsworth
9/5/65(H)	N.Y.	3–0	2	8	3	McGraw
5/10/66(A)	Chi.	8–0	6	7	2	Faul
6/11/66(A)	Phi.	2–0	9	7	2	Bunning
6/15/66(H)	Pit.	1–0	3	8	2	Veale
7/23/66(A)	Chi.	4–0	6	4	5	Roberts
8/23/66(A)	Hou.	3–0	3	5	2	Dierker
4/11/67(H)	S.F.	6–0	5	12	0	Marichal
5/2/67(H)	Cin.	5–0	2	12	2	Maloney
6/6/68(A)	Hou.	4–0	3	5	2	Wilson
6/11/68(A)	Atl.	6–0	5	4	2	Kelley
6/15/68(H)	Cin.	2–0	4	13	0	Nolan
6/20/68(H)	Chi.	1–0	5	6	1	Jenkins
6/26/68(H)	Pit.	3–0	4	7	0	McBean
7/6/68(A)	S.F.	3–0	6	9	4	Marichal
7/21/68(H)	N.Y.	2–0	7	12	0	McAndrews
7/25/68(H)	Phi.	5–0	5	6	1	Short
8/9/68(A)	Atl.	1–0	4	5	0	Niekro
8/19/68(A)	Phi.	2–0	2	11	2	Fryman
8/28/68(A)	Pit.	8–0	4	14	3	Veale
9/2/68(A)	Cin.	1–0	4	8	3	Abernathy
9/27/68(H)	Hou.	1–0	6	11	0	Dierker
5/6/69(H)	S.F.	3–0	5	8	2	Sadecki
5/20/69(A)	S.F.	3–0	4	6	4	McCormick
5/25/69(A)	L.A.	4–0	6	9	3	Osteen

The Great Shutout Pitchers

Date	Team	Score	Hits	S.O.	Walks	Loser
9/28/69(A)	Mon.	2–0	9	4	2	Stoneman
6/17/70(A)	S.D.	8–0	1	13	2	Coombs
6/26/70(H)	Phi.	7–0	4	5	3	Wise
8/22/70(A)	S.D.	7–0	2	4	0	Coombs
7/22/71(H)	Phi.	8–0	5	6	3	Fryman
7/26/71(A)	N.Y.	4–0	5	4	2	Sadecki
8/14/71(A)	Pit.	11–0	0	10	3	Johnson
8/28/71(H)	Cin.	4–0	3	13	1	Nolan
9/12/71(A)	Chi.	4–0	4	8	0	Holtzman
5/31/72(A)	Chi.	1–0	3	5	2	Jenkins
6/4/72(A)	L.A.	4–0	5	6	1	Osteen
7/12/72(H)	Atl.	7–0	6	6	2	Schueler
8/21/72(A)	L.A.	4–0	7	6	2	Sutton
5/26/73(H)	Atl.	2–0	4	8	2	Niekro
6/24/74(H)	Pit.	4–0	4	11	3	Demery

Year	Home	Away	Total
59	0	1	1
61	0	2	2
62	0	5	5
63	1	1	2
64	1	1	2
65	3	3	6
66	1	4	5
67	2	0	2
68	6	7	13
69	1	3	4
70	1	2	3
71	2	3	5
72	1	3	4
73	1	0	1
74	1	0	1
	21	35	56

Bob Gibson's Shutouts by Team

Atl.	Chi.	Cin.	Hou.	L.A.	Mon.	N.Y.	Phi.	Pit.	Stl.	S.D.	S.F.	Total
6	11	7	3	3	1	4	7	6	0	2	6	56

Shutouts by Team Finish

1	2	3	4	5	6	7	8	9	10	Total
3	5	8	9	7	7	4	6	1	6	56

Steve Carlton
Mr. Lefty

When it comes to selecting great left-handed pitchers, the names of Warren Spahn, Eddie Plank, Rube Waddell, Lefty Grove, Sandy Koufax, and Whitey Ford are mentioned along with Steve Carlton. Carlton was the top left-hander to emerge after the retirement of Sandy Koufax. When Carlton retired he became the second winningest left-hander (329 victories) behind Spahn. He had 4,136 strikeouts, the most of any southpaw, and is only one of three men to surpass the 4,000 mark in that category. He amassed 55 career shutouts. Only Eddie Plank and Warren Spahn topped him as a left-hander. This made him one of six pitchers to be a member of the exclusive 300 club who had over 3,000 strikeouts and 50 or more shutouts.

When Carlton was first signed, the St. Louis Cardinals didn't regard him that highly because his fastball wasn't of major league caliber. Steve, a dedicated worker, conditioned himself and improved his repertoire of pitches. Given a $5,000 bonus, he was assigned in 1964 to Rock Hill of the Class A Western Carolina League. He was outstanding and posted a 10–1 mark with an eye-opening 1.03 E.R.A. He then moved up to Winnipeg of the Northern League, another Class A circuit. He came in at 4–4 but his E.R.A was 3.36, which was not bad considering he had to adjust to batters of a new league. During the latter part of the year, he was moved up to Tulsa of the Class AA Texas League, where he was 1–1 in four games.

In 1965, the Cardinals called him up, and he appeared in 15 games showing no record. In the 25 innings he pitched, he allowed 27 hits and struck out 21 while posting an E.R.A. of 2.52. He made his major league debut on April 12 in a game versus the Chicago Cubs in Wrigley Field, which ended in a 10–10 tie.

In 1966, St. Louis felt he needed more seasoning and sent him to Tulsa of the Triple A Pacific Coast League. At Tulsa, he sported a 9–5 record with a 3.59 E.R.A. striking out 108 batters in 128 innings but allowing only 110 hits in that span. Near the end of the year, he was recalled to the parent club and appeared in nine games. On August 5, he posted his first major league win in defeating the New York Mets 7–1 on six hits. Later that month on the 22nd he spun his first major league shutout, defeating the Houston Astros 3–0, giving up seven hits.

In 1967, the Cardinals assembled one of their better teams as they captured the pennant by 10½ games over second-place San Francisco. Led by Orlando Cepeda on the field and Bob Gibson on the mound, the team was a solid contingent. In the middle part of the year, Gibson was felled by a line drive off the bat of Roberto Clemente, which sidelined him for eight weeks. Everyone thought the Cards would crumble without Gibson, but with the addition of Steve and newcomer Dick Hughes, they stayed afloat and put more distance between themselves and the rest of the league.

Steve finished the year with a 14–9 mark and his E.R.A. was a respectable 2.90 with two shutouts. In the World Series, the Cardinals met the "Impossible Dream," the Boston Red Sox, who were ninth-place finishers the previous year. In game five, with the Red Birds holding a 3–1 game edge, Steve was given the start in hope that the Cards would clinch the Series. He battled Cy Young winner Jim Longborg through six innings, yielding only an unearned run in the third. Steve was extremely sharp in a losing effort, giving up only three hits and two walks. St. Louis prevailed in seven games when Gibson subdued Boston and their ace, Longborg.

The "Year of the Pitcher" exploded in 1968. The batters witnessed diminished batting averages as only five men in the National League broke the .300 mark during the year and would qualify for the batting championship. Carl Yastrzemski was the lone hitter in the American League to hit over .300, and that was a meager .301. Dennis McLain broke the 30-win mark with 31 victories, the first time that barrier was scaled since 1934. Bob Gibson posted 13 shutouts, the most since Grover Alexander set the record at 16 in

1916. Gibson also had the lowest E.R.A. since Hubert "Dutch" Leonard set the all-time standard at 1.00 in 1914. The cause of all this could be attributed to the rise of the pitcher's mound to 15" and a widening of the strike zone.

Steve's record was not as impressive as the year before, but he did manage a 13–11 mark. His E.R.A. was still under 3.00 and stood at 2.99. He did manage to pitch five shutouts. One of them was his best game of the year when on June 19 he blanked the Cubs 4–0 on one hit. Glen Beckert spoiled a no-hit attempt with a single in the fourth. Only two others got on base, one by an error and the other being hit by Steve.

In the World Series, Steve was used twice in relief as the Detroit Tigers battled back from a 3–1 game deficit and dethroned the Cardinals. Steve did not fare well and he was roughed up by the Bengals. He gave up seven hits in four innings for a 6.75 E.R.A.

The next year, 1969, saw the second expansion during the decade by both leagues, which created divisional arrangements. The N.Y. Mets shocked the baseball world by capturing the world championship. Everything seemed to go their way, as they became the team of destiny during the year. Evidence of this came on September 15 when the Mets, batting against Carlton, defeated him 4–3 on the strength of two two-run homers by Ron Swoboda. In this game, Steve set a new strikeout record, fanning 19 Mets! It was meant to be for the New Yorkers, regardless of which outstanding obstacles they had to confront.

Steve had his best year at 17–11 sporting a 2.17 E.R.A., which was second behind Juan Marichal's 2.10. He manufactured two shutouts, one being his best game of the year when he defeated the Dodgers on May 23, 1–0 on five hits. In that game, his control was impeccable as he walked none.

The following year, 1970, Steve held out for more money and missed spring training. His record collapsed to 10–19 and his E.R.A. skyrocketed to 3.72. The team fell out of the first division as they witnessed a losing season. Included in Steve's victories were two shutouts, both by the score of 3–0.

Steve's competitiveness and pride were exemplified the following year in 1971 when he had a reversal of fortune and became a 20-game winner for the first time in his career. His 20–9 mark helped boost the Cardinals back to a winning record as they finished second in the National League East, seven games behind the Pittsburgh Pirates. His E.R.A. was 3.56, which can be blamed on his hits per inning statistic (above 1.00). Still, he managed four shutouts.

During the off-season, he again held out for more money, which drew the wrath of the Cardinal management. This precipitated his trade to the Philadelphia Phillies, who exchanged Rick Wise for Carlton. The Phillies were doormats in the National League East, and their prospects didn't look any brighter for 1972, even with the acquisition of Carlton.

Steve responded with the best year of his career as he posted 27 wins versus 10 losses for the last-place Phils. His victories tied Koufax's record for the most wins as a left-hander in the National League for one season. He also struck out 310 men, giving him the distinction, along with Koufax, as the only southpaw to achieve that mark in the National League. Steve's total victories were 46 percent of the team's total. He threw eight shutouts, which gave him a phenomenal E.R.A. of 1.98. Included in his shutouts was a 3–0 victory versus the San Francisco Giants on April 25. He gave up a leadoff hit to Chris Spier for the only Giant safety as he struck out 14 batters.

This outstanding year won Steve the first of his four Cy Young Awards. The vote was unanimous and at the time placed him in the company of Koufax and Bob Gibson as the only National League hurlers to win it unanimously. His winning of the Cy Young Award made him the first pitcher to win a major award while playing for a last-place team.

In 1973, it would have been presumptuous to believe that Steve could duplicate his 1972 year. Steve had a difficult year at 13–20 and a 3.90 E.R.A. He did manage three shutouts, with his first of the year on May 26 versus the San Diego Padres, whom he beat 4–0 on four hits. This was a notable one as it was his 25th career blanking.

The Phillies were still a few years away from assembling the team that would blossom into a contender with the arrival of Mike Schmidt to go along with Larry Bowa, Bob Boone, and Greg Luzinski from the previous year. The Phillies again claimed the basement abode of the National League East but improved their won-loss record. They finished only 11⅓ games back of the New York Mets, who edged their way into the World Series with the worst winning percentage ever (.509).

In 1974, Carlton again rebounded with a 16–13 mark, helping Philadelphia to rise to third, two games under .500 but only eight games behind the division winner, Pittsburgh. Steve again led the league in strikeouts (240), but his control was a little shoddy as he led the league in walks with 136. His E.R.A. was improved at 3.22 with only one shutout.

Philadelphia broke through in 1975 with a winning record (86–76) for the first time since 1967. They finished in second place, 6½ games behind Pittsburgh, who claimed their fifth National League East title in six years.

Steve had compiled a 15–14 record with an E.R.A. of 3.56 that went along with three shutouts. His victory total led the club. More impressive, his 0.85 hits per inning indicated that he was competitive in most of his games. His best effort of the year was on June 7th in a game where he defeated the Dodgers 1–0 on two hits. The Dodgers had captured the National League pennant the previous year with basically the same team they fielded in 1975. Better days lay ahead for Philadelphia and Carlton.

The Phillies won the National League East title with relative ease in 1976 as they won 101 games while losing 61. They outdistanced the Pirates by nine games. This was the best percentage and victory total the team had in its history.

Carlton returned to the 20-win club as he sported a 20–7 mark with a 3.13 E.R.A. His shutouts totaled two, both by the scores of 5–0. As good as Steve's totals were for the year, they left him short in the Cy Young voting. Randy Jones of the San Diego Padres won the award.

In the National League championship series, Steve opened at home against Cincinnati's "Big Red Machine" and was defeated 6–3. It was his first taste of post-season play since the 1968 World Series. He was down by 3–1 as he entered the eighth inning, but the Reds iced the game by scoring three times in that frame. Cincy went on to sweep the Phils in three games.

The following year Philadelphia proved that their win in 1977 was not an aberration as they duplicated their record of the previous year. They faced a stiffer test from the Pirates but still prevailed by five games. Carlton's record was 23–10 with an E.R.A. of 2.64. His shutout totals were again at two. One was a 1–0 win over the Montreal Expos in which he gave up four hits. His efforts for the season were outstanding and he was rewarded with his second Cy Young Award, making him only the second left hander to win the award twice (Koufax was the other).

In the National League championship series, he again opened the series but this time versus the Los Angeles Dodgers at Chavez Ravine. Steve held them at bay, carrying a 5–1 lead into the seventh inning when the Dodgers exploded for four runs to tie the score. He wasn't around for the final decision as the Phils rallied to win. In game four, with the Dodgers leading two games to one, he tried valiantly to even the series, but his mound opponent (Tommy John) pitched exceptionally well, giving up only five hits as the Dodgers clinched the pennant. This loss in the league championship series made the Phillies the only team in baseball history to win 100 or more games in consecutive years and not come home with the bacon.

In 1978, the Phils triumphed again, edging out Pittsburgh by a game and a half. Steve also slumped to a 16–13 mark, but he still was able to lead the team in victories. His E.R.A. was a credible 2.84 aided by three shutouts. One of his whitewashings was versus the San Francisco Giants, defeating them 3–0. This was a valiant effort as he allowed ten hits to the heavy-hitting Giants kept them from scoring.

Steve did not open the National League championship series versus the Dodgers because the closeness of the division race required that he pitch late-season games. He started the third game in Los Angeles and finally won his first post-season game by a score of 9–4, defeating Don Sutton. He allowed eight hits in the only game Philadelphia captured during the Series. The Dodgers clinched the flag the next day, again earning them the opportunity to face the New York Yankees for the world championship.

In 1979, the Phillies could not hold on to the top spot and they fell into fourth place, 14 games behind Pittsburgh, who had edged out the Expos by two games for the division title. Steve improved his record to 18–11 with an E.R.A. of 3.62, while he carved out four shutouts. This was his highest total since his outstanding year in 1972. On June 5, he blanked the Houston Astros 8–0 in a one-hitter. Jeff Leonard prevented Steve from acquiring a no-hitter.

One significant move made by Philadelphia was in obtaining free agent Pete Rose to add extra leadership to the team. Pete responded well by hitting .331, but it wasn't enough to elevate the Phillies above a fourth-place finish.

The following year, 1980, both divisions saw down-to-the-wire finishes, with Philadelphia gaining the top rung over Montreal by one game. In the National League West, Houston and Los Angeles battled for the title in a one-game playoff. It was the first playoff for a playoff in league history. Houston emerged with their first title ever when Joe Niekro's knuckle ball stymied the Dodgers.

Steve had another exceptional year, to which his 24–9 record would attest. His E.R.A. of 2.34 was his lowest since 1972. As he led the league in victories, he also topped the list in strikeouts (286) and innings pitched (304). He had three shutouts. The first of the year on April 26 was a 7–0 one-hitter versus the St. Louis Cardinals. Ted Simmons marred that effort with a single.

In the National League championship series the two teams met for a memorable battle. In the first game, Steve defeated Houston 7–1 but dealt out seven hits. Houston had scored in the third and held the lead until Philly pushed across two runs in the sixth. That was all Carlton needed because he had command of the game.

The next four games were decided in extra innings. Houston took game two 7–4, breaking a 3–3 tie in the tenth when they scored four runs. The next three games were played indoors, the first time any post-season contests were played under enclosed surroundings. The Astrodome rocked with excitement for the next three days.

The third game was the best-pitched game in the series. The Astros pushed over a run in the 11th inning, winning 1–0. The next two games were confrontations where the Phillies had to rally spectacularly. Steve started game four and was relieved with one out in the fifth, losing 2–0. The Phils scored three runs in the eighth making it a 3–2 edge, but Houston tied it in the bottom of the ninth. In the top of the tenth, Philly scored two runs to win 5–3, creating a fifth and final showdown.

With Nolan Ryan on the mound, Houston held a 5–2 lead going into the eighth. It wasn't enough; the Phils erupted for five runs to take a 7–5 lead, but Houston tied it in the bottom of the ninth. Again they went into extra innings. The Phillies scored in the top of the tenth with a run that gave them their first pennant since 1950.

The World Series saw the Kansas City Royals capture the American League pennant and challenge the Phillies for the supremacy of the baseball world. Steve started the second game and trailed the Royals 3–2 until the Phils bombarded Kansas City's ace reliever, Dan Quisenberry, for four runs in the bottom of the eighth. Steve got credit for the win as Ron Reed held the Royals in the ninth.

Steve started the sixth game, hoping to clinch the first world championship in the Phillies' history. He did it with a strong performance, as he had Kansas City shut out until the eighth inning. He was relieved but got credit for the win, his second for the Series. Steve again was rewarded for his efforts during the year by earning his third Cy Young Award, placing him in exclusive company along with Sandy Koufax, Tom Seaver, and Jim Palmer.

The strike season of 1981 created havoc in the baseball world and the season was divided into halves. The winner of each half would meet to determine who played in the league championship series and the winner of that would earn the right to play in the World Series.

Steve had a fantastic year at 13–4, leading the Phillies to first place in the East before the strike halted play for almost two months. When play was resumed, the Phils were declared the first-half winners while Montreal captured the second half. Steve, with his 13 wins, was second in that department. His E.R.A. was a strong 2.34 with one shutout coming on September 1 as he defeated the Atlanta Braves 3–0 on three hits.

In the Eastern Division series, Montreal edged the Phillies out three games to two. Carlton lost two games in that series mainly because his teammates were able to score only one run for him in those two games. He faced off both times versus the Expos' ace, Steve Rogers.

In 1982, manager Dallas Green left the Phillies to take over as general manager of the Chicago Cubs. Pat Corrales took over the reins, and the team fell to second place, three games behind the St. Louis Cardinals, who would win the world championship.

Steve, at 37, had another outstanding year as he finished at 23–11. His total victories led the league along with his complete games (19), innings pitched (296), strikeouts (286), and shutouts (6). His E.R.A. was a sound 3.10. When he shut out the Dodgers on July 25, he gained his 50th career shutout. His Herculean efforts gained him his fourth Cy Young Award. This was the first time that any player achieved that distinction. This would be duplicated by Greg Maddux when he won four consecutive Cy Young Awards and Roger Clemens who received his fourth in 1997. Randy Johnson and Pedro Martinez would eventually add their names to the list.

In 1983 Carlton witnessed his first losing season since 1973, but he did contribute to the success of the team. The Phils replaced Pat Corrales in mid-season with Paul Owens, and it seemed to be the elixir for success. The Phils put on a late-season spurt to give them the division title, six games ahead of Pittsburgh. Steve was 15–16 but led the league in K's (275) and innings pitched (284). He managed to pitch three shutouts, which kept his E.R.A. at 3.11. On August 3 he shut out the Chicago Cubs 5–0. It was the last of his career. Teammate John Denny led the staff with a 19–6 record, which garnered him the Cy Young Award.

In the National League championship series Steve opened against the Los Angeles Dodgers and made a first-inning run hold up as he defeated them 1–0. He was relieved in the eighth inning by John

Holland, who preserved the victory. In the fourth game, he again was victorious as the Phillies clinched the pennant, sealing the fate of the Dodgers 7–2 and giving Philadelphia the right to meet the Baltimore Orioles for the world championship.

In the World Series, he started game three with the Series tied at one game apiece. He pitched courageously, losing 3–2 to Jim Palmer, who came in in relief. Steve completed the game, doling out six hits. Incidentally, this was the last game to date where two Hall of Fame pitchers faced each other in a World Series game. The Orioles subdued the Phillies in five games.

The year 1984 saw Philly fall to fourth place at an even .500. Steve had a good year at 13–7, but his E.R.A. bulged to 3.58. He did not notch a shutout, the first time that that had happened to him in his career. He started 33 games but completed only one. Regardless of his physical fitness credo, he was starting to show his age.

In 1985 his record plummeted to 1–8 and he was placed on the disabled list with a sore shoulder. This was the first time he had any injury during his career. Steve returned in 1986 but could show only a 4–8 record, which induced the Phillies to release him. For the remainder of the year, he wandered first to San Francisco where he posted a 1–3 mark and was waived to the American League to the Chicago White Sox, posting a 4–3 record. The following year, with the Cleveland Indians, he was 5–9, and he was later picked up by the Minnesota Twins. With Minnesota he appeared in nine games for pennant insurance, but it was apparent it was all over for "Mr. Lefty." He could only muster one win out of six decisions.

He finally called it quits in 1988 when he lost his only decision with the Twins. His great career was studded with remarkable achievements. In his first year of eligibility, he was inducted into the Hall of Fame on the first ballot.

Steve Carlton

Date	Team	Score	Hits	S.O.	Walks	Loser
8/22/66(A)	Hou.	3–0	7	7	1	Bruce
9/9/67(A)	Pit.	6–0	7	9	1	Blass
9/15/67(A)	Cin.	4–0	2	8	1	Nolan
5/8/68(H)	N.Y.	2–0	4	5	2	Jackson
5/15/68(A)	Pit.	1–0	4	6	1	Blass
5/30/68(H)	S.F.	6–0	8	5	1	Sadecki
6/19/68(H)	Chi.	4–0	1	9	0	Nye
7/27/68(A)	Pit.	4–0	6	4	2	Moose

Date	Team	Score	Hits	S.O.	Walks	Loser
5/23/69(A)	L.A.	1–0	5	8	0	Foster
7/16/69(H)	Phi.	5–0	5	12	4	Champion
5/11/70(H)	Phi.	3–0	4	10	1	Bunning
6/21/70(A)	Chi.	3–0	6	7	2	Holtzman
4/17/71(A)	S.D.	4–0	4	5	5	Pheobus
5/2/71(H)	Mon.	1–0	9	2	1	Morton
5/20/71(H)	L.A.	5–0	5	5	3	Singer
9/19/71(A)	Mon.	11–0	4	2	5	McAnally
4/19/72(H)	Stl.	1–0	3	5	0	Gibson
4/25/72(A)	S.F.	3–0	1	14	1	Marichal
6/25/72(A)	Mon.	1–0	4	8	3	McAnaly
7/23/72(A)	L.A.	2–0	5	6	1	John
7/28/72(H)	Chi.	2–0	4	7	1	Pappas
8/5/72(A)	Stl.	5–0	5	7	1	Cleveland
8/9/72(A)	Pit.	2–0	3	12	1	Blass
9/3/72(A)	Atl.	8–0	5	4	3	Hardin
5/26/73(A)	S.D.	4–0	4	12	4	Caldwell
7/14/73(H)	Hou.	7–0	3	5	5	Reuss
7/30/73(A)	Pit.	1–0	6	10	1	Moose
6/12/74(A)	Hou.	3–0	5	8	4	Wilson
5/14/75(H)	Cin.	4–0	7	3	3	Darcy
6/7/75(H)	L.A.	4–0	2	3	3	Rau
7/22/75(H)	Atl.	1–0	3	8	3	Morton
5/26/76(H)	N.Y.	5–0	3	1	1	Matlack
7/10/76(H)	S.D.	5–0	7	5	2	Foster
5/10/77(H)	S.F.	3–0	4	3	0	Cornutt
9/24/77(A)	Mon.	1–0	4	4	7	Holdsworth
6/16/78(A)	S.D.	5–0	5	8	2	Jones
8/6/78(A)	Pit.	5–0	3	3	3	Bibby
8/19/78(H)	S.F.	3–0	10	4	1	Montefusco
5/16/79(A)	Chi.	13–0	3	4	0	Reuschel
6/5/79(A)	Hou.	8–0	1	4	4	Williams
7/4/79(H)	N.Y.	1–0	4	9	0	Hassler
9/30/79(A)	Mon.	2–0	3	12	3	Rogers
4/26/80(H)	Stl.	7–0	1	5	1	Fulgham
5/23/80(H)	Hou.	3–0	4	8	3	Ryan
10/1/80(H)	Chi.	5–0	2	10	2	Lamp
9/1/81(A)	Atl.	3–0	3	4	1	Mahler
5/14/82(H)	S.F.	2–0	2	8	1	Gale
6/28/82(H)	Stl.	1–0	6	4	4	Mura
7/16/82(A)	S.F.	1–0	4	5	3	Laskey
7/25/82(A)	L.A.	1–0	5	8	0	Reuss
9/13/82(H)	Stl.	2–0	3	12	0	Forsch
9/29/82(H)	Mon.	4–0	2	3	1	Smith
4/20/83(H)	Chi.	2–0	4	10	3	Rainey
7/4/83(H)	N.Y.	4–0	4	9	1	Terrell
8/15/83(A)	Chi.	5–0	6	4	1	Trout

Steve Carlton

Year	Home	Away	Total
66	0	1	1
67	0	2	2
68	3	2	5
69	1	1	2
70	1	1	2
71	2	2	4
72	2	6	8
73	1	2	3
74	0	1	1
75	3	0	3
76	2	0	2
77	1	1	2
78	1	2	3
79	1	3	4
80	3	0	3
81	0	1	1
82	4	2	6
83	2	1	3
	27	28	55

Steve Carlton's Shutouts by Team

Atl.	Chi.	Cin.	Hou.	L.A.	Mon.	N.Y.	Phi.	Pit.	Stl.	S.D.	S.F.	Total
3	7	2	5	5	6	4	2	6	5	4	6	55

Shutouts by Team Finish

1	2	3	4	5	6	7	8	9	10	Total
5	9	8	11	12	8	0	1	1	0	55

Mordecai "Three Finger" Brown
The Mainstay of the Cubs

Mordecai Peter Centennial Brown was born in 1876, the centennial year of our country's birth. Hence, his second middle name. He became better known as "Three Finger" when he started playing professional baseball. This moniker can be traced to the time when Brown was seven years old and suffered a mishap on his uncle's farm by getting his right hand caught in a corn grinder. His forefinger was badly mangled. A few days later, it required amputation which left him with only a one-inch stub for his index finger. Because of this injury, Brown was able to throw a baseball that had a peculiar breaking motion. Brown was not a gigantic man, standing at 5'11" (175 lbs.), but his ability to make the ball do tricks made him an awesome pitcher for his time. Brown started out as an infielder but later was switched to pitching because of his ability to make the ball travel in unique paths.

Before going on with Brown's career highlights, it is important to discuss some of the statistical differences found in the various books needed by researchers combing through the records. When it came to his shutout totals, all of the books differ slightly. Brown was a contemporary of the great Christy Mathewson, another pitcher whose records were not always agreed upon. This can be traced back to poor record keepers of the time, who were not as accurate as those of today.

The Macmillan Baseball Encyclopedia shows a total of 57 shutouts for Brown while *Total Baseball* gives Brown credit for 55. Neft and Cohen's book shows Brown with 56 shutouts while *The Sporting News* record book has Brown with 50. *The Sporting News* did not recognize any records of the Federal League, which Brown played in for two years recording five shutouts. Given that number and adding it to 50 matches *Total Baseball* exactly. While Macmillan erroneously gives Brown credit for one extra shutout in 1906 and 1910, Neft and Cohen credited him with an extra shutout in 1910. The error in 1906 was that in one game Brown was credited with the win but did not complete the game, and in 1910 he won a 1–0 game in relief which, in that case, also was incorrectly recorded as a complete-game shutout. Therefore, Brown's career total should be 55 shutouts.

Three Finger started his professional career late after playing local ball with some of the teams around the coal mines of Indiana. The nickname "Miner" was also an appellation that was attached to him. As stated before, his ability to make the ball deviate from its normal route thrust him into the pitching corp when he started out in 1901 with Terre-Haute of the Three I League at the age of 24. He posted a 23–8 mark, leading the league in victories. Minor league stats were poorly kept and not held in high regard, so many of the pitching categories are nonexistent. The following year he was promoted to the more competitive Western League, which saw him carve a 27–15 record with Omaha.

In 1903, he was promoted to the St. Louis Cardinals as a 26-year-old rookie. St. Louis finished last in the league that year with a 43–94 mark, giving them a paltry .314 winning percentage. Only the Washington Nationals in the American League matched them in futility. Brown did not raise any eyebrows with his performance that year, as his efforts produced a 9–13 record. The nine victories gave him a share of the team's lead with Charles McFarland. He gave up 231 hits in 201 innings pitched. He did log the first shutout of his career on April 19 when he stopped the Cubs 3–0. This was a five-inning game curtailed by rain. Brown allowed only one hit, which was by Bobby Lowe, who will always be known as the first man to hit four home runs in one game.

After the season, Brown, along with Jack O'Neill, was traded to the Cubs for 21-game winner, Jack Taylor. The irony of this was that Taylor, three years later, would be traded back to the Cubs leaving the Cardinals with only dreams of what might have been.

Three Finger relished his years with the Cubs, as he became an integral part of a sprouting Cub dynasty that lasted until 1910. In 1904, he was the number-five starter, winning 15 versus 10 losses. His E.R.A. was a sparkling 1.87—second only to "Ironman" Joe McGinnity (1.61). Brown spun four shutouts during the season. He finished 21 of 23 games he started and was used in relief three times. His doubling as a reliever was frequent, as he would save 39 games for them during the years. The Cubs had assembled their fabled infield of Tinker, Evers, and Chance and needed another year to wait for the McGraw-led Giants to fade.

In 1905, the New York Giants won their second consecutive pennant, by nine games over Pittsburgh. The Cubs finished third, 13 games back, which was the same distance they finished in 1904 when they came in second. Brown had an 18–10 record, sharing the team lead in wins with Jake Weimer and Ed Ruelbach. He had finished with a respectable 2.17 E.R.A. based on four shutouts. On June 13, he matched serves with the legendary Christy Mathewson and lost this game of inches. Matty pitched his second no-hitter in defeating Three Finger 1–0. Brown matched him inning for inning but he weakened in the ninth by allowing two singles that delivered the only run that "Big Six" needed. This was the beginning of the classic duels the two protagonists made famous during their careers. Brown, after that loss, defeated Matty nine straight times over the years. It must be acknowledged that Brown completed all of the games he started that year (24 for 24). He was also used six times in relief. He suffered 13 defeats but that was offset by the same number of victories.

Near the latter part of the year, Manager Frank Seele resigned and was replaced by first baseman Frank Chance, who improved the team's percentage from .578 to .635. This was the onset of Chicago's dominance in the National League for the next five years.

In 1906, the Cubs produced the winningest team of all time when they won 116 games versus 36 losses for a winning percentage of .763. They vaulted over the second-place Giants by 20 games. Their infield now had Harry Steinfeldt, who they procured from Cincinnati for Hans Lobert and Jake Weimer. Steinfeldt was the answer to one of baseball's most frequently asked trivia questions: Who played third base for the renowned Chicago Cub infield of Tinker, Evers and Chance?

This team was loaded with outstanding pitching and led by Brown, who sported a 26–6 mark. He led the league in E.R.A. with an incredible 1.04. This was the major-league record until it was toppled by

Mordecai "Three Finger" Brown

Hubert "Dutch" Leonard in 1914 with a 1.00. In fairness to Brown, Leonard only pitched 225 innings while Brown had 277. Brown can still claim the National League mark. Two other members of that incredible pitching staff had E.R.A.'s under 2.00 (Jack Pfester had 1.56 and Ed Ruelbach had 1.65). The staff's E.R.A. was a combined 1.76, a good barometer of why they captured 116 victories.

The Cubs' pitching staff was outstanding. Over the next five years, from 1906 to 1910, they had 30, 32 (a major league record they shared with the 1906 White Sox who they met in the World Series), 29, 32, and 25 shutouts respectively. Brown had over 25 percent of these himself.

Brown's low E.R.A. could be traced to his league-leading nine shutouts. The only team to escape his blanking were the seventh-place Cardinals. He shut out the Pirates three times by the score of 1–0. In all three games, he defeated "Lefty" Leifeld, with two of the games being one hitters. The game on July 4 was a 1–0 thing of beauty as the Cubs scored the only run in the top of the ninth. The only hit off of Brown was by his opposing moundsman, Leifeld. Amazingly, Leifeld also pitched a one-hitter.

On September 6, he again one-hit Pittsburgh by the score of 2–0. In that game, Tom Sheenan broke the Bucs' lethargic attempts when he singled in the fifth inning. He was quickly erased on a double play.

The World Series of 1906 would be the first time two teams from the same city would face off for the world championship. The Cubs' crosstown rivals, the White Sox, had witnessed a hard-fought pennant race with the New York Highlanders. The White Sox sported a team batting average of .230 with six home runs. This prompted the enduring nickname the "Hitless Wonders." Pitching was their strong point and it carried them to a 19-game winning streak, an American League record, which was tied by the Yankees in 1947. The Cubs were overwhelmingly favored to win the championship as they outshined the American Leaguers in every category.

The first game saw a matchup of Brown versus Nick Altrock, one of the Sox's 20-game winners. Both spun four-hitters but Altrock prevailed with 2–1 decision. After three games, the surprising Chisox had a 2–1 game lead with the fifth game scheduled on their home turf. Brown was again matched up with Altrock, with Three Finger coming out on top with a stunning 1–0 two-hitter.

Two days later with the Cubs facing elimination, they rushed Brown back with one day's rest. The White Sox showed no mercy on him as they drove him from the mound in the second inning with seven runs and eight hits. This shocked the baseball world, as no one expected the Cubs to lose.

The following year of 1907 saw the Cubs romp to their second consecutive pennant, this time by 17 games over second-place Pittsburgh. This team also had a winning percentage of over .700, the only team in modern baseball to have two years in a row of .700 or better ball. Brown again had another 20-game-win season and an E.R.A. that was a stunning 1.39. This was aided by six shutouts—two of them in August against their archrivals, the Giants. He started the two games on the Giants' last trip to the Windy City. He beat Mathewson on August 2 by 5–0 and four days later he defeated Luther "Dummy" Taylor 2–0. During this year, he had a ten-game winning streak.

The Cubs matched off versus the Detroit Tigers, who won out in a hard-fought photo finish against the Philadelphia Athletics. They were be led by the notorious Ty Cobb, who vowed he would create havoc against the Chicago pitching staff. His boasts were hollow words as the Cubs held him to a measly four hits in 20 at-bats. Detroit was held to six runs for the entire Series. The Tigers were humbled four games to zero with their best effort a 3–3 tie on the opening game. This was the first tie game in World Series history. In the fifth game, Brown shut the Detroiters out 2–0 on seven hits. After this game Cobb claimed that Brown was the toughest pitcher he ever faced.

The year 1908 saw a down-to-the-wire finish in both leagues. In the American League the Tigers won out over the Cleveland Naps by one half of a game and over the White Sox by a game and a half. It was also a three-team race in the National League with the Cubs prevailing by a game over the New York Giants and Pittsburgh Pirates. The Giants were buoyed by Mathewson, who was 37–11, but Brown's effort could not go unnoticed because he went 29–9. Mathewson had 11 shutouts while Brown spun 9. Matty's E.R.A. was a league-leading 1.43, followed by Three Finger at 1.47. Both did double duty—Brown with 13 relief appearances and Christy with 12. Both had five saves, which gave them a share of the lead in that department.

The first of Brown's shutouts in 1908 was his 25th career blanking on May 17 when he defeated Brooklyn 5–0 on one hit. Bill Berger, the catcher, singled in the 3rd inning, spoiling Brown's gallant effort. During the month of July, Brown posted four shutouts with two coming in successive starts versus the Pirates at Pittsburgh (July 2 and July 4). His shutout on July 17 of the New York Giants was a 1–0 beating of their ace, Mathewson.

In September, he hooked up in a classic duel with Pittsburgh's Vic Willis, who edged him out 1–0. This game preceded the famous Merkel game, which will be discussed in detail in the chapter on Vic Willis. The Merkel game, mentioned in the chapter on Mathewson, led to a replay after the season ended. It determined the pennant winner. The game was scheduled for October 8 and matched Mathewson versus Jack Pfiester. Brown, who came in and relieved in this game, declared that this was his finest hour in baseball. The intensity before the game was deep, and Brown revealed later that he had received many death threats prior to the game. (For more see "1908— Chicago Cubs 4, N.Y. Giants 2," by Mordecai Brown as told to Jack Ryan, in the *Fireside Book of Baseball*, edited by Charles Einstein.) Three Finger had shown the death-threat letters to Manager Frank Chance, begging him to start the game. Brown, who had pitched only two days prior and who had done yeoman work down the stretch (he pitched 11 of the last 14 games and 14 of Chicago's last 19) craved the challenge of the death threats.

Chance stood with his original choice, Pfiester, but kept Brown in the bullpen in case he needed him. In the top of the first, Matty retired the Cubs without much effort. In the bottom of the first, the Giants battered Pfiester for a run and had him reeling with two on and two out. Chance then decided to bring in Brown to quell the Giants and keep the game close. It was a sound decision as Three Finger retired the Giants without any further damage. He allowed only one run and that came in the 7th inning. The Cubs had slammed Matty for four runs earlier, giving them a lead that they never relinquished. Basking in the warmth of their victory, the Cubs now geared themselves to meet the Detroit Tigers once again for the world championship. Detroit also had a hard-fought drive for the pennant, winning on the last day of the season when they defeated the Chicago White Sox.

In the Series, the Cobb-led Bengals showed more of an effort than the previous year but succumbed to the Cubs four games to one. Cobb had an excellent Series, going 7 for 19, a .368 average. In the first game, the Cubs had to score five runs in the top of the ninth to cement the victory 10–6. Brown, the third Cub pitcher, got credit for the victory as he pitched the last two innings with two unearned runs scored against him. With Chicago leading in the Series two games to one, Brown was called to solidify the lead, which he did with an artistic touch by painting a 3–0 whitewashing. In that game, he doled out four hits. More noteworthy, he tied Christy Mathewson for the most World Series shutouts with three.

In 1909, the Cubs' string of pennants was interrupted by the Pirates, who captured the flag by 6½ games with a 110–47 record. The Pirates had to play .724 ball to assure themselves of the pennant because the Cubs won 104 games, making it the first time in the game's history that a team didn't win the pennant while winning over 100 games.

Brown had another fabulous year. He showed a 27–9 record with 1.31 E.R.A., finishing second behind the great Mathewson, who had a 1.14 mark. They both had eight shutouts but finished second in that department behind Three Finger's teammate, Orval Overall, who had nine.

In Brown's list of shutouts for the year, he recorded two one-hitters. On August 1, he blanked the Phillies 3–0 with "Kitty" Bransfield getting a single in the seventh inning. On September 14, he stopped the Cincinnati Reds 4–0 with Dick Egan singling in the fifth inning for the Reds' only safety.

In 1910, the Pittsburgh Pirates relinquished the pennant back to the Cubs, who romped over the second-place Giants by 13 games. The Cubs boasted 104 wins, making it the fourth time in five years that they broke the 100-victory mark. In 1908, they won 99 games. Their 530 wins in that five-year span averaged out to 106 wins per year and in all probability will never be duplicated. Brown, who posted a 25–13 record for 1910, was the mainstay of the staff. His 127 victories over that five-year period can attest to that fact. This was almost 25% of the team's total wins for that same period. Over that stretch of time, the team's percentage was an outstanding .696, while Brown's was even more extraordinary at .747. If it wasn't for Mathewson, the Cub ace would have no doubt been the leading pitcher in the National League during the first decade of the 20th century.

During the year, Brown forged six shutouts. Top research resources disagree about his total for the year. The error lies in the fact that Brown was credited with a 1–0 victory that he attained while relieving Jack Pfeister on June 17th versus Brooklyn. He pitched three innings in that game and got the win because the Cubs scored while he was on the mound. Another game that he was in that resulted in 1–0 victory was on June 24, when he relieved Ed Ruelbach versus Cincinnati. In that game, he was credited with a save. In neither case would he have been credited with a shutout, so his total for the year is six, which tied him with three others for the lead (Earl Moore of Philadelphia, Nap Rucker of Brooklyn, and Al Mattern of Boston).

Over this period, Brown had an E.R.A. that was so remarkable it only once rose to 1.80, in 1910. From 1906 to 1909 he had E.R.A.'s of 1.04, 1.39, 1.47, and 1.31 respectively. During this time frame, he pitched 38 of his 50 National League shutouts.

In the World Series the Cubs met the first of Connie Mack's dynasties and groveled to the Philadelphia A's in five games. This was the first time an American League team won over 100 games, and that two teams met in the World Series that each had 100 victories. The Cubs, known for their pitching strength, were outgunned by the A's staff, which was anchored by 31-game-winner Jack Coombs. The A's used only two pitchers in the five games and Coombs notched three of Philadelphia's four wins. After "Chief" Bender stymied the Cubs in the opener 4–1 on three hits, it was Coombs versus Brown in the second game. The "Mackmen" racked up Three Finger by the score of 9–3, in which he gave up all of the runs. Brown came back in the fourth game in relief and got credit for the victory when Chicago scored a run in the bottom of the tenth to squeak by the A's 4–3. Frank Chance was ejected in this game, making him the second manager to be ousted from a World Series game. Brown started the fifth game and held his own until the A's erupted for five runs in the top of the eighth, sealing Chicago's fate. Brown was below average this Series as he gave up 23 hits in 18 innings with a bloated E.R.A. of 5.50.

In 1911, John McGraw's Giants started a string of three consecutive pennants. The Cubs finished 7½ games back in second place. The famed infield was now showing signs of breaking up as Chance appeared in only 31 games due to an ankle injury. Evers participated in 46 games and was out the majority of the year due to an undisclosed illness. Brown, now 34 years of age, led the staff with a 21–11 mark, his sixth straight year of 20 or more wins. He didn't throw a shutout, which pushed his E.R.A. to 2.80, the first time it was over 2.00 since 1905. Along with his victories, he saved a league leading 13 games, which made him a participant in 37% of Chicago's wins. Brown's best years were obviously behind him.

In 1912 Brown dropped out of the starting rotation. He appeared in only 15 games, of which he started only eight and finished five for a 5–6 record. This was his first losing season since his rookie year.

He did manage two shutouts, both six-hitters, and his E.R.A. was a healthy 2.63 despite his poor record. The Giants again won the pennant but Chicago had fallen to third, 11½ games off the pace but only 1½ behind Pittsburgh.

In 1913, Frank Chance was replaced as manager by Johnny Evers. Brown was released but picked up by the Cincinnati Reds, who were now managed by Three Finger's old teammate Joe Tinker. Brown pitched credibly for the Reds as he showed an 11–12 mark and an E.R.A. of 2.92. He pitched one memorable shutout, his 50th career blanking. Ironically, this was a brilliant six-hitter versus his ex-team, the Cubs, as he subdued them 4–0. This was his last National League shutout.

In 1914, the newly formed Federal League began play and Brown was lured over by the fledgling league's flow of cash. He did double duty as a player/manager, posting a 50–63 mark for the St. Louis team, and then showed a 12–6 record as a pitcher. Near the end of the year, he was traded to the Brooklyn team where he was 2–5. St. Louis finished dead last while Brooklyn came in fifth at an even .500. He spun his first shutout in the new league on July 4, which was a 1–0 blanking of Kansas City on five hits. The game lasted only eight innings because of darkness. He shut out the Chicago team 4–0 on two hits 11 days later.

In 1915, he wound up with the Chicago Whales and was reunited with his old teammate and manager, Joe Tinker. He helped pitch them to the pennant by contributing a 17–8 mark, making him an integral part of the team. This was the last year of the new league, and it was a showcase of parity because the Whales beat out the St. Louis Terriers by one percentage point. The Pittsburgh Rebels were only half a game back in third; sixth place Buffalo was 12 games out.

Brown sported a 2.10 E.R.A., aided by three shutouts. His first shutout was on June 18 when he defeated Buffalo 8–0 on one hit. Jack Dalton was the culprit who deprived Brown of his last moment of glory by getting a single in the eighth inning. Brown blamed himself for the hit by making a 2–0 pitch too good. He faced only 31 men, 21 of whom were retired on infield outs.

On August 22, the Chicago fans honored him with a day to show their appreciation for his constantly outstanding work. Brown responded with a four-hit shutout of Buffalo, giving up only two hits. This was his last career shutout. At the end of the year, the Federal League would not exist and Brown would return to the Cubs for the 1916 season. The 1916 season was the last for Brown as he appeared in only 12 games, winning two and losing three. In one game, which was a promotional gimmick, he was matched up with Christy Mathewson, now the manager of the Cincinnati Reds. Matty prevailed in a 10–8 match with both pitchers going the route. This win enabled Matty to square his record with Brown at 13–13.

Brown's record was remarkable over the years, for he was the major factor in bringing his teams to five pennants and two World Series championships. His outstanding career was recognized in 1949 when he was enshrined in baseball's Hall of Fame.

"Three-Finger" Brown

Date	Team	Score	Hits	S.O.	Walks	Loser
4/19/03(H)	Chi.	3–0	1	2	1	W. Williams (5 inns)
5/12/04(H)	Phi.	4–0	5	4	3	Duggelby
7/14/04(H)	Bos.	14–0	3	3	3	Fisher
7/19/04(H)	Phi.	1–0	6	4	1	Suthoff
8/26/04(H)	N.Y.	5–0	5	4	1	Elliot
4/23/05(H)	Pit.	1–0	4	1	5	Phillipi
8/26/05(A)	Phi.	4–0	6	5	0	Duggelby
9/1/05(H)	Cin.	3–0	3	2	2	Overall
9/11/05(H)	Cin.	12–0	2	2	1	Chech
4/28/06(H)	Cin.	1–0	4	3	0	Weimer
6/5/06(A)	N.Y.	6–0	3	2	4	McGinnity
7/4/06(A)	Pit.	1–0	1	5	0	Leifeld
7/7/06(A)	Pit.	5–0	4	2	3	Leifeld
7/28/06(A)	Bos.	8–0	7	8	2	Dorner
8/3/06(A)	Phi.	1–0	6	5	2	Lush
8/10/06(A)	Brk.	2–0	3	5	1	Stricklett
8/28/06(H)	Cin.	8–0	8	1	2	Ewing
9/6/06(H)	Pit.	2–0	1	1	2	Leifeld
4/29/07(A)	Cin.	1–0	4	3	0	Ewing
6/21/07(H)	Stl.	2–0	8	2	2	Lush
7/8/07(A)	Brk.	5–0	6	0	0	Pastorious
7/12/07(A)	Phi.	3–0	4	3	1	Corridon
8/2/07(H)	N.Y.	5–0	4	4	1	Mathewson
8/6/07(H)	N.Y.	2–0	3	6	1	Taylor
5/17/08(H)	Brk.	5–0	1	4	0	Rucker
6/13/08(A)	Phi.	1–0	3	1	0	McQuillan
6/25/08(H)	Cin.	7–0	6	6	1	Dubec
7/2/08(A)	Pit.	3–0	6	3	0	Young
7/4/08(A)	Pit.	2–0	2	4	1	Leever
7/17/08(H)	N.Y.	1–0	6	1	1	Mathewson
7/29/08(A)	Bos.	6–0	4	3	0	Finherty
8/12/08(A)	Pit.	3–0	3	5	1	Willis
10/2/08(A)	Cin.	5–0	4	7	1	Roman

Date	Team	Score	Hits	S.O.	Walks	Loser
6/25/09(H)	Cin.	7–0	8	2	3	Dubec
7/2/09(A)	Pit.	8–0	5	3	1	Camnitz
7/19/09(A)	Brk.	2–0	2	6	2	Rucker
8/1/09(H)	Phi.	3–0	1	3	0	McQuillan
8/8/09(H)	Brk.	7–0	3	7	0	MacIntyre
8/15/09(H)	N.Y.	9–0	4	4	0	Crandall
8/31/09(A)	N.Y.	2–0	5	3	1	Wiltse
9/14/09(A)	Cin.	4–0	1	5	0	Gasper
6/23/10(H)	Pit.	9–0	3	4	1	Adams
7/1/10(A)	Stl.	2–0	4	8	1	Harmon
7/21/10(H)	Bos.	3–0	9	3	2	Frock
8/15/10(A)	Brk.	14–0	11	4	0	Barger
9/28/10(A)	Bos.	11–0	6	6	1	Mattern
10/7/10(H)	Pit.	1–0	2	8	1	Leifeld
6/25/12(A)	Cin.	11–0	6	1	0	Keefe
7/4/12(A)	Stl.	2–0	6	2	1	Sallee
7/4/13(A)	Chi.	4–0	6	0	2	Smith
7/4/14(A)	K.C.	1–0	5	1	0	Harris
7/15/14(A)	Chi.	2–0	4	1	4	Hendrik
6/18/15(A)	Buf.	8–0	1	3	3	Kropp
6/29/15(A)	Nwk.	1–0	4	4	0	Moseley
8/22/15(H)	Buf.	4–0	2	1	3	Kropp

Year	Home	Away	Total
03	1	0	1
04	4	0	4
05	2	2	4
06	3	6	9
07	3	3	6
08	3	6	9
09	4	4	8
10	3	3	6
12	0	2	2
13	0	1	1
	23	27	50

Federal League

	Home	Away	Total
14	0	2	2
15	1	2	3
	1	4	5
	24	31	55

Three Finger Brown's Shutouts by Team

National League

Bos.	Brk.	Chi.	Cin.	N.Y.	Phi.	Pit.	Stl.	Total
5	6	2	10	7	7	10	3	50

Mordecai "Three Finger" Brown

Federal League

Buf.	Chi.	K.C.	Ind. Nwk.	Total
2	1	1	1	5

(Both Leagues) 55

Shutouts by Team Finish

National League

1	2	3	4	5	6	7	8	Total
2	3	13	8	7	8	3	6	50

Federal League

1	2	3	4	5	6	Total
1	1	0	0	1	3	5

Jim Palmer
From Oblivion to Greatness

Jim Palmer got his baptism into major league baseball when most his age were preparing for a career in college. At the tender age of 19 he was to become the most successful of all the "Kiddie Korps" pitchers that Baltimore was grooming during the early 60s.

Pitchers like Steve Barber, Jack Fisher, and Wally Bunker had glimpses of greatness, but Palmer's career was etched with the immortals of the game. He was one of history's elite when his days on the mound ended, but it looked precarious for awhile.

The way his career started, it looked as if history was repeating itself when almost 30 years prior to Jim's emergence, another teenager (named Bob Feller) erupted on the scene to become the dominant right-handed pitcher of the American League. Both Palmer and Feller won five games in their abbreviated rookie years. Feller's start was meteoric while Jim's grew in intensity as he went along game to game and season to season. Jim's second year produced 15 wins before he was of legal age. He did not pitch a shutout during those victories, but he achieved one in the second game of the 1966 World Series against the Los Angeles Dodgers. Fitted against the legendary Sandy Koufax, he outpitched the man who many consider the very best pitcher in the 1960s. This game also marked the final appearance in major league baseball for the stylish left-hander. Jim, who was nine days short of his 21st birthday, dazzled the Dodgers with just four hits, while leaving the Los Angeles fans in disbelief. Although the Orioles were aided by Willie Davis' notorious play in center field, Palmer's masterful performance would prevail 6–0. He needed no one to assist him except national television, which propelled him to majestic heights. With the whole baseball world watching, somewhat like the Israelites and Philistines, David slew the awesome Goliath! The world was now his oyster.

The following year, 1967, he started out with a rush just like a thoroughbred breaking from the gate in a high-stakes race. His 3–1 record included his first major league shutout on May 12, when he beat the once-proud Yankees and their future Hall of Famer, Whitey Ford. This was only a shell of the once mighty Bombers, but the lineup still included Mantle, Howard, and Pepitone. He had plenty of support and won 14–0, giving up one single to Horace Clark. He faced the minimum 27 men as he waltzed through the batting order.

Soon after, there was a downward detour on his road to greatness. After only nine games, he developed a sore arm that plagued him for the next two years. Minus his contributions, the Orioles nose-dived to below .500, and they floundered the remainder of the year.

During 1967, the Orioles sent him to Rochester of the International League to straighten out his arm problems. He proved ineffective at that level and dropped further to Miami of the Class A Florida State League. To go from the World Series phenom to Class A was like going from the penthouse to the basement without an elevator.

In 1968, starting out with Rochester, his sore arm did not respond. Again he was demoted, but this time he went to Elmira (Class AA Eastern League). His bright career seemed to be like a nova whose brilliant illumination faded into a dying ember. Would he be just another Orioles pitcher who tasted glory but who would shortly wind up on the junk heap? But fate, along with his determination not to become discouraged, brought him back to the majors. He was only 23 when the 1969 season started and his arm trouble seemed to be in the past. By June 7, he had fashioned four shutouts when more problems plagued him in the form of back trouble. He overcame this injury after 42 days on the disabled list and again became a member of the starting rotation. In his second start off the disabled list, he pitched his only no-hitter! This was against the Oakland A's, who were on the brink of becoming a dynasty themselves. The ominous likes of Reggie Jackson, Joe Rudi, and Sal Bando were there in the lineup. Jim struck out eight but walked six. Three of these bases on balls occurred in the ninth inning, but a force-out preserved this masterpiece.

By the end of 1969 he had thrown a total of six shutouts out of his 16 victories. He seemed like the mystical Phoenix rising from the ashes and ascending to his promise. His appearance in the post-season was one win against Minnesota in the American league championship series. He clinched the pennant and the right to face the Miraculous Mets in the World Series. In the first inning of game three, he gave up his first Series run as the Mets coasted to a 5–0 victory. Jim could not be faulted because his teammates could only scrape four hits against Gentry and Ryan. Losing the Series was probably the greatest upset in World Series history, but the Orioles emerged with a plethora of hope for the coming decade. His name was Jim Palmer.

In 1970 Jim broke into the 20-game-winner's bracket for the first time. Included in his wins were five shutouts, tying him with Gaylord Perry of the San Francisco Giants and Chuck Dobson of the Oakland A's for the major league lead. In 1971, Jim recorded three whitewashes. His third made him a 20-game winner a second time. This Baltimore team produced two tying distinctions in major league history. They accomplished the feat of winning 100 games or more for three consecutive seasons, duplicating the precedents set by the Philadelphia A's of 1929–1931 and the St. Louis Cardinals of 1942–1944. This etched fame for the team in the annals of the game while Jim was a major contributor.

Another notable accomplishment was that the pitching staff showcased four 20-game winners: Palmer, Mike Cuellar, Dave McNally, and Pat Dobson. Only once in history did a team boast of that many stalwarts on the mound, the 1920 Chicago White Sox. Their fame did not last because of the infamous 1919 season. The Oriole team won a pennant whereas the Chicago team failed.

In 1972 the Orioles slipped to third place mainly because half of their four-man rotation had losing years. Palmer was the only 20-game winner, as he became the ace and anchor of the staff.

In 1973 Baltimore was on top in the Eastern Division due to Palmer's spectacular pitching. He forged six shutouts and captured the earned run title with a 2.40 E.R.A. One was a one-hitter versus Cleveland in which George Hendricks spoiled Jim's no-hitter. In the American League championship series, he threw a 6–0 shutout versus the Oakland A's, besting Vida Blue. He alone couldn't get Baltimore over the top and into the World Series, but his effort could not go unnoticed. This was his first post-season shutout since that memorable 6–0 game against Koufax and the Dodgers in 1966. His splendid season earned him the first of three Cy Young Awards.

In 1974, Jim was beset by the injury jinx again. He won only seven games (and his first losing record) but he was the deciding factor at the end of the season. He helped Baltimore to edge out the Yankees by spinning two shutouts in September. On September 4, he blanked the Boston Red Sox for his 25th career shutout. Later that month, he stopped the hard-charging Yankees 4–0. That game was the difference for the division title. If the Yankees had won, it would have been a flat-footed tie at season's end. Even with a sore arm and a low victory total, his presence was felt in the final victory. In the American League championship series, he was the loser against Oakland and Vida Blue (1–0).

After his disappointing year in 1975, he exploded with a spectacular flair that won him his second Cy Young Award. This was his career year as he recorded his highest win total with 23. He almost pitched Baltimore to another championship but his efforts could not erase a stubborn Boston lead. In those 23 victories he pitched 10 shutouts to give him another E.R.A. title (2.09). Those ten shutouts placed him in an elite class that includes Cy Young, Walter Johnson, Christy Mathewson, Grover Alexander, Ed Walsh, Carl Hubbell, Sandy Koufax, Juan Marichal, and Bob Gibson. All of these men are enshrined in baseball's Hall of Fame. The significance of ten shutouts in one year is that it has been accomplished 19 times since 1900. Some of those mentioned have achieved that milestone twice. One of his shutouts was a one-hitter against Kansas City, which was building one of the most fierce hitting machines. George Brett, John Mayberry, and Hal McRae were members of that lineup. McRae spoiled Palmer's no-hit bid.

Now the premier pitcher in the American League, he again flashed another award-winning year by notching his third Cy Young Award in 1976. Another 20-win season with six shutouts cemented it for him. He missed leading the league in shutouts by falling to Nolan Ryan by one. The three Cy Young Awards put him in select company—with Sandy Koufax and Tom Seaver—as the only pitchers to win three awards at that time. He was the only American Leaguer to claim that distinction until Roger Clemens duplicated the feat in the 80s and 90s.

In 1977 he won another 20 games, but his shutouts were down

to three. He started the year with a blast by posting two of them in April—one of them a stunning 1–0 two-hitter against Milwaukee. The Orioles finished a close second to the Yankees, but Palmer couldn't be blamed for any lack of effort on his part. He exhibited durability by leading the league with 319 innings pitched, making it three consecutive years of 300 or more innings toiled. This is another statistical category that will not be embraced in the coming years.

In 1978 he broke the 20-game column again, for the seventh time in eight seasons. He pitched another six shutouts, including the milestone 50th, which was a brilliant 1–0 win versus Oakland. His control was impeccable, as he allowed no walks and conceded just three hits. He just missed 300 innings pitched, but he still led the league in that category. If it wasn't for Ron Guidry having his career year, Palmer might have copped his fourth Cy Young Award!

In the ensuing years, he started to decline. He was now the seasoned veteran coming to the end of the line. He still had wins left in his arm, but he went three years without a shutout. In 1982 he had enough left to pitch two whitewashes—the last coming against Minnesota on September 4. This was another thing of beauty in which he allowed only one hit. He had retired the first 11 batters with two outs in the fourth. A single by Gary Gaetti spoiled the effort. Ironically, his first and last shutouts were one-hitters.

In 1983, he had his last fling of glory as an active player. This occurred in the World Series against the Philadelphia Phillies and Steve Carlton when he relieved the starter, Mike Flanagan, in the fifth inning. He slammed the door on Philadelphia, which was leading 2–0 at the time. Jim was spectacular, shutting out the Phils, which enabled the Orioles to regroup and salvage the win 3–2. This gave Baltimore the lead in the Series, which they never relinquished. It also gave Palmer the distinction of being the only pitcher to win a World Series game in three different decades.

The end of the road was now inevitable, and in 1984 he called it a career. He was the best the franchise ever had, including the years of the St. Louis Browns who gave birth to the Baltimore Orioles.

Jim Palmer

Date	Team	Score	Hits	S.O.	Walks	Loser
5/12/67(A)	N.Y.	14–0	1	1	0	Ford
4/13/69(H)	Wash.	2–0	5	8	3	Coleman

Jim Palmer

Date	Team	Score	Hits	S.O.	Walks	Loser
4/21/69(H)	Cle.	11–0	3	5	4	McDowell
5/11/69(H)	K.C.	5–0	3	6	2	Nelson
6/7/69(H)	Sea.	10–0	2	9	3	Brabender
8/13/69(H)	Oak.	8–0	0	8	6	Dobson
9/1/69(A)	Chi.	8–0	5	6	3	Wynne
5/23/70(H)	Bos.	3–0	7	6	0	Culp
7/1/70(H)	Cle.	3–0	8	5	1	Austin
7/5/70(H)	Det.	2–0	3	7	3	McLain
8/5/70(A)	Bos.	3–0	4	7	2	Siebert
9/20/70(H)	Cle.	7–0	4	8	3	Paul
6/10/71(H)	Min.	12–0	6	5	1	Perry
7/30/71(H)	K.C.	1–0	7	4	1	Drago
9/26/71(A)	Cle.	5–0	3	8	2	Foster
8/2/72(A)	Cle.	7–0	4	5	2	Dunning
8/28/72(A)	Min.	2–0	5	6	2	Woodson
9/10/72(H)	Mil.	2–0	2	7	1	Lockwood
5/6/73(H)	Cal.	5–0	5	3	0	Ryan
5/11/73(A)	N.Y.	3–0	3	3	0	Kline
6/26/73(A)	Mil.	6–0	4	5	5	Colborn
7/27/73(H)	Cle.	9–0	1	5	3	Bosman
9/16/73(H)	N.Y.	3–0	2	6	4	Peterson
9/20/73(A)	Det.	9–0	5	3	1	Fryman
9/4/74(H)	Bos.	6–0	3	6	1	Moret
9/17/74(A)	N.Y.	4–0	7	3	0	Medich
4/10/75(A)	Det.	10–0	3	4	0	Coleman
4/22/75(A)	Mil.	1–0	6	6	4	Broberg
5/16/75(H)	Cal.	1–0	9	5	1	Tanana
5/30/75(A)	Cal.	5–0	4	6	1	Figueroa
6/8/75(H)	K.C.	1–0	1	4	3	Busby
6/21/75(H)	Bos.	3–0	5	8	3	Pole
8/5/75(A)	Bos.	3–0	2	8	1	Tiant
8/13/75(H)	K.C.	3–0	2	6	0	Pattin
8/17/75(H)	Tex.	4–0	4	4	3	Perzanowski
9/28/75(H)	N.Y.	3–0	8	4	0	May
5/5/76(H)	Chi.	2–0	2	6	2	Gossage
6/15/76(A)	Chi.	4–0	5	3	1	Gossage
7/15/76(H)	Cal.	4–0	3	2	2	Ross
8/10/76(H)	Min.	2–0	1	5	1	Goltz
8/27/76(H)	Tex.	3–0	7	10	0	Perry
9/22/76(A)	N.Y.	2–0	4	2	0	Ellis
4/12/77(A)	Mil.	1–0	2	6	1	Travers
4/17/77(A)	Tex.	5–0	3	6	2	Blyleven
9/8/77(A)	Det.	4–0	4	3	1	Sykes
4/15/78(H)	Mil.	7–0	2	7	1	Augustine
5/24/78(H)	Det.	1–0	6	3	2	Sykes
5/28/78(H)	Cle.	3–0	8	4	1	Paxton
6/1/78(A)	N.Y.	1–0	2	2	5	Beatty

The Great Shutout Pitchers

Date	Team	Score	Hits	S.O.	Walks	Loser
6/11/78(A)	Oak.	1–0	3	4	0	Renko
8/23/78(A)	Oak.	11–0	3	5	3	Renko
8/31/82(A)	Tor.	1–0	4	3	1	Leal
9/4/82(H)	Min.	3–0	1	7	2	Castillo

Year	Home	Away	Total
67	0	1	1
69	5	1	6
70	4	1	5
71	2	1	3
72	1	2	3
73	3	3	6
74	1	1	2
75	6	4	10
76	4	2	6
77	0	3	3
78	3	3	6
82	1	1	2
	30	23	53

Jim Palmer's Shutouts by Team

Bos.	Cal.	Chi.	Cle.	Det.	K.C.	Mil.	Min.	N.Y.	Oak.	Sea.	Tex.	Tor.	Total
										Sea.		Wash.	
5	4	3	7	5	4	6	4	7	3	0	5	0	53

Shutouts by Team Finish

1	2	3	4	5	6	7	8	9	10	Total
4	6	10	9	8	14	7	0	1	0	53

Gaylord Perry
The Master of Deception

When following the career of Gaylord Perry, one is often amazed how frequently he was accused of tampering with and doctoring the baseball. Constant searches for hidden or alien objects and substances that might be a part of this arsenal dotted his career. No paraphernalia was ever found, although many still accused him of somehow manipulating the flight of the ball. As batters approached the plate, they were wary of the tall pitcher. His various gyrations confused them and they lost their concentration. Perry would go to his hat and rub his hand across his shirt, touch his pants legs, and finally throw a pitch the opposition claimed was a spitter or was coated with some foreign substance. Nothing was ever found, so Mr. Perry must get credit for being one hell of a pitcher to use psychology to throw the hitter off stride. There was nothing illegal about that!

Perry was signed by the San Francisco Giants on June 3 in 1958 for a reported $90,000, which was big money back then. He started his professional career right after signing, and he pitched for St. Cloud Class A Northern League where he was 9–5 with an excellent E.R.A. of 2.39. This promoted him the following year to Corpus Christi of the Class AA Texas League. His stay was not impressive as he had a 10–11 record with a bulging E.R.A. of 4.05. This could be attributed to 218 hits he gave up in 191 innings pitched.

In 1960, he was still on the Texas League roster but the name was changed to Rio Grande Valley. His record was 9–13 but his E.R.A. was a much improved 2.82, which led the league. His hit total (164) in 195 innings pitched lent credence to his improvement. His success in these two areas got him promoted in 1961 to Tacoma of the Triple A Pacific Coast League, where he led the league in victories (16) and innings pitched (219). His E.R.A. was a healthy 2.55.

He started 1962 with the Giants, winning three and losing one, and with a high E.R.A. (5.23). He made his debut on April 14 versus Cincinnati and won his first game on April 25, defeating the Pittsburgh Pirates 8–3. He was sent back to Tacoma where he won 10 and lost 7 and led the league with a 2.48 E.R.A.

In 1963, he was back at Tacoma where he pitched one game and won it. He was recalled by the Giants, where he appeared in 31 games mainly as a relief pitcher. His 1–6 record and 4.03 E.R.A. gave no indication that a talented pitcher was on the road to Cooperstown.

In 1964, Gaylord saw himself woven into the starting rotation and finished the year at 12–11. His victory total was good enough to be second to Juan Marichal's 21. His E.R.A. of 2.75 was also second best on the team. He pitched two shutouts with his first coming on June 30, defeating the Mets 5–0 while dealing the "Amazin's" three hits.

In 1965, Perry had a poor year, winning eight and losing twelve with a bloated E.R.A. of 4.18. His failure to pitch a shutout didn't enhance his E.RA., but he did allow slightly less than a hit per inning. By the end of the year, with two full seasons and part of two others under his belt, his career record stood at 24–30, which did not raise any eyebrows.

While the 1965 campaign was frustrating—not only to him but to the team—they lost out to the Dodgers by a scant two games. Perry's disappointment and his achievement was erased in 1966. He started the year with a flourish that lasted to August. By that time, he had secured his first 20-win season with a record of 20-2. Along with Juan Marichal, he formed a potent 1-2 pitching punch, which rivaled the Dodgers' Koufax/Drysdale combo. Perry then slumped the last month of the season, winning only one of seven decisions, which finalized his record at 21-8. He and Marichal carried the team as far as it went. The rest of the staff contributed meagerly. This was probably the reason the Giants were again second best, finishing 1½ games behind the hated Dodgers. Perry's E.R.A was a commendable

2.99 with three shutouts. The first of these was on May 1 when he hooked up in a pitching duel with Bob Gibson, defeating the Cardinals 2–0. In that game he distributed four hits while walking none. On June 26, he stopped the Cincy Reds 10–0 on two hits and bested their ace, Jim Maloney.

The Houston Astros felt Perry's sting on August 12 as he defeated them 1–0 on three hits. The Astro's ace lefty hurler, Mike Cuellar, was his opponent that day. He was drawing an assignment that paired him up against the aces of the other team's staff.

The next year, 1967, he slumped to 15–17. But his record shows he did not pitch all that badly. He had an E.R.A. of 2.61 and allowed only 231 hits in 293 innings pitched, slightly over seven hits per nine innings. Marichal was hampered by a leg injury, which definitely put pressure on the remainder of the staff to compensate for the loss of the "Dominican Dandy." Gaylord spun another three shutouts in which the most hits that he gave up in a game was four. Regardless of his record, he was a steady fixture on the Frisco staff. The Giants wound up a distant second behind St. Louis.

In 1968, the year that the pitchers dominated, Perry was back on the winning track with a 16–15 mark. This was with an aging Giant team that again finished second, eight games off the pace. He had his best E.R.A. at 2.44, one point higher than Marichal (2.43). He again matched up with the opposition's best, as was shown in his three shutouts.

On May 19, he defeated the Chicago Cubs and their ace, Ferguson Jenkins, 1–0. Against the Cubs, this time on August 26, he blanked them 3–0 on one hit, defeating their number-two man, Bill Hands. Glen Beckert marred his performance by getting a hit in the third inning. His final shutout of the year was on September 17. He had to be exceptional that night because he drew Bob Gibson as his pitching foe. Gibson manufactured 13 shutouts that year. Perry defeated the Cardinals and Gibson 1–0 on a no-hitter. This was only the second Giant no-hitter since Carl Hubbell turned the trick in 1929. Perry's teammate, Juan Marichal, created the other one in 1963. The Cardinals, not to be outdone, reciprocated the following night when Ray Washburn no-hit the Giants 2–0. This was the only time that opposing teams no-hit each other in a series during the season.

A division arrangement was started during the 1969 season due to the new expansion. The San Diego Padres and the Montreal Expos were now a part of the National League scene. The Giants, for the fifth consecutive time, finished second, three games behind the division-winning Atlanta Braves. Gaylord emerged as the workhorse of the league, toiling a total of 325 innings. His 19–14 mark with a 2.49 E.R.A. supplemented Marichal's efforts in keeping the Giants in the thick of the race until the last weekend. In his collection of wins were two shutouts.

In 1970, Gaylord had another gratifying year as he took over the role as ace on the staff. Marichal witnessed sickness that throttled him for the year. Perry salvaged the Giants' year, as they slipped into third place. Without him, they would, at best, be a .500 team. The difference of his 23–13 record was exactly the amount of games by which the Giants finished over .500. He tied for the league lead in victories with Bob Gibson. He also led the league in innings pitched (328) for the second consecutive year. His E.R.A. might have been higher if it wasn't for the five shutouts, which also was top in that department. All of them came after July started. His last four were consecutive in September, which gave him a string of 39 scoreless innings. In those four games he gave up a total of fifteen hits and allowed only three hits in his last whitewashing.

In 1971 the Giants won their division for the first time. Marichal came back and contributed 18 wins while Perry showed his usual steadiness at 16–12. His winning percentage was higher than the team's. His E.R.A. (2.76) was the best on the team. His two shutouts helped keep it below 3.00. The Giants waited until the last game of the season to secure their title.

The National League championship series opened at the Giants' home at Candlestick Park and Perry was given the starting assignment. He battled the heavy-hitting Pirates, who led the league in home runs, the whole way. After the Pirates scored two in the seventh inning, he triumphantly nursed a one-run lead the rest of the game for a final verdict of 5–4. It was the last time Perry participated in a post-season game.

Over the winter, he was traded with Frank Duffy to the Cleveland Indians for Sam McDowell. The Giants felt confident that they had the best of the deal since "Sudden Sam" was four years younger than Perry. It turned out to be an embarrassment for Frisco. McDowell was 10–8 with a shoulder injury while Gaylord had a career year that won him the Cy Young Award in the American League.

Perry did not have a strong contingent of ballplayers supporting him and the Indians finished fifth in the American League East. He finished the year at 24–16, which made his victory total exactly one-third of the team's winning total. He pitched five shutouts, which helped to lower his E.R.A. to 1.92. Amazingly, he didn't win that crown because Louis Tiant edged him out with a 1.91. Included in his shutouts was one on July 14 when he went 14 innings against the Texas Rangers, beating them 2–0. When he shut out the Orioles on September 27, it was a milestone 25th career shutout. Gaylord also led the league with 29 complete game and his innings pitched (343) was a surprising second to Wilbur Wood (377). Those totals during the 1990s were two years' totals for a good many pitchers. It wasn't unexpected when he was awarded the Cy Young Award.

When he led the American League in victories, he was the third man, at the time, to lead both leagues in that category. He joined select company with Cy Young and Jack Chesbro as the only ones previously to do it. Young did his deed in the National League prior to the 1900s, so Chesbro and Perry were the only ones to do it in the 20th century. Two years later, Fergy Jenkins joined the group.

Cleveland occupied the basement in 1973, and Perry had a 19–19 mark for the year with an E.R.A. of 3.38, despite having seven shutouts to his credit. He again led the league in complete games with 29 and worked 344 innings, which was, again, second-best to Wilbur Wood. In his game on August 22, he zeroed the Chicago White Sox 1–0, going 12 innings to get credit for the win.

Cleveland acquired Gaylord's brother, Jim, for the 1974 season, and between them they won 38 of Cleveland's 77 wins, which comes out to 49 percent. The two of them raised the Indians to fourth place, giving the team its best record since 1968.

Gaylord opened the season versus the New York Yankees on April 6. He was treated to a 6–1 pounding, losing to their ace, Mel Stottlemyre. From then on he was unbeatable as he ticked off 15 consecutive victories. In that streak, he divided his wins evenly with eight at home and seven on the road. Not all of the scores were laughers because seven of the games were decided by less than two runs. He defeated 10 out of 11 league opponents. Only the Minnesota Twins escaped the notch on his gun handle.

On July 8, he set out to tie the league record of 16 straight that was held by four pitchers. His opposition was the two-time world champion Oakland A's in their own ball park. Perry carried a 3–2 lead into the bottom of the ninth when Joe Rudi tripled. The next batter, Gene Tenace, hit a sacrifice fly to bring home the tying run. The game entered the bottom of the tenth, when, with two outs and bases loaded, rookie Claudell Washington singled home the winning run and shattered Perry's chance for lasting fame.

Included in that streak were three of his four shutouts. Perry had another splendid E.R.A. at 2.52, covering 322 innings. This was his third year in a row breaking the 300-inning mark and the fifth time in six years. He completed 28 of his 37 starts. In his three years with Cleveland, he completed 86 out of 118 starting assignments, which translates to 73 percent. Modern pitchers do not obtain that in a decade!

Cleveland hired the first black manager in 1975. Frank Robinson led them to a 79–80 record. Perry saw his last games with the Indians, as they traded him to the Texas Rangers for Jim Bibby, Jackie Brown, and Rick Waits. With the Indians, Perry was 6–9 with one shutout against Baltimore. With Texas he went 12–8 with four shutouts, three of which came in July. On July 18, he hooked up in a duel with the Yankees' Jim "Catfish" Hunter and bested him 1–0. He only allowed two hits and walked two. His combined E.R.A. for the year was 3.24 for two losing teams.

In 1976, he went 15–14 for Texas, giving him the team lead in victories. The Rangers were a losing team, so his record was good considering what he had backing him. Again, his E.R.A. was 3.24 with two shutouts, both against the Twins.

The Rangers made great strides in 1977 despite having four different managers leading them. Frank Lucchesi started the season and led them for 62 games with a .500 percentage. He was let go and replaced by Eddie Stanky, who resigned after one game. Connie Ryan was the interim manager until Billy Hunter took hold of the reins permanently. Under Hunter, they played .645 ball and rose to second place. They finished with a .580 percentage, the best in their franchise history. Perry had another winning season at 15–12 with a 3.37 E.R.A., which was still lower than the team's. He was able to toss four shutouts, beating the two eventual division winners in May. He stopped the Kansas City Royals 2–0 with four hits while edging the Yankees 1–0 on six hits.

During the year, he was able to secure his 100th American League win, which, along with his 134 victories in the National League, placed him in a small group to claim that distinction. Notables such as Cy Young and Jim Bunning were among the elite.

Prior to spring training in 1978, Perry was traded by the Rangers to the Padres for Dave Tomlin and $125,000. He was now 39, and it seemed that he might be at the proverbial end of the road, so the deal looked good for Texas. But Perry fooled everyone by going 21–6 with a 2.72 E.R.A. He led the league in victories and pitching percentage and because of his surprising effort, he was awarded the Cy Young. This made him the first man to win the coveted trophy in both leagues. In his victory total, he managed two shutouts, both four-hitters during June. His efforts elevated the Padres to fourth place, with their first winning season in team history. They finished only 11 games behind the Los Angeles Dodgers, who went to the World Series.

In 1979, over 40 years of age, he fell to a 12–11 mark, but his E.R.A. was a respectable 3.05. There were no shutouts in his win total, making it the first time since 1965 he didn't accomplish that feat. This precipitated a trade in 1980 to Texas that acquired Willie Montanez for the Padres.

In 1980, Gaylord split the season between the Rangers and the Yankees. He had a 6–9 mark for Texas and pitched two shutouts. His first on April 19 versus the Boston Red Sox was his 50th career shutout. In that game he gave up five hits in defeating Dennis Eckersley. In mid-August, the Rangers traded him to the Yankees for Ken Clay. He was 4–4 with the New Yorkers but had an extremely high E.R.A. of 4.41.

At the end of the season, he was granted free agency and signed with the Braves in 1981. During the strike season, his efforts were curtailed for another milestone, his 300th career win. He finished the season with Atlanta at 8–9, which was considered good because the Braves were below .500 for both halves. Gaylord did have a high E.R.A. at 3.93 and no shutouts. He was released at the end of the season and was signed to the Seattle Mariners where he was 10–12 in 1982. They finished fourth with a sub-.500 record. His E.R.A. was a hefty 4.40 and again he didn't master a shutout. His third win of the season was against the Yankees, which gave him his 300th career win.

In 1983, he started the year with Seattle but was released after going 3–10. He was signed by the Kansas City Royals who needed pitching help. He could only contribute with a 4–4 mark. He achieved his most significant victory when he spun his last shutout on September 3, blanking the Texas 5–0 on six hits.

In his career, he had 314 victories, 52 shutouts, and 3,534 strikeouts. This made his credentials for the Hall of Fame obvious for enshrinement. In 1991, his induction into Cooperstown became a reality. The only question one could raise is why did the Baseball Writers Association of America wait two years to induct him?

Gaylord Perry

Date	Team	Score	Hits	S.O.	Walks	Loser
6/30/64(H)	N.Y.	5–0	3	4	1	Cisco
8/8/64(A)	Cin.	1–0	2	7	0	Nuxhall
5/1/66(H)	Stl.	2–0	4	7	0	Gibson
6/26/66(A)	Cin.	10–0	2	2	0	Maloney
8/12/66(H)	Hou.	1–0	3	5	0	Cuellar
4/13/67(A)	Atl.	2–0	4	4	1	Cloninger
8/28/67(H)	L.A.	7–0	3	9	3	Sutton
9/6/67(H)	Hou.	2–0	3	9	3	Giusti
5/19/68(H)	Chi.	1–0	6	5	2	Jenkins
8/26/68(H)	Chi.	3–0	1	3	0	Hands
9/17/68(H)	Stl.	1–0	0	9	2	Gibson
5/17/69(A)	Phi.	5–0	8	9	4	Wagner
7/6/69(H)	Atl.	5–0	4	6	2	Jarvis
7/8/70(A)	Atl.	13–0	5	5	0	Niekro
9/6/70(A)	Atl.	1–0	4	5	1	Reed
9/10/70(H)	Hou.	11–0	4	6	2	Blasingame
9/15/70(H)	Atl.	8–0	4	2	0	Reed
9/19/70(A)	S.D.	3–0	3	7	0	Kirby
4/12/71(H)	S.D.	5–0	3	11	0	Kirby
8/31/71(H)	Atl.	9–0	7	5	1	Stone
5/6/72(H)	Chi.	12–0	3	4	3	Bradley
5/23/72(A)	N.Y.	3–0	4	5	1	Stottlemyre
6/1/72(H)	Det.	1–0	7	3	0	Coleman
7/14/72(A)	Tex.	2–0	9	9	3	Panther
9/27/72(A)	Bal.	3–0	7	5	5	McNally
4/15/73(A)	Det.	7–0	2	7	1	Timmerman
5/8/73(H)	Cal.	2–0	4	5	3	Wright
8/2/73(H)	Bal.	6–0	5	6	3	Hood
8/18/73(H)	Min.	5–0	3	5	3	Woodson
8/22/73(H)	Chi.	1–0	6	8	5	Acosta
8/30/73(A)	Det.	3–0	6	3	0	Coleman
9/26/73(H)	Bos.	1–0	5	7	2	Lee
5/23/74(A)	Bal.	2–0	3	7	0	Palmer
5/28/74(A)	Tex.	8–0	5	6	5	Hargan
6/22/74(A)	Bos.	11–0	4	8	1	Lee
9/15/74(A)	Bal.	1–0	5	4	3	Grimsley
4/26/75(A)	Bal.	3–0	5	7	6	Grimsley
7/6/75(A)	Min.	7–0	7	9	3	Wiley
7/18/75(H)	N.Y.	1–0	4	4	2	Hunter
7/22/75(H)	Cle.	4–0	2	13	1	Raich
8/11/75(A)	Det.	7–0	5	7	1	LaGrow
8/6/76(H)	Min.	6–0	5	4	1	Redfern
9/28/76(A)	Min.	7–0	6	6	0	Singer
5/12/77(A)	K.C.	2–0	4	5	2	Leonard
5/25/77/(A)	N.Y.	1–0	6	2	0	Torrez
6/29/77(A)	Oak.	4–0	6	4	2	Norris

Gaylord Perry

Date	Team	Score	Hits	S.O.	Walks	Loser
7/28/77(A)	Tor.	3–0	11	8	2	Garvin
6/14/78(A)	Mon.	1–0	4	5	0	Fryman
6/23/78(H)	Hou.	3–0	4	4	1	Dixon
4/19/80(A)	Bos.	8–0	5	3	2	Eckersley
6/27/80(H)	Min.	5–0	4	2	0	Redfern
9/3/83(A)	Tex.	5–0	6	4	1	Darwin

National League

Year	Home	Away	Total
64	1	1	2
66	2	1	3
67	2	1	3
68	3	0	3
69	2	1	3
70	2	3	5
71	2	0	2
78	1	1	2
	15	8	23

American League

Year	Home	Away	Total
72	2	3	5
73	5	2	7
74	0	4	4
75	2	3	5
76	1	1	2
77	0	4	4
80	1	1	2
83	0	1	1
	11	19	30
	26	27	53

Gaylord Perry's Shutouts by Team

National League

Atl.	Chi.	Cin.	Hou.	L.A.	Mon.	N.Y.	Phi.	Pit.	Stl.	S.D.	S.F.	Total
6	2	2	4	1	1	1	2	0	2	2	0	23

American League

Bal.	Bos.	Cal.	Chi.	Cle.	Det.	K.C.	Mil.	Min.	N.Y.	Oak.	Sea.	Tex.	Tor.	Total
5	3	1	2	1	4	1	0	5	3	1	0	3	1	30

Shutouts by Team Finish

National League

1	2	3	4	5	6	7	8	9	10	Total
2	1	3	2	6	3	2	2	1	1	23

American League

1	2	3	4	5	6	7	Total
6	4	10	5	1	2	2	30

Juan Marichal
The Dominican Dandy

Just as Lou Gehrig was overshadowed by Babe Ruth, Juan Marichal felt the presence of Sandy Koufax blanketing him when it came to being the dominant pitcher of the 1960s. Koufax copped three Cy Young Awards to Marichal's none. When Sandy retired prematurely with an arthritic elbow, Bob Gibson eclipsed Juan for the remainder of the Dominican's career, winning two Cy Young Awards to Juan's none. One thing that can be ascertained is that Marichal was a formidable opponent on the mound, as his stats will verify.

Known for his high leg kick, which became his trademark throughout his career, he had no difficulty finding the plate consistently with his unorthodox motion. Marichal was signed out of the Dominican Air Force by the New York Giants in September 1957, a month before his 19th birthday. The following year he started his career with Michigan City of the Class D Midwest League. He led the league in victories (21), innings pitched (245), and E.R.A. (1.87). He struck out 246 batters during that year.

His excellence at Michigan City got him promoted to Springfield of the Class A Eastern League in 1959. He again was the league leader in victories (18), innings pitched (271), E.R.A. (2.39), and also led in strikeouts (208). This again boosted him to a higher level as 1960 saw him at Tacoma of the Class AAA Pacific Coast League. At 21, he showed an 11–5 mark with a strong 3.11 E.R.A., which was quite good considering the league was geared predominantly for hitting. He was summoned to the Giants, and on July 19 he made his major league debut with a spectacular flash as he shut out the Philadelphia Phillies 2–0 on one hit. In that game he struck out the first two batters he faced, with a total of 12 for the game. He was so dominant that he retired the first 19 batters in order until an error and a walk broke the string. With two outs in the eighth inning, the Phils sent up Clay Dalrymple to pinch hit, and he succeeded by getting a single.

Juan appeared in 11 games for the remainder of the season. He compiled a 6–2 mark with an excellent 2.67 E.R.A. He had served notice on National League batters that he was here to stay. In 1961, the Giants hired Al Dark to manage the team and try to get the right chemistry flowing into one of the most potent hitting attacks in the majors. With a lineup that included Willie Mays, Willie McCovey, Orlando Cepeda, and Felipe Alou, the nucleus was there for a contender. The team's fault was in its fielding. In the previous year, they led the league in errors and were dead last in the majors in that category. Ironically, their pitching was second only to the Dodgers. They had to find replacements for two former veterans. John Antonelli was traded to the Cleveland Indians for Harvey Kuenn, and Sam Jones, who was showing his age, was dealt to Detroit. This would be a challenge thrust upon Dark. The acquisition of Kuenn gave them five former Rookies of the Year (Mays in 1951, Kuenn in 1953, Jack Sanford in 1957, Cepeda in 1958, and McCovey in 1959).

In 1961, the Giants improved to finish third and rise up two notches in the standings. They improved their won-loss record by six games. They finished eight games behind the Cincinnati Reds who captured their first pennant in 20 years.

Juan finished the season with a 13–10 record with an E.R.A. of 3.89, which was the highest he had until the end of his career when he was all but through. He tossed three shutouts. All of them came late in the season and on the road.

On August 2, he stopped the Los Angeles Dodgers 6–0 in a one-hitter. Tommy Davis singled in the fifth. The Dodgers had just won eight straight games and had held first place. The loss to Marichal knocked them out of the lead and gave it to the Reds, who never relinquished it.

The 1962 season started with two new teams, the New York Mets and Houston Colt .45's, due to the first expansion by the National League during the 20th century. The American League had started theirs the previous year. The Giants acquired the services of former Chicago White Sox lefty Billy Pierce, which gave them a solid starting rotation with Sanford, Billy O'Dell, Marichal, and Pierce. The hitting was outstanding and the team led in several categories, including home runs with 204. This was only the fifth time in major league history that a team scaled that height (1947 New York Giants, 221; 1956 Reds, 221; 1961 Yankees, 240; and 1962 Tigers, 209).

The pitching staff contributed mightily as the starting four responded with solid efforts. Sanford won 16 games in a row and finished the year with 24 victories. O'Dell gathered 19 while Marichal had 18 and Pierce had 16. Juan started the year for the Giants on the right track as he shut out the Milwaukee Braves and their ace, Warren Spahn, 6–0. He meted out three hits while fanning ten. He finished the year with three shutouts and had an E.R.A. of 3.35. In September, he had an 18–8 mark when he injured his foot, which caused him to miss some starts. This might have given him a 20-win season. When he returned, he lost his last three decisions and finished with an 18–11 record.

As the year progressed, the Giants seemed to be cast in the role of bridesmaids as they painstakingly trailed the Dodgers. In the last two weeks, the Dodgers' lead dwindled. They could only win three games. This gave the Giants the opportunity they sought, and they closed the gap and tied for the lead on the final day. The St. Louis Cardinal's sweep of the Dodgers with Gene Oliver hitting a home run in the final game created the pennant tie and set up another three-game playoff between the two arch rivals. It was the fourth time this scenario occurred in league history with the Dodgers appearing in all four, while the Giants made their second appearance.

In game one, Billy Pierce shut out Los Angeles 8–0 at Candlestick Park, defeating Koufax, who was having circulatory problems in his finger during the year. The Dodgers won the second game 8–7, which set up the tie-breaking game. Marichal started the finale and was trailing 4–2. His foot injury started to act up on him. As in 1951, the Giants rallied for four runs in the ninth to salvage their comeback drive for the pennant. They would now face the New York Yankees for the world championship.

The 1962 World Series had a unique outcome when the Yankees won all of the odd-numbered games and the Giants took all of the even-numbered games. In the first game, the Giants stopped Whitey Ford's consecutive scoreless inning streak at 33, when they dented the plate in the second inning.

In game four, Juan was given the starting assignment and had the Yankees groveling with two hits after four innings. He attempted to bunt and his finger was smashed. He had to come out and thereby lost his chance at a World Series win. Former Yankee hero, Don Larsen, picked up the win in relief. The Yankees edged the Giants 1–0 in the seventh and deciding game, as Willie McCovey lined out to Bobby Richardson with two outs and the bases loaded. It was a stunning climax to a highly exciting season.

In 1963, the Giants slid down to third place, 11 behind the pennant-bound Dodgers, who went on to humiliate the Yankees in a four-game sweep in the World Series. San Francisco's decline could be attributed to the poor year that three of the four starters had. Only Marichal performed above expectation as he tied for the league lead in victories with Koufax at 25. Juan lowered his E.R.A. to 2.41, which was almost a run less than the previous year. He threw five shutouts with the first coming on June 11 when he stopped Los Angeles 3–0 in defeating the previous year's Cy Young winner, Don Drysdale. He ceded seven hits but walked no one.

Four days later, he tossed another shutout, defeating the Houston Colt .45's 1–0 with his only no-hitter. Willie McCovey, who was playing left field and who was not known as a solid outfielder, made a tremendous catch off the bat of Bob Aspromonte in the 7th inning. The Giants would push a run across in the eighth to give Juan the victory. Incidentally, it would be the first Giants no-hitter since Carl Hubbell wove his on May 8, 1929, versus the Pittsburgh Pirates, 11–0. This was a span of 34 years between Giants no-hitters.

On July 2, Juan pitched another 1–0 shutout, this time against the Milwaukee Braves. This game was notable because he and opposing moundsman, Warren Spahn, dueled 16 innings in a courageous effort. Spahn, at the time, was 42 years of age!

Because of Koufax's brilliant year, he was given the Cy Young Award unanimously. This was the first time that anyone received all first-place votes. Juan had to sit back and see the laurels given to his rival.

The 1964 season saw a four-team race down to the final weekend of the season. The Giants finished fourth, only three games from the lead. The St. Louis Cardinals soared to the top of the perch thanks to the catastrophic collapse of the Philadelphia Phillies. The Phils, in their last 12 games, lost ten in a row before they tasted victory in their last two. It was too late to lock the barn because the horse had already been stolen.

Juan managed another 20-win season as he finished at 21–8. His E.R.A. was a commendable 2.48, and was aided by four shutouts.

The year 1965 was a cat-and-dog fight between the Dodgers and the Giants. The Giants would replaced Al Dark with longtime coach and minor league manager, Herman Franks. At the final stage, the Dodgers prevailed over the Giants by two games. Juan logged in at 22–13 with a league-leading 10 shutouts, which helped him lower his E.R.A. to 2.14. This was only good for second place behind Koufax's 2.04. His shutout efforts were the 17th time that ten or more were achieved in major league history and only the seventh time in National League history that that level had been reached. Four of his shutouts were versus the lowly New York Mets, but still they had enough hitters capable of scoring at least one run a game.

On June 5, he battled Cincy's ace, Jim Maloney, and edged him 1–0 while giving up five hits. Later in that month he blanked the Dodgers and Don Drysdale 5–0. On August 18, he defeated the Mets 5–0, but more importantly, he had his 25th career shutout. His next start would become infamous and synonymous with Juan.

On August 22, while dueling Koufax and trailing 2–1, all hell broke loose. The fierce rivalry of the two teams was festering at the start of the three-game series, and the closeness of the pennant race acted as a catalyst in fanning the intensity of the two teams. A throwback from Dodgers catcher, John Roseboro, almost found its way to Marichal's cranium, which made Juan respond with some harsh words. Roseboro felt that Marichal had intentionally thrown at a couple of his teammates. He removed his catcher's mask and confronted the Giants ace with some angry words of his own. The heated argument continued. Then Marichal swung his bat, hitting Roseboro in the head and giving the Dodgers backstop a concussion. This precipitated one of the most violent baseball brawls of all time. The final result was that Juan was fined $2,000 and suspended for a week. He lost two starts. It had further repercussions when Marichal was eligible for induction into the Hall of Fame. He was shunned for two years when he should've been voted in on his first year of eligibility. Roseboro and Marichal had patched up their differences years after the incident, but it left an angry memory in many baseball fans' minds regarding the Dominican Dandy.

The Dodgers won the pennant by two games. It is possible that the two times Juan was suspended could've been the two games that made the difference in the standings. One will never know if the game of August 22 cost the Giants the pennant.

In 1966, Juan again led the Giants to a close finish behind the Dodgers, a meager 1½ games out, but no one could blame Marichal. Koufax had his winningest year, thereby earning his third Cy Young Award. Juan had a 25–6 record and led the league in percentage at .806. His E.R.A. was a healthy 2.23 to go along with his four shutouts, which all came before June 1. On May 22, he blanked the Mets, which gave him a perfect 15–0 versus the New Yorkers. Four days later on May 26, he hooked up versus Jim Bunning of the Philadelphia Phillies. They matched goose eggs for ten innings, when Bunning was relieved. The Giants scored in the 14th inning to help Marichal record a 1–0 win.

Koufax retired at the end of 1966, thereby leaving Marichal with a chance to dominate the league's pitching union in 1967. But Marichal suffered a leg injury that hampered him throughout the season. He finished at 14–10 with only two shutouts but had a fine E.R.A. of 2.76. This was the first year the Cy Young Award was offered in both leagues, which was due to the dominance of the award by Koufax. The National League winner, ironically, went to Juan's teammate, Mike McCormick, who sported a 22–10 record. The Giants again finished second, 10½ games behind the Cardinals.

In 1968, the year of the pitcher, Juan had his winningest season as he posted a 26–9 record. He completed 30 of 38 starts and had a healthy 2.43 E.R.A. His shutout total was five. His best effort occurred on August 13 when he shut out Pittsburgh on two hits. From the third inning on, he kept the Pirates hitless. Juan also led the league in innings pitched with 326. Bob Gibson emerged as the recipient of the Cy Young based on his 22–9 mark, 13 shutouts, and a remarkable 1.12 E.R.A. As good as Juan was, it seemed that he was snakebitten and received no justice for his performances year after year. The Giants captured second place for the fourth straight year.

The second expansion in 1969 created two new teams and a divisional arrangement where the two winners would meet in a championship series to determine who earned the right to go to the World Series. The Giants were placed in the West and wound up second. Juan had another 20-win season, finishing at 21–8. He led the league with a 2.10 E.R.A., the first time he came out on top there. His league-leading eight shutouts aided him immensely. Six of his shutouts were against teams that finished no lower than third. The closest rivals for the Western Division title were the Atlanta Braves, who won the division by three games over San Francisco, and Cincinnati, who finished third, one game back of the Giants.

On September 12, Juan stopped the Reds on one hit, defeating them 1–0. Tommy Helms spoiled his shot for a no-hitter. In his next start, versus the Atlanta Braves, he defeated them 2–0 on four hits. Tom Seaver emerged in pitching dominance. He copped the Cy Young Award for the year.

The year 1970 saw the San Francisco Giants break with tradition and wind up third, 16 games behind the Reds. One reason could be attributed to Juan's collapse. He posted a 12–10 record with only one shutout, and his E.R.A. ballooned to a hideous 4.11. In fairness to his poor year, it could be said that his downfall was caused by sickness, a reaction to penicillin that caused an arthritic condition. He also injured his back during the season, which compounded his poor performance.

The Giants finally shed the role of runner-up when they won the Western Division by one game over the Dodgers. Juan pitched the game that clinched the title on the last night of the season.

In the National League championship series he started game three versus Pittsburgh and held his own. Going into the eighth inning, the game was tied up when the Pirates pushed a run across the plate to win by a score of 2–1. Juan finished the game allowing only four hits. His season was a good one as he compiled an 18–11 mark and a respectable E.R.A. of 2.94. Included in his victories were four shutouts, with the one on August 10 versus the Montreal Expos being his 50th career shutout. He gave up two hits, defeating them 1–0.

The Giants fell apart in 1972, which was evident by their fifth-place finish and their sub-.500 percentage. Aging stars like Willie Mays were traded to the New York Mets. Gaylord Perry was swapped for Sam McDowell, who fell short of expectations at 10–8 and wound up with a sore shoulder.

Willie McCovey, along with Marichal, was now 34 years old. McCovey hit just about his weight that year with a meager 14 home runs. Juan witnessed his first losing season at 6–16 with an E.R.A. of 3.71 and no shutouts. The once-strong nucleus of the Giants was only a shell of its former self. In 1973, Juan again floundered, this time at 11–15. His E.R.A. was 3.83, but he did manage two shutouts. The last one of his career was thrown on July 15, when he defeated the Pirates 12–0 on four hits. After the season, he was sold to the Boston Red Sox where he became a spot starter. His record for 1974 was 5–1 but his E.R.A. was a disheartening 4.89. He was given his release and was signed by, ironically, the Los Angeles Dodgers. He appeared in six games and lost his only decision. Wisely, he realized it was over and called it a career.

As stated before, he should've been elected to the Hall of Fame when eligible in his first year, but the awful debacle of August 22, 1965, poisoned the minds of many sportswriters, postponing the inevitable for two years. Regardless of how people felt about him, he earned and deserves to this day the honor of enshrinement bestowed upon him. He was a man who was constantly overshadowed by others, but he was at least equal to them.

Juan Marichal

Date	Team	Score	Hits	S.O.	Walks	Loser
7/19/60(H)	Phi.	2–0	1	12	1	Buzhart
7/27/61(A)	Pit.	2–0	5	8	3	Mizell
8/2/61(A)	L.A.	6–0	1	11	2	Podres
8/23/61(A)	Cin.	14–0	3	1	0	Jay
4/10/62(H)	Mil.	6–0	3	10	6	Spahn
5/12/62(A)	Hou.	11–0	4	3	3	Woodeschick
6/16/62(A)	Stl.	5–0	2	4	3	Jackson
6/11/63(A)	L.A.	3–0	7	4	0	Drysdale
6/15/63(H)	Hou.	1–0	0	5	2	Drott
7/2/63(H)	Mil.	1–0	8	10	4	Spahn
8/9/63(A)	Phi.	4–0	7	6	2	Culp
9/12/63(A)	N.Y.	6–0	4	13	1	Stallard
5/8/64(H)	L.A.	3–0	5	3	3	Ortega
5/12/64(A)	Hou.	6–0	5	3	0	Brown
6/23/64(A)	Cin.	4–0	7	5	2	Maloney
9/2/64(A)	N.Y.	4–0	4	9	0	Stallard
4/17/65(A)	N.Y.	4–0	4	6	2	Parsons
4/25/65(H)	N.Y.	5–0	5	9	2	Jackson
6/5/65(A)	Cin.	1–0	5	9	0	Maloney
6/10/65(A)	N.Y.	3–0	7	6	0	Kroll
6/28/65(H)	L.A.	5–0	6	5	1	Drysdale
7/2/65(A)	Chi.	4–0	5	9	0	Koonce
7/10/65(A)	Phi.	7–0	2	5	1	Culp
7/17/65(H)	Hou.	7–0	5	7	0	Farrell
8/18/65(H)	N.Y.	5–0	3	7	4	L. Miller
9/9/65(H)	Hou.	4–0	4	5	1	Bruce
4/28/66(H)	Cin.	3–0	4	3	0	Ellis
5/12/66(A)	Pit.	3–0	6	6	1	Veal
5/22/66(H)	N.Y.	5–0	3	5	1	Bernarth
5/26/66(H)	Phi.	1–0	6	10	1	Knowles
4/29/67(A)	L.A.	5–0	5	11	1	Miller
5/3/67(A)	N.Y.	8–0	4	9	1	Denehy
6/10/68(H)	Pit.	8–0	4	8	1	Veal
7/2/68(H)	Atl.	5–0	5	4	1	Jarvis

Juan Marichal

Date	Team	Score	Hits	S.O.	Walks	Loser
7/18/68(A)	Stl.	3–0	4	5	0	Carlton
8/1/68(A)	L.A.	2–0	3	5	0	Drysdale
8/13/68(A)	Pit.	3–0	2	7	3	Veal
4/30/69(H)	L.A.	3–0	2	6	2	Singer
5/14/69(A)	Pit.	3–0	4	6	0	Bunning
6/17/69(H)	Cin.	4–0	5	7	3	Culver
7/10/69(A)	L.A.	3–0	9	6	3	Sutton
8/15/69(H)	Chi.	3–0	4	9	3	Holtzman
8/29/69(H)	N.Y.	5–0	4	7	1	Gentry
9/12/69(H)	Cin.	1–0	1	5	1	Arrigo
9/16/69(H)	Atl.	2–0	4	9	1	Reed
9/21/70(A)	L.A.	7–0	6	2	1	Moeller
4/6/71(A)	S.D.	4–0	5	8	1	Phoebus
4/16/71(H)	Chi.	9–0	2	5	1	Jenkins
5/15/71(H)	L.A.	1–0	6	2	2	Singer
8/10/71(H)	Mon.	1–0	2	8	3	Stoneman
4/25/73(A)	Chi.	5–0	8	4	0	Jenkins
7/15/73(H)	Pit.	12–0	4	6	1	Moose

Year	Home	Away	Total
60	1	0	1
61	0	3	3
62	2	1	3
63	2	3	5
64	1	3	4
65	5	5	10
66	3	1	4
67	0	2	2
68	2	3	5
69	6	2	8
70	0	1	1
71	3	1	4
73	1	1	2
	26	26	52

Juan Marichal's Shutouts by Team

Mil. Atl.	Chi.	Cin.	Hou.	L.A.	Mon.	N.Y.	Phi.	Pit.	Stl.	S.D.	S.F.	Total
4	4	6	5	10	1	9	4	6	2	1	0	52

Shutouts by Team Finish

1	2	3	4	5	6	7	8	9	10	Total
6	5	6	5	4	8	2	4	5	7	52

Rube Waddell
The Man-Child of Major League Baseball

When it comes to discussing the so-called flakes in baseball history, you can go through the each decade and find out that one stands out exclusively for that period. In the 1930s Dizzy Dean made headlines with some of his antics while playing for the "Gashouse Gang." "Dizz" had a supporting cast in that crew that egged him on. In the 1950s, a talented right-hander for the Brooklyn Dodgers named Billy Lowes denounced the virtues of winning 20 games because it was less stressful than winning 15 games. In the 1960s, Joe Pepitone squandered his God-given talents to carouse the nightspots of every town he entered. Spaceman Bill Lee was the prime character of the 1970s while pitching for Boston and Montreal. The most famous of them all was the most talented. This was George "Rube" Waddell. Rube pitched around the turn of the century and displayed performances that were the talk of the baseball world back then. He had no concept of responsibility and, feeling that life was one constant good time, sought out excitement with a childlike glee, chasing fire engines, marching in a parade twirling a baton, or wrestling an alligator when he was scheduled for pitching assignments. Inside his masculine body (he was big for his day), which stood 6'1½" and weighed around 200 pounds, was the spirit of an impish child.

Rube Waddell

He was born in Bedford, Pennsylvania in the north-central part of the state on October 13, 1876. Bradford is small town close to the New York state line, and you wonder how a community that thrives on calmness with an unassuming demeanor could produce someone who was erratic as a pinball machine. Waddell was completely eccentric.

Because of Waddell's nature, stories of him that are handed down through the generations get distorted as the years pass. This is illustrated in a 1955 essay by Ray Robinson that appeared in *The Fireside Book of Baseball*, edited by Charles Einstein. Mr. Robinson alludes to a story about Waddell's zany heroics in which he describes Rube pitching in 1904 versus the Cleveland Blues. Leading the Blues by a 1–0 score in the ninth inning, with bases loaded, he had to face the heart of the Cleveland lineup which consisted of Napoleon Lajoie, Elmer Flick (both Hall of Famers), and Bill Bradley. Waddell, with a wave of his hand, summoned his outfielders in on the sidelines. The story claims he struck out the three batters on nine pitches, preventing Cleveland from scoring. This is purely a myth. There is no record Waddell ever accomplished this in a major league game. He might have staged the deed in the minors, but this cannot be substantiated. The truth of the matter is that Rube did not pitch a shutout versus Cleveland in 1904. This tale somehow germinated in the minors and was transplanted as a deed done in a major league game. Besides, manager Connie Mack would not have tolerated Rube's tactics in a game.

In reality, Rube got his baptism in the game pitching for small towns in western Pennsylvania. There he drew the attention of scouts for the Louisville Colonels of the National League in 1897. He was offered $500 to pitch the remainder of the season. That was a fantastic sum for the unpredictable Waddell, who was scarcely 21 and who had acquired a taste for liquor and the ladies (he married three times). This would only increase his clownish ways. His first major league manager was Fred Clarke, who took over the managerial reins of the Colonels in mid-season, and they would finish eleventh out of a 12-team league. Clarke was enshrined in Cooperstown in 1946 both for his abilities as a player and a manager. On September 8, 1897, Rube made his debut and finished with an 0–1 record, losing the only game he started. He was able to complete it, showing that he did have endurance.

The following year he was demoted to Detroit of the Western League (this was the forerunner of today's American League) where he went 4–4 in nine games. He jumped the team and wound up in Chatam in Ontario, Canada, pitching semipro ball. This is revealed in an article entitled "Rube Arrives" by Joe. A. Scott that appeared in SABR's *National Pastime* (#10).

In 1899, Rube was assigned again to the Western League, but this time to Columbus. The franchise was transferred later that year to Grand Rapids. Rube was under the tutelage of Tom Loftus, who realized his potential and accepted the pitcher's bizarre behavior. Somehow he was able to get Waddell to contribute a 27–13 record before being called up to Louisville, where he went 7–2 with an E.R.A. of 3.08. At Louisville he pitched his first major league shutout, of defeating Cincinnati 4–0 on six hits.

In 1900, the National League cut back to eight teams with Louisville's best ballplayers being absorbed by the Pittsburgh Pirates. This is how the Pirates got the likes of Honus Wagner, Fred, Clarke, and Rube Waddell.

In 1900, he started the season with Pittsburgh. In his first start of the season, he shut out Cincinnati 6–0. Even with the promise and potential he held as a pitcher, he continued to fray the patience of manager Clarke, who suspended him and later reassigned him to Milwaukee of the American League. At Milwaukee, he came under the watchful eye of Connie Mack, who wet-nursed him through a 10–3 record. Connie utilized psychology in dealing with the immature hurler by allowing him time off between pitching assignments. Rube had to return when his next assignment was due, and the perceptive Mack had someone close by watching him.

Waddell was summoned back to Pittsburgh, where he had good results. He pitched his second shutout of the year as he defeated St. Louis 8–0 on four hits. For the year, his 9–11 record was not all that impressive for a second-place team, but he did lead the league in E.R.A. with a strong 2.37. When it comes to his strikeout totals, there is some contradiction on his stats. *Total Baseball* and *Macmillan's Baseball Encyclopedia* give him 130 for 1900 while *The Sporting News* shows him at 133. *The Baseball Encyclopedia* and *The Sporting News* give him the league lead with different totals while *Total Baseball* has Frank Hahn heading the list. If one credits him with the league lead, then Waddell would be the first man who led the two leagues in strikeouts (Jim Bunning and Nolan Ryan are the other two on this short list).

In 1901, he went 0–2 with Pittsburgh when Fred Clarke decided he had enough of Waddell. Rube was sold to the Chicago Orphans (the next year they became the Cubs). With the Orphans he was 14–14 (although this total is again disputed by major research sources) when he decide to jump the team and again was toiling in the semipro circuits. The end of the season saw him migrate to the Pacific coast, and he settled in the Los Angeles area.

During these first years at the turn of the century, the National League and the fledgling American League were at war with each other. This led to constant raiding by each league of the other teams' players. Connie Mack, who had achieved the services of Napoleon Lajoie, Elmer Flick, and pitcher Bill Bernhard, lost them due to an injunction by their crosstown rival, the Philadelphia Phillies, and issued by the Pennsylvania courts. This hampered Mack and his A's as the court decision barred the players from playing any games for the A's in Pennsylvania. This caused Mack to trade the trio to Cleveland, which weakened the "Mackmen." While all this legal palavering and manipulation was going on, Waddell was content during 1902 while in California. He was pitching for Los Angeles of the Pacific Coast League and was the local hero. He was sporting a 12–8 record and doing double duty as an outfielder. The A's were mired in sixth place because of the loss of the players involved in the court order. Mack heard about Waddell's success in California and also knew about him in Milwaukee and decided to secure his services once again. Mack sent an agent to offer a lucrative contract to bring the vacillating pitcher back East. The Los Angeles manager found out about it and talked Rube out of his decision. Mack, in dire need of Waddell, sent another agent with a bonus and snuck him out at night with the aid of Pinkerton agents.

Waddell finally reported to the A's and made his first American League start on June 26, which was inauspicious at best as he lost 7–3 to the last-place Baltimore Orioles. This was not an omen of things to come.

Waddell's shining glory came in 1902. In fact, he only pitched two-thirds of a season and hung up numbers that boggle the mind. Peter Palmer, whose article "Rube Waddell in 1902" appeared in SABR's *Baseball Research Journal* for 1979, gives the most accurate and precise account of Waddell's spectacular performance. With all credit due to Mr. Palmer, I would like to employ the research he made known; starting July 1, Rube pitched his first American League shutout, defeating the Orioles 2–0. He allowed only two hits, striking out 13 with no walks. In that game, he faced the minimum 27 batters. The next start, he outlasted the Washington Senators 12–9.

On July 8, he was called on in relief in the fifth inning with Philadelphia leading Boston 9–6. As Palmer states, the Macmillan research team credited Rube with a victory, as he came out in the sixth inning when the A's scored 12 runs. Mack found it unnecessary to waste his efforts, and it was a wise decision, as the record shows. On July 9, he started versus Boston, defeating them 4–2 in 17 innings. He chalked up wins on July 12, again defeating Boston (3–2), and on July 15, stopping the Chicago White Sox 15–3. He had a struggle on July 18, defeating the Chisox 7–6. He relieved on July 21 against Cleveland with the score tied 10–10, and got the decision when Philly scored in the bottom of the ninth. On the 22nd, he relieved versus Cleveland again and picked up another win as Philly overcame a 4–1 deficit. He started on July 26, beating the St. Louis Browns. Three days later, the Brownies stopped his ten-game winning streak. Two days later, he, wound up in a 4–4 tie with St. Louis.

In August, he lost his first two starts (one versus Chicago and one versus Cleveland). He stopped his losing streak on August 11th by shutting out Detroit 1–0, going 13 innings. He doled out four hits in that superhuman effort and scored the only run by getting a triple. Two days later, he still had the master's touch when he blanked the Tigers again. He had more to work with this time and defeated them 8–0. Against the White Sox, he split two decisions. He defeated them on August 11th by a score of 2–1, putting the A's in first place. On August 19, Chicago turned the tables on him (5–2). He took over in relief in St. Louis with the "Mackmen" down 3–0 after one inning. He picked up the win in that game as his teammates responded with a 12–4 victory. On August 28, he stopped Chicago 5–4 and defeated them two days later with a 6–5 decision.

On September 1, the Browns defeated him 5–1. He came back with wins versus Detroit on September 2, defeating them 5–1 and on September 4, defeating them by a score of 13–4. The victory on September 4 was his 20th! On September 6 and 8, he defeated Cleveland by scores of 3–2 and 8–5. He relieved on September 10 in both games of a doubleheader versus the St. Louis Browns, winning 9–5 and 5–4. He was defeated by Cy Young and Boston on September 12 by a score of 5–4. He and Young met in some classic confrontations in their careers. He defeated Boston for his last three victories (September 15, 9–2; September 19, 6–4; and September 22, 5–3). Other research resources, such as Mr. Palmer's *Total Baseball* and Neft and Cohen's *Baseball Encyclopedia*, credit him with a 24–7 record while *Macmillan's Baseball Encyclopedia* has him at 25–7.

The Sporting News gives him a 23–7 mark. If given the benefit of doubt, Rube would in July have set a new record for modern baseball, getting ten wins during a single month. Rube also struck out 210 batters to lead in that category.

It can be assumed that Waddell's heroics turned the season around dramatically in the American League. It gave Connie Mack his first pennant ever. The legendary Waddell exploded on the scene in a meteoric arrival. He finished second in victories and might have made over 30 if he pitched the whole season.

In 1903, the A's set out to defend their championship but fell 14½ games off the pace to the Boston Pilgrims (the forerunners of the Red Sox). Rube could not match his performance of the previous year but still had an excellent record at 22–16. He was now part of a pitching rotation that included left-hander Eddie Plank, who had been with the team since 1901. Connie Mack would employ the services of right-hander Albert "Chief" Bender, from Carlisle Indian College. This trio collaborated to give the A's one of the most formidable pitching staffs created. This was contingent upon Rube not pulling any of his antics. The three of them eventually were admitted to the Hall of Fame. Plank and Waddell were enshrined in 1946 while Bender made it in 1953.

In 1903, Rube had an amazing 34 complete games in 38 starts. His E.R.A. was an excellent 2.44 with four shutouts. On July 14, he defeated the White Sox 2–0 on seven hits, but the important feature was the 14 strikeouts he had. His total for the year was 302 K's which again gave him the league lead, for the second consecutive year. The 300-plus mark was the first time in league history and the first time at the 60'6" distance. So Rube will always have that distinction of accomplishing those two feats.

In 1904 the A's slid into fifth place, 12½ games behind Boston. Their record was commendable at 81–70. Plank and Waddell had identical records at 26–17. This accounted for 64 percent of the team's total wins. Together they pitched 15 of the team's 26 shutouts with Rube having eight, two behind league leader Cy Young. His first shutout came versus the Boston Pilgrims on April 25 defeating Cy Young 2–0. On May 2, he again blanked Boston by 3–0. In that game, he allowed just one hit. Patsy Dougherty spoiled his attempt at a no-hitter. Boston, on May 5, got revenge on Rube when Cy Young whitewashed him and the A's 3–0. Most significantly, Young pitched a perfect game versus the A's. There is no way to beat perfection—even if your name is Waddell.

Rube just missed leading the circuit with his 1.62 E.R.A., but Cleveland's Addie Joss won it with 1.59. In all fairness to Waddell, Joss only pitched 192 innings while Waddell threw 383 innings. Included in Waddell's stats for the year was a league-leading 349 strikeouts. This made him the first pitcher to have back-to-back years breaking the magic 300 strikeout barrier. That accomplishment was not made again until Sandy Koufax of the Los Angeles Dodgers did it in 1965 and 1966.

In regard to Rube's totals, there were disputes about his actual figures. The original record total was at 343 strikeouts and was supposedly broken when Bob Feller chalked up 348 in 1946. Some diehard fans delved into the records and came up with Waddell's total of 349. It didn't matter, because Koufax set a new major league record when he struck out 382 in 1965, which was broken by Nolan Ryan of the California Angels with 383 in 1973. Waddell has the American League record for left-handers.

In 1905 Philadelphia won their second pennant by a scant two games over the Chicago White Sox. Rube led the league with 26 victories while Plank chipped in with 25. Included in Rube's victories were seven shutouts, which won him his first E.R.A. title (1.48). He zeroed the White Sox twice and his efforts on August 15 defeated the St. Louis Browns 2–0 on no hits. The game went only five innings with Rube getting credit for a shutout but not a no-hitter. He came through in the pennant stretch as he totaled four shutouts in August. The one on August 31, beating Cleveland 2–0, was the 25th of his career. He again led the league in strikeouts for the fourth consecutive time, with 287. He continued to do yeoman work with another year of over 300 innings pitched.

Waddell pitched a game on July 4 versus Boston, locking horns with Cy Young. The game, at the time, set a record for longevity as it took 20 innings to decide the outcome. Waddell gave up two runs in the first inning while the A's tied it in the sixth. Goose eggs went up constantly until Philadelphia broke the deadlock by scoring two runs on an error, hit batter, and two singles. Waddell pitched the last 19 innings, shutting out Boston the rest of the way. This was equivalent to a doubleheader shutout! It was observed that he did cartwheels after recording the final out.

It's ironic that Waddell, who was the dominant pitcher in the American League, did not make it to the World Series to meet the dominant National League pitcher, Christy Mathewson. All eagerly awaited that confrontation, but it never materialized. Right after the pennant was clinched, Rube got into some horseplay with Andy Coakley and injured his shoulder, which kept him on the sidelines. We don't know if Rube's participation in the World Series would have stemmed the tide of events, but the 1905 World Series was won by the New York Giants, with all games being shutouts.

The A's failed to defend their American League championship in 1906 by finishing a disappointing fourth (78–67). This placed them 12 games behind the pennant-bound "Hitless Wonders," the Chicago White Sox. Even more discouraging was Rube's 16–16 record. He did manage to post a 2.25 E.R.A., backed up by eight shutouts. Included in those games were four blankings of Boston, which was only a remnant of the pennant-winning teams of two years previous. In two of those wins, he defeated Cy Young, giving him a measure of satisfaction over his nemesis. Another shutout was versus the Detroit Tigers, who now had the ferocious Ty Cobb in his first full year of major league ball. He defeated the Tigers 5–0 on one hit. The brash young Cobb laid down a bunt in the first inning to mar Waddell's efforts. Rube again led the league in strikeouts with 196.

The year 1907 saw the pennant race in the American League go down to the wire between the A's and the Tigers. This marked the fourth consecutive year that the pennant was decided by three games or less. Detroit eked by the A's by a minute 1½ games, and the irony of the race was that second-place Philadelphia lost one less game than Detroit. During the early years of the American League, postponed games were not required to be made up. This is the reason why Philadelphia had one less loss. The Tigers played five games more, giving them four wins over the A's total.

The pennant went down to the last week of the season with a crucial series between the two contenders. The Tigers won the first game of the series, giving them the lead. Two days later a classic confrontation occurred as the two teams battled to a 9–9 tie in 17 innings. The Tigers left town with a slim lead they never relinquished. Waddell came into that game in relief but could not hold what was a so-called safe lead. In fact, one cause of Philadelphia's collapse was Waddell's slump during the end of the year. It was the failure of Rube that finally drained the patience of Connie Mack, who sold him the following year. Rube did pitch seven shutouts, which was one behind teammate Plank, who led the league. One of Waddell's shutouts was a 0–0 tie versus Boston and Cy Young. The match-up lasted 13 innings with darkness finally causing it to be halted. Rube gave up only four hits while Young ceded only six safeties. Rube also led the league in strikeouts, with 232, for the sixth year in a row.

In February 1908, Mack sold Waddell to the St. Louis Browns. He felt deeply that Waddell was a major factor in Philadelphia's failure to take the flag in 1907. Regardless of the change of venue, Rube did quite well for the Browns by keeping them in the pennant race until September, when they faded, losing out by 6½ games. He contributed a 19–14 mark with a brilliant 1.89 E.R.A. braced by five shutouts. His first shutout of the season, he defeated the White Sox 1–0 on one hit. That was made by Jakey Atz, the second baseman, who got a scratch hit leading off the second inning. Third baseman Hobe Ferris attempted to make the play and prevented Bobby Wallace, who had the better shot of throwing Atz out at first, from coming up with the ball. Rube had another memorable game on July 29 versus his old teammates, the A's, when he struck out 16 batters in a nine-inning game, a new major league record for the time.

The Browns, who made an amazing rise in 1908, went back to reality in 1909 as they finished seventh. It looked as if the 32-year-old Waddell was showing his decline much too early in his career, which, in all probability, was due to his burning the candle at both ends. He finished his first losing season in the American League at 11–13. His E.R.A. was a strong 2.37, which could be traced to the five shutouts he pitched through the year. He threw three of them in May. On July 25, he stopped the Washington Senators 6–0, besting their new phenom, Walter Johnson. The last shutout he threw in the majors was on September 10 (his 50th) when he halted the Chicago White Sox on three hits. Better days did not lie ahead for Waddell.

The year 1910 was his last at the major league level, and he had a 3–1 record when he was released. His contract was picked up by Newark of the Eastern League, where he went 5–3. In 1911, he had one last shot of fame, with Minneapolis of the American Association. An old friend, Joe Cantillon, managed the club and gave Waddell a free hand. He rewarded Cantillon with a 20–17 mark. At the end of the season, Rube went home with Cantillon, who lived in Kentucky. It was just about the end of the line for him. During the winter, the Mississippi River flooded the area where Rube was staying in Kentucky. He, along with others, stood in the frigid waters to repair a broken levee. Rube contracted a horrible cold, which eventually led to tuberculosis. Rube did pitch briefly for two more years. In 1912, he was 12–6 with Minneapolis, and the following year he finished his professional career with a 3–9 mark with Virginia in the Northern League.

The spring of 1914 saw him lying in a hospital in San Antonio, Texas. The dreaded disease had laid claim on his once powerful physique. He was down to a shell of his former self. Rube finally passed away on April Fool's Day in 1914, which seemed appropriate for the most famous of baseball's zanies. He was penniless, and someone who remembered him saw it fitting to place a headstone by his grave. Rube had lived for only 37 years, but his mark upon the game will live for eternity. In 1946, he was elected to the Hall of Fame as a tribute to his short but remarkable career.

Rube Waddell

Date	Team	Score	Hits	S.O.	Walks	Loser
10/5/99(A)	Cin.	4–0	6	2	1	Frisk
4/23/00(A)	Cin.	6–0	3	6	0	Scott
10/8/00(A)	Stl.	8–0	4	4	3	Jones
7/1/02(H)	Bal.	2–0	3	13	0	Cronin
8/11/02(A)	Det.	1–0	4	7	5	Siever
8/13/02(H)	Det.	8–0	2	7	1	Murcer
6/1/03(A)	Wash.	1–0	2	6	2	Townsend
7/14/03(H)	Chi.	2–0	7	14	4	White
7/27/03(H)	Wash.	3–0	5	6	1	Orth
8/21/03(A)	Det.	1–0	3	6	2	Donovan
4/25/04(H)	Bos.	2–0	6	3	0	Young
5/2/04(A)	Bos.	3–0	1	7	2	Tannehill
5/26/04(H)	Det.	3–0	4	12	3	Donovan
5/30/04(A)	N.Y.	1–0	7	8	0	Hughes
7/9/04(H)	Wash.	3–0	3	8	2	Patten
7/27/04(H)	Det.	5–0	3	11	2	Stovall
8/15/04(A)	Det.	2–0	2	5	2	Kitson
9/29/04(A)	Stl.	1–0	2	7	1	Morgan
5/4/05(H)	Wash.	6–0	8	5	0	Jacobson
5/18/05(A)	Chi.	3–0	7	9	2	Smith
6/23/05(H)	Cle.	3–0	6	7	1	Rhoades
8/15/05(H)	Stl.	2–0	0	7	0	Howell (5 inns)
8/22/05(A)	Chi.	4–0	6	9	0	Patterson
8/29/05(A)	Cle.	6–0	3	5	2	Donahue
8/31/05(A)	Cle.	2–0	4	8	3	Joss
4/25/06(H)	Bos.	5–0	6	13	0	Young
5/7/06(A)	Bos.	4–0	7	8	0	Winter
5/12/06(H)	Chi.	4–0	5	9	1	Owen
5/17/06(H)	Det.	5–0	1	8	1	Siever
6/19/06(A)	Cle.	2–0	7	5	3	Joss
6/25/06(H)	Bos.	1–0	7	11	3	Dineen
8/13/06(A)	Stl.	8–0	6	3	2	Powell
9/14/06(H)	Bos.	4–0	6	3	0	Young
5/21/07(A)	Det.	3–0	6	7	0	Willetts

Date	Team	Score	Hits	S.O.	Walks	Loser
6/6/07(H)	Chi.	3–0	5	11	3	Walsh
6/10/07(H)	Stl.	3–0	4	11	2	Glade
6/29/07(A)	Bos.	3–0	8	12	0	Glaze
8/22/07(A)	Chi.	2–0	2	13	0	Walsh
8/25/07(A)	Stl.	1–0	2	10	1	Peity
9/9/07(A)	Bos.	0–0	4	6	0	Young
4/17/08(A)	Chi.	1–0	1	5	4	Owen
6/8/08(H)	Phi.	10–0	8	2	0	Vickers
7/10/08(A)	Phi.	6–0	9	9	2	Dygert
8/31/08(H)	Chi.	4–0	6	10	1	Walsh
9/24/08(H)	Bos.	3–0	3	6	1	Morgan
5/23/09(H)	Bos.	1–0	5	4	1	Arellane
5/26/09(H)	Bos.	5–0	4	8	1	Steele
5/30/09(H)	Cle.	2–0	6	7	1	Berger
7/25/09(H)	Wash.	6–0	5	7	1	Johnson
9/10/09(H)	Chi.	2–0	3	7	1	Olmstead

Year	Home	Away	Total
02	2	1	3
03	2	2	4
04	4	4	8
05	3	4	7
06	5	3	8
07	2	5	7
08	3	2	5
09	5	0	5
	26	21	47

National League

99	0	1	1
00	0	2	2
	26	24	50

Rube Waddell's Shutouts by Team

American League

Bos.	Chi.	Cle.	Det.	Bal. N.Y	Phi.	Stl.	Wash.	Total
11	9	5	8	2	2	5	5	47

National League

Cin.	Stl.	Total
2	1	3

Shutouts by Team Finish

American League

1	2	3	4	5	6	7	8	Total
4	3	7	1	6	7	9	10	47

National League

5	6	7	Total
1	1	1	3

Vic Willis
Ultimate Recognition at Long Last

In 1986 the Hall of Fame's Veteran's Committee decided on their selection of old-timers to be enshrined in the pantheon of baseball. It came down to three men: Bobby Doerr, Ernie Lombardi, and Vic Willis. Doerr and Lombardi were selected, which left Willis on the outside looking in. It could be that the Veteran's Committee knew more about Doerr and Lombardi. Some might have even participated against them in games, causing them to opt for the more modern players. The majority of Doerr and Lombardi's careers spanned the 1930s and 1940s while Willis' career started in 1898 and ended in 1910. Therefore, his lack of familiarity with the selectors was the basic reason for his not being chosen at that time. Finally, in 1995, after many years of neglect, Vic Willis was given the delayed consideration that he was entitled to when he was selected by the Veteran's Committee. Only a purist of the game could know about Vic Willis and his splendid achievements on the mound.

Standing 6'2" tall and weighing over 180 pounds, he was an ominous sight. He was considered big for a man during this early era of the game. In comparison, "Big Ed" Walsh stood 6'1". Vic broke in with the Boston Beaneaters, who along with the Baltimore Orioles were the scourge of the league during the 1890s. During this decade, they won eight pennants, with Boston capturing five. This Boston team had Charles "Kid" Nichols, who anchored the pitching staff through the 1890s with seven 30-win seasons. In 1898 Boston won for the fifth time, with Nichols chalking up 31 victories. He had Jack Stivitt and "Parson" Ted Lewis to help him through the years, but in 1898 Vic Willis emerged to contribute 25 victories as a rookie. Without Willis, Boston would have succumbed to the second-place Orioles. If there was a Rookie of the Year Award back then, Vic would have notched that without any questions being asked.

On April 20, Vic made his debut in relief of Mike Sullivan versus Baltimore. His performance was inauspicious in a game already lost, giving up eight runs. Baltimore coasted to a laughable 18–3 win. This was not a harbinger of things to come. He made his first start a winning one against the Washington Nationals 11–4, besting the National's ace, Gus Weyhing. During the year, he carved his first shutout by blanking the Cleveland Spiders 6–0. He gave up six hits and threw six strikeouts. He showed flawless control by walking none. His control was a bit of a problem during his career. He walked 100 or more batters in 6 of his 13 years. The Spiders' team was still a formidable opponent with Jessie "the Crab" Burkett, "Rody" Wallace, and the great Cy Young. This was the Cleveland team, minus its stars, that became baseball's worst in the following year. In 1898 Vic Willis was here to stay and was someone to respect.

The last year of the 19th century was his greatest winning season, with 27 victories. He would duplicate that in 1902 but his 1899 winning percentage of .771 was his best ever. Included in that victory total were five shutouts, which made him the league leader. Willis emerged as the ace of the staff, with Nichols showing the strains of past campaigns. But Vic's efforts were not enough to enable the Beaneaters to capture the pennant. The Brooklyn Superbas enjoyed that distinction, but when facing Vic, they were blanked twice. Willis had beaten their two aces in "Brickyard" Kennedy and Jim Hughes. He pitched his only no-hitter that year against Washington on August 7. His wildness in the first inning cost him a shutout. With one out, Vic walked Jack O'Brien, who proceeded to steal second. A wild throw by battery mate Marty Berger enabled O'Brien to reach third. Another walk to Dan McGann, who was thrown out attempting to steal on the ensuing play, allowed O'Brien to score. Vic settled down and went on to win 7–1.

The new century started out as a disappointment for Boston as they fell under .500. Vic, along with Kid Nichols, suffered losing seasons, but he still managed two shutouts—one against pennant-bound Brooklyn. He seemed at his best when facing the champion Superbas, posting three shutouts in two years against them.

In 1901 he boosted Boston back to a .500 record while leading the team in victories and earned run average. Spinning six shutouts, he won the E.R.A. title. One of the shutouts, on September 13th, was a one-hitter versus the Chicago Cubs. The spoiler was third baseman Charlie Dexter. He was the Beaneaters' main hope against the aces of the other seven teams.

His winning percentage wasn't his highest, but he was now pitching for a team whose glory days were behind them. Coupled with "Togie" Pittenger, he raised Boston back into the first division. During 1902, he led his league in eight different categories, including losses (19). That unappealing mark could be attributed to the number of game appearances he had compiled (51). His victory total was one short of Jack Chesbro's league lead, but his three saves in relief made him a contributor to 30 of his team's 73 wins. Vic started 46 games and finished 45. In comparison to Chesbro, who had one save to go along with his 28 wins, Vic's performance was better. "Happy Jack" had the luxury of pitching for the pennant-winning Pirates who romped through the league. They cakewalked their way to the top by 27½ games, which is still a major-league record. Vic's importance to his team is more appreciated than Chesbro's. While completing his 45 games, he surpassed the 400 innings mark for the first time in his career. This Herculean feat eclipsed his previous year's total by 105 and made him the first pitcher to pitch over 400 innings in the 20th century. His record would be short-lived because Ironman Joe McGinnity set the league record at 434. This was shattered in 1904 by Chesbro in the American League and later by Ed Walsh's record of 464 in 1908. These four are the only men to break this barrier, with McGinnity and Walsh doing it twice.

In 1903, the war between the American and National Leagues was in full heat. Willis could have jumped for the big money offered by the American League, with the possibility of landing with a contender, but he declined all offers and stayed with the Beaneaters. This portrayed a glowing character trait. He felt his obligation was more important than the mighty dollar that many of the superstars of the era grabbed with glee. A good many players whose plaques hang in Cooperstown cannot exhibit the character that Vic Willis showed. Statistical achievement alone does not make one outstanding on the playing field.

The 1903 season saw Boston fall back to the second division and finish a dismal sixth. Vic's record also fell below the break-even point when he logged a 12–17 record. His winning percentage was slightly lower than the team's, but his 2.98 E.R.A. (two shutouts) was considerably lower than the combined staff's. In 1904, the team fell even lower, this time to seventh, with Vic leading the league with 25 losses. Regardless of this, he still had a higher percentage than the team and a highly respectable E.R.A of 2.85. He twirled another two shutouts, which enabled him to keep his E.R.A. below 3.00. The Beaneaters were a pathetic lot, as the next year would attest to.

During the 1905 season, Vic set the modern major-league record for most losses in a season when he finished with an 11-29 record. This could be due to the atrociousness of the team. They lost 103 games that year, which was one less than Brooklyn and the reason they escaped the cellar. Regardless, Boston's National League entry had fallen on hard times. Vic still threw four shutouts and his E.R.A. was 3.21, which was quite good given the lack of talent that surrounded him. His third shutout that year was his 25th career whitewash, which came against Cincinnati 12–0. At the end of the season on December 15, he was traded to Pittsburgh for Dave Brain, Del Howard, and Viva Lindaman. After eight years with Boston, he left with a 150–146 record which came out to be almost 19 wins a year.

In Pittsburgh, Vic was resurrected and again became one of the best right-handers in the league. He was now part of a contender with a nucleus of Honus Wagner and player/manager Fred Clarke (both Hall of Famers). He led the team in victories for three consecutive years, and during his four-year tenure his win total did not fall below 22. In his first year with the Pirates, he pitched six shutouts and posted a sparkling 1.73 E.R.A. The Bucs finished third with 93 victories, but because of the unbelievable pace of the Cubs in 1906, winning 116 games, there was no contending for the pennant. Setting the major league record for winning percentage, this Cubs team boasted the noted Tinker to Evers to Chance infield along with stalwart Three Finger Brown. But 1906 showed a promising Pirates team. In 1907 the Bucs finished second with 91 victories and closed the gap between them and the Cubs to 17 games. Vic notched 22 wins among them with six shutouts and now he was the ace of the staff. He knew that he had steady support and could pitch with reassurance, something he lacked in his last years with Boston.

The following year (1908) was a year that would never be duplicated. Both leagues saw the pennant decided on the last days of the season. Focusing on the National League race, it was a three-way dogfight (Cubs, Pirates, Giants) where the teams were jockeying for the lead throughout the year. They were so close you could cover them with a postage stamp! Vic chimed in with 23 wins, 7 shutouts. Three of them were against the Cubs, with two of those being 1–0 shutouts. The game he pitched on September 4 was not only a classic but highly significant because of the impact it had on the pennant race and the way the game would be played for all time.

Pitted against the Cubs' ace, Three Finger Brown, Vic had to be at his best. The game was a showcase with two masterful pitchers dueling for a pennant, similar to two swordsmen locked in mortal combat for the hand of a fair maiden. Willis started out shaky with his control off in the beginning of the game. Chicago might have won it in the second when they had Vic on the ropes after he gave up two hits. The Cubs fouled up a hit-and-run play which was followed by the hits. With a man in scoring position, Jim Slagle lined out to Shannon who made a circus catch in center field. The two combatants matched blanks inning after inning with the Pirates almost scoring in the fourth. If they were successful, the dramatic climax with the lasting result would not have materialized. Brown, being the competitor he was, (this was the man who broke even in head-to-head encounters with the great Mathewson) pitched out of the dilemma when he faced Leach and Wagner (two of the Pirates heavy hitters) with one out and a runner on third. Striking out Leach was only a temporary reprieve because the menacing Wagner stood waiting. Brown was able to get him to fly-out routinely to right field.

The game had to be played to its predestined conclusion as if staged by Olympus deities. Extra innings were now essential and the Cubs went meekly in the top of the tenth. The Pirates took their turn in the bottom of the inning. Manager Fred Clarke singled past Harry Steinfeld (who is noted in trivia quizzes as the fourth man in the Cub infield). Clarke was sacrificed to second by Leach; Wagner hit an infield single that Evers stopped from going into the outfield, which temporarily prevented the run from scoring. Brown then walked Warren Gill, who became the protagonist in the unfolding drama. The bases were now loaded when Brown faced Eddie Abbaticchio and successfully struck him out. Two outs and it looked like Three Fingers would escape another predicament. Owen Wilson singled, scoring Clarke, making the game come to a decision, but Gill stopped midway between first and second, turned, and headed toward the dugout. Feeling the game was over, he did not advance to second which was a constant practice during the early years of the game. Evers, the astute competitor that he was, noticed Gill's blunder of omission, called for the ball, and touched second causing a force-out to end the inning. Evers screamed for umpire Hank O'Day to make the obvious call, but O'Day did not see the play, therefore causing a storm of protest from the Cubs. The Pirates were the victors but had to hold on for a few days until the protest was decided by league president Pulliam. The final decision declared the Pirates the ultimate winners with Willis gaining the victory, but the repercussions were heard three weeks later when the Cubs and the Giants played a game with a similar scenario. Evers and O'Day were the central characters in that one. O'Day was alert to the situation at hand, ruling in favor of the Cubs this time who eventually won a replay of the game and the pennant. This game labeled Fred Merkle as "Bonehead" for all time.

Although the Pirates didn't win the pennant, they were right there to the last days, finishing in a tie for second place with the Giants, one game from the lead. Willis was a determining factor with his 23 wins, 7 shutouts, and brilliant 2.07 E.R.A.

The following year the Pirates played consistently throughout the season and won the pennant by a comfortable 6½ games over the Cubs. They had to be steady because the Cubs won 104 games, making them the first team to win over 100 games and not win a pennant. Vic had another productive year where he made the 20-game win circle for the eighth time. He logged four shutouts with a commendable E.R.A. of 2.23. One of those shutouts was a one-hitter against Brooklyn, with Zack Wheat denying Vic his masterful game.

During the World Series, he appeared in relief in game two, giving up two runs in 6⅓ innings. He started game six where he relinquished a 3–0 lead and was taken out in the sixth inning, charged with a loss. This was a tenacious Tigers team whose ferocity was exemplified by Ty Cobb, the real bite for the Bengals. The Bucs were able to defang Cobb, enabling them to wear the cloak of champions when in the seventh game "Babe" Adams shut out the Detroiters. Vic was now a member of a world champion team and he had made a substantial contribution to sport the crown of baseball's highest acclaim. His basking in glory lasted for a short while, because during the off-season he was sold for cash to the St. Louis Cardinals. The Cardinals were much like the Beaneaters in Vic's last years with Boston. They were dreadful as they finished seventh in 1910. Vic, now in his mid–30s, could no longer perform miracles by moving his new club to loftier heights. It would have been similar to changing water into wine because there was a lack of talent on St. Louis. Still he posted a 9–12 record, which was a better percentage than his team. He pitched his last shutout, which was a memorable one against the

Philadelphia Phillies, and number 50 for his career. He gave up five hits in stymieing the Phils 2–0. At the end of the season, he called it a career. He finished his career with a final record of 248 wins and 205 losses for a .548 winning percentage. His lifetime E.R.A. was a noteworthy 2.63, which surpassed many of the Hall of Famers. After many years, he was finally recognized for his glorious achievements. On March 7, 1995, he was selected by the Veteran's Committee to be inducted into the Hall of Fame. The winds of time finally eroded the forgetfulness of the committee, and Vic Willis is rightly honored along with his contemporaries who must have been echoing the same sentiments throughout the decades.

Vic Willis

Date	Team	Score	Hits	S.O.	Walks	Loser
8/15/98(H)	Cle.	6–0	4	6	0	Jones
5/8/99(H)	Brk.	5–0	5	1	2	Hughes
5/18/99(A)	Lou.	6–0	5	2	2	Cunningham
7/15/99(H)	Pit.	1–0	7	4	4	Tannehill
8/19/99(H)	Brk.	9–0	6	2	4	Kennedy
10/11/99(H)	Phi.	2–0	5	2	2	Fraser
8/4/00(A)	Cin.	2–0	4	3	2	Scott
8/25/00(H)	Brk.	8–0	4	4	4	McGinnity
6/3/01(A)	Chi.	3–0	4	4	0	Hughes
6/20/01(H)	Chi.	2–0	5	3	2	Taylor
7/31/01(H)	N.Y.	5–0	5	1	0	Denzer
8/26/01(A)	Brk.	2–0	2	5	3	Donovan
9/13/01(H)	Chi.	1–0	1	7	1	Taylor
9/20/01(A)	Chi.	7–0	3	8	0	Eason
5/1/02(H)	Brk.	5–0	5	3	4	Kitson
5/28/02(H)	N.Y.	1–0	6	3	1	Taylor
7/23/02(H)	Phi.	3–0	3	9	3	Iberg
10/03/02(H)	N.Y.	6–0	5	2	1	Miller
6/3/03(A)	Cin.	6–0	4	0	3	Harper
9/9/03(A)	Brk.	1–0	8	7	2	Garvin
6/18/04(H)	Phi.	7–0	3	3	3	McPherson
7/30/04(A)	Brk.	6–0	3	4	3	Jones
7/5/05(H)	Brk.	7–0	3	3	2	Scanlon
8/7/05(A)	Pit.	3–0	4	4	3	Flaherty
8/18/05(H)	Cin.	12–0	8	7	2	Walker
9/2/05(A)	Brk.	1–0	3	8	3	McIntyre
5/16/06(H)	N.Y.	11–0	7	4	2	Ames
5/21/06(H)	Bos.	8–0	7	5	1	Young
5/25/06(H)	Brk.	2–0	6	3	2	Eason
8/8/06(A)	Bos.	2–0	4	3	2	Young
9/26/06(A)	Phi.	5–0	6	3	0	Richey

Vic Willis

Date	Team	Score	Hits	S.O.	Walks	Loser
9/29/06(A)	Brk.	3-0	3	5	3	Stricklett
5/18/07(A)	Brk.	1-0	2	3	0	McIntyre
6/6/07(H)	Bos.	6-0	3	6	1	Lindaman
7/12/07(A)	Brk.	5-0	7	4	1	McIntyre
7/17/07(A)	N.Y.	2-0	2	3	4	Mathewson
8/6/07(H)	Brk.	8-0	3	3	1	Bell
9/17/07(A)	Stl.	2-0	4	6	0	Fromme
5/3/08(A)	Cin.	1-0	5	2	3	Campbell
5/10/08(A)	Chi.	1-0	2	3	2	Pfiester
6/8/08(A)	Phi.	5-0	4	1	1	Moren
7/3/08(H)	Chi.	7-0	5	4	2	Overall
8/31/08(A)	Cin.	5-0	2	1	1	Spade
9/4/08(H)	Chi.	1-0	4	4	5	Brown
9/26/08(A)	Bos.	5-0	6	3	1	Mattern
5/27/09(A)	Bos.	7-0	7	1	4	Lindaman
6/9/09(H)	Phi.	6-0	6	4	4	Sparks
8/27/09(A)	Brk.	5-0	6	1	0	Wilhelm
9/18/09(H)	Brk.	6-0	1	3	3	Rucker
7/17/10(H)	Phi.	2-0	5	3	3	McQuillan

Year	Home	Away	Total
98	1	0	1
99	4	1	5
00	1	1	2
01	3	3	6
02	4	0	4
03	0	2	2
04	1	1	2
05	2	2	4
06	3	3	6
07	2	4	6
08	2	5	7
09	2	2	4
10	1	0	1
	26	24	50

Vic Willis' Shutouts by Team

Bos.	Brk.	Chi.	Cin.	Cle.	Lou.	N.Y.	Phi.	Pit.	Stl.	Total
5	16	7	5	1	1	5	7	2	1	50

Vic Willis' Shutouts by Team Finish

1	2	3	4	5	6	7	8	9	10	Total
6	3	2	5	11	8	5	9	1	0	50

Jim Galvin
The "Little Engine That Could"

When writing this book, I purposely omitted Jim Galvin even though he qualified with 57 shutouts. My reasoning was that he is the only one of the 20 pitchers with 50 or more shutouts who never threw from the present 60'6" distance. In fact, most of Galvin's career paralleled the evolution of the pitching rules. For instance, in 1880 eight balls instead of nine would entitle a batter to first base. In 1881 the pitching mound was moved back from 45' to 50'. The present-day distance did not come into effect until 1893. During Galvin's time, the pitcher could now throw overhand. That began in 1884. Prior to that, the pitcher could only throw from waist level and then shoulder level. During this period, the pitcher had to stand facing the batter.

When submitting my manuscript to the publisher, they wanted me to include him regardless of his not pitching from the present distance. I felt strongly that researching Galvin would be rather difficult—which it was. The record keeping during the 1800s was not precise and cross-referencing data showed frequent contradictory facts. This sometimes would be frustrating and leave one in a state of confusion. During my research on Galvin, I realized that my interest grew in studying this period of our national pastime. This was highlighted by my finding an extra shutout that was not included in Galvin's totals. This is comparable to an archaeologist finding a relic of a lost civilization. I will go into more detail of this find when I present Galvin's history. I present this to the Society of Baseball Research (SABR) Record Committee Chairman, Lyle Spatz. I will wait for SABR to confirm this game in question.

Jim Galvin, like many ball players, has more than one nickname. The most frequently used was "Pud"—rhyming with "could"—because he would turn the hitters' bats into pudding. He was also called "Gentleman Jeems" because of his even disposition. Another name dubbed on him was the "Little Steam Engine." One thing about Galvin, who stood at 5'8", was that he was taller than the average height for his generation. One must remember that the number one pitcher of that period, Charles "Old Hoss" Radbourne, stood only 5'9".

Galvin's life spanned the worst crisis our nation ever faced. Born on Christmas Day in 1856, Galvin witnessed the Civil War, Lincoln's assassination, and the period of Reconstruction in the South before his 21st birthday. Being born on Christmas Day did not guarantee him any blessing of a prosperous life. When he died in 1902 at the age of 46, only a pauper's state followed him to the grave.

In 1879 when Galvin entered the National League for the first time, the league was represented by a small strip from Boston and Providence to Buffalo. Small cities like Troy and Syracuse were among them. Three cities in the Midwest were part of the circuit with Chicago being the farthest west. At this time, "Old Glory" was batted with only 38 stars. Near the end of Pud's career, six new states were admitted to the Union.

Galvin made his national debut on May 1, 1879, for Buffalo against the Boston Red Caps (who were, years later, re-baptized as the Boston Braves). He lost that game 5–0. The pitching rule of the day was that the pitcher must face the batter when delivering the ball. His first victory was against the same Boston team on May 3, 1879, who bowed before Pud 6–4. This was the era of one primary starter for each team. On May 20, Pud recorded his first shutout. He humbled the Syracuse Stars 8–0 while doling out six hits. He totaled six shutouts for the year. His best performance was on July 1 as he defeated the Cleveland Blues 9–0 on one hit. Tom Carey, the Blue's shortstop, ruined his bid for no-hit fame by singling.

At the end of the year his record was 37–27. His victory total was only good for fourth because the three hurlers ahead of him all won 40 games or more. Galvin had started 66 of Buffalo's 78 games. He completed 65 of his starts.

The following year, Galvin didn't start the season with the Bisons. He was toiling in the California League for the San Francisco entry. He was offered more money than Buffalo was willing to pay. The Buffalo team was floundering and realized their mistake in not signing Pud.

The Bisons offered him a contract, which he gladly accepted. This meant that he would have to dishonor the contract with San Francisco. A big problem arose because the California club had advanced Pud $200 on his salary. On his sojourn back East he was arrested and jailed. He wasn't released until he agreed to repay the money. This he did, but the financial snafu delayed his rejoining Buffalo.

Even with Galvin's presence, the Bisons could only rise to seventh place. His record was a dismal 20–35 while the team staggered in with a 24–58 mark. Jim fashioned five shutouts and three came at the expense of the Worchester Ruby Legs. Worchester replaced the Syracuse Stars and they would eventually became the Philadelphia Phillies. His finest performance during the year came on August 20, 1880, when he threw his first no-hitter. He defeated Worchester 1–0.

The year 1881 brought one dramatic change in the pitching rules. The distance of the pitching box was moved from 45 feet to 50 feet. The Detroit Wolverines replaced the Cincinnati Reds. It was a good year for both Pud and the Bisons. He finished the year at 28–24 while Buffalo finished in third place. His best game pitched was on June 9 when he went 13 innings, topping the Redcaps and their ace Jim Whitney 1–0 on six hits. Whitney led the league in victories with 31. He had four other shutouts during the year.

In 1882 the National League was challenge by the newly formed American Association. The rivalry between the leagues lasted ten years. A world championship started in 1882 consisting of two games. Both leagues agreed to a more formal arrangement in 1883.

During 1882 Galvin had another successful season as he went 28–23, aiding Buffalo in securing third place for the second consecutive year. He blanked the opposition three times. He pitched 445⅓ innings, which was the lowest number he had in his four-year National League career. This would change the next two years.

Another pitching rule change occurred in 1883. The pitcher now could deliver the pitch at shoulder height. It seemed to help his performance. He amassed 40 wins which made him runner-up behind Charles "Old Hoss" Radbourn's 48. Buffalo finished fifth, but it wasn't any fault of Jim's. He became a league leader in several categories for the first time in his career.

He led the league in games (76), complete games (72), innings pitched (656⅓), and shutouts (5). His most outstanding game pitched was on June 21 versus the Chicago White Stockings. He stymied them 12–0 on one hit, which was obtained by his opposing moundsman Larry Corcoran. Back in that ERA pitchers often were offensive threats and batted higher that the ninth hole in the lineup.

In every player's career, there is that one year classified as the career year. In 1884 Pud would have been a prime candidate for the Cy Young Award if it existed. Pud would not have won it. It would have gone to Old Hoss Radbourn, who won 60 games for the Providence Grays. Some historians and resource books credit him with only 59. Regardless of what number you select, it still is the all-time record for victories. Besides all that, 1884 was Galvin's shining moment. His achievements were as Herculean as well. He claimed 46 victories of the Bisons' 64 wins. He whitewashed the opposition 12 times and four of those were against the Detroit Wolverines. Champion Providence bit the dust in two of those games with Old Hoss victimized once.

His first shutout of the year was the 25th of his career. He bested Larry Corcoran and the Chicago White Stockings while spreading out eight hits and walking none. At the end of July he had only three shutouts, which didn't indicate what was to come.

On August 2 he stopped Detroit on one hit, which was posted by catcher Charlie Bennett. Two days later he spun his second career no-hitter as Buffalo pummeled Detroit 18–0. On August 7 he repeated his shutout mastery over Detroit 9–0. The following day, in the second game of a doubleheader, Galvin finally ceded a run. He had blanked Detroit going into the bottom of the 12th inning when the Wolverines scored a run on a error by right fielder Jim Lillie. In a period of six days, he pitched almost 39 innings, giving up twelve hits and one unearned. The three-shutout performance would only be duplicated by Walter Johnson in 1908 against the New York Highlanders. To his credit he pitched all of the games on the opponents' turf. He finished the month with five shutouts. In September he added three more to his total. On October 1 he pitched his 12th of the season, stopping the league champion Providence 2–0. This game ended Providence's 18 game winning streak.

His total innings pitched were 636⅓ and his complete games totaled 71. Both were second best to Radbourn, but his 12 shutouts bested Radbourn by one.

A new rule change in pitching might have aided the hurlers in the National League. The pitcher now could deliver the ball without any restraints, except he must face the batter and be in the lines of the pitching box. Overhand pitching was now allowed except in the American Association and the Union Association.

The Union Association was a 12-team league formed to challenge the National League and American Association. They dropped the reserve clause to attract talent from the two established leagues. Its demise came quickly as there was a great deal of manipulation within the league.

The year 1885 was the last year of Buffalo's National League existence. The team had shown the aging of several players. There was talk the franchise would be disbanded around the middle of the season. Rumors persisted that the team wouldn't complete its season. N. E. Young, secretary of the National League, sent a note to team secretary George Hughson asking if the rumors had any validity. Hughson replied in a memo back to Young that the team would honor its commitment in completing the season, which it did. The franchise was in financial straits and was replaced along with Providence by Kansas City and Washington the following year.

Galvin had his worst season when he won only 13 of 32 decisions. Buffalo finished its final season at 31–74, barely edging out St. Louis for seventh place. Pud's three shutouts were against St. Louis.

Gavin's downfall might have been the lack of talent or the past two years' workload or a combination of the two. He pitched a total of 1292⅔ innings, starting 147 games and completing 143 of them. The little engine that could couldn't as he ran out of steam.

Jim also tried his hand at managing, but that too was disheartening. His record was only 7–17. In July he was released to the Pittsburgh Allegiance of the American Association. He did not improve with the change of venue, as he only produced a 3–7 record.

Starting 1886 in the American Association with Pittsburgh, Pud rebounded dramatically by sporting a 29–21 record. He supplemented staff leader Ed Morris who led the league in wins (41) and shutouts (12). Between Morris and Galvin, the team moved up to second place, 23 games over .500. They trailed the St. Louis Browns by 12 games. These were the same Browns who won four consecutive pennants (1884–1887), giving the association its only dynasty during the league's short history.

Before I go on, I would like to take the time to debate some of Galvin's shutout totals. All records show Galvin's total for 1886 as two. But in researching his shutouts, I came across a game on August 26, 1886, for which he should be given credit for pitching a shutout.

In that game Pittsburgh played Louisville at Louisville. During this period of baseball history, the home team didn't always bat last. This was decided prior to the start of the game. This particular game was interrupted by rain after five innings with Pittsburgh leading 7–0. With the rain subsiding, the umpire allowed the game to continue up until the eighth inning. In the top of the eighth Louisville scored three runs off of Galvin when the rain again came down in torrents, which prevented Louisville from completing its turn at bat. The umpire called the game according to league rules stated in rule 34.4 of the rules guide of 1886.

The rules state that when an umpire calls a game on account of darkness or rain at any time after five innings have been completed by both sides, the score shall be that of the last equal inning played. Since the eighth inning was not completed because of the deluge, the score would be that of the seventh inning when Pittsburgh was leading 7–0. I have researched this by getting accounts of the game from both the Pittsburgh *Commercial Gazette* and the Louisville *Courier Journal*. Both papers state that the game's score will revert back to the 7–0 score with seven complete innings. *The Sporting News* also shows it as 7–0. The *Reach Guide* for 1887 also lists the game as 7–0. This would enable Galvin to have three shutouts and a career total of 58, placing him in a tie for tenth place all time. I disagree with the SABR Record Committee who refuse to accept the findings of that game. Regardless, I will list Galvin's totals with an asterisk. In 1887 Galvin found himself back in the National League because the Pittsburgh Alleghenys decided to drop the American Association and become part of the older league. The move didn't hamper Pud because he wound up with a 28–21 record. This placed him fourth in victories. The team didn't fare as well as they floundered in sixth place, 14 games under .500. He did toss three shutouts during the season.

In 1888 Jim won 23 games but lost 25. He managed to pitch six shutouts, which placed him third in the league. Pittsburgh fumbled in sixth again but improved their record to only two under .500.

Galvin obtained two historical milestones during the season making him the first pitcher to achieve those levels of greatness. Depending on which game you consider—July 27, 1888, or August 23, 1888—one of those was his 50th career shutout. This is muddled somewhat by the game of August 26, 1886, which is still in question.

At the time of this writing, Galvin should be credited with a shutout. Prior to this milestone achievement, his shutout game of July 13 was a one-hitter. Third baseman Bill Nash of Boston prevented him from getting his third no-hitter, which would have tied him for the record at the time with Larry Corcoran.

The other milestone occurred October 5 when he posted his 300th career win. He defeated the Washington Nationals 5–1 on four hits. I must give credit for this piece of information to John O'Malley of SABR Baseball Records Committee who, along with his associates Bill Deane, Frank Williams, and Bob Richardson, gave me the date to find that significant game.

The year 1889 was Pud's last big year as well as his last winning season. He logged in at 23–16 with four shutouts. Pittsburgh rose to fifth but finished the season ten games under .500. He was nearing 33 years old and it seemed the number of pitches during his career were resulting in some wear and tear on his arm.

In the following year of 1890, a protest league emerged to voice their dissent against management. This was the Player's League, which lasted one year. In its brief existence, it was the nail in the coffin of the fragile American Association. The association lasted through the 1891 season, giving the National League complete control of the game until the arrival of the American League in 1901.

Galvin, like many others, jumped to the maverick league. He toiled for the Pittsburgh Burghers. He could only manage a 12–13 record with one shutout. That whitewash job was against the Chicago Pirates, defeating them 6–0 on three hits. The oddity of this was that when Pud returned to the National League in 1891, he joined Pittsburgh, who renamed themselves the Pirates. In his one-year stint with the Player's League, the Burghers could only rise to sixth place, which seemed to be a trend for Galvin's team.

Back in the National League for 1891, he broke even at 14–14. He couldn't be blamed for Pittsburgh's last-place finish. He recorded his last two shutouts. The last came on September 4 against Brooklyn 6–0.

In 1892 the end of his career was in sight when the Pirates traded him to St. Louis. He posted identical 5–6 marks for both teams and then was out of baseball for 1893. In 1894 he tried a comeback with Buffalo of the Eastern League. That convinced him there was nothing left. He tried umpiring for a while, then opened a bar. This was not a success and he eventually went broke. On March 7, 1902, at the age of 45, he died in a rooming house without enough money to pay for his burial. This was the way one of the most consistent players of the 19th century would exit life.

Galvin set the records that would be challenged and surpassed by some of the greats of the game. He still ranks second in innings pitched and complete games behind Cy Young. He was the first 300-game winner and likewise the first 50-career shutout pitcher. His record might have been more impressive if he didn't toil for mediocre and poor teams. He gave them all he could.

Pud Galvin

Date	Team	Score	Hits	S.O.	Walks	Loser
5/20/79H	Syr.	8–0	6	2	0	McCormick
6/14/79A	Syr.	10–0	2	5	2	Purcell
6/25/79H	Cle.	3–0	3	0	0	McCormick
7/1/79A	Cle.	9–0	1	1	0	McCormick
8/26/79A	Cin.	4–0	5	2	2	White
9/22/79H	Cin.	3–0	4	3	0	Purcell
6/12/80A	Bos.	5–0	3	1	0	Bond
7/5/80H	Wor.	1–0	5	5	1	Richmond (10 inn)
7/16/80A	Pro.	1–0	9	1	0	Ward 14 inn
8/6/80A	Wor.	4–0	2	6	1	Corey
8/20/80H	Wor.	1–0	0	2	0	Corey
5/11/81H	Bos.	1–0	4	5	1	Whitney
5/20/81H	Wor.	7–0	3	2	0	Corey
6/9/81A	Bos.	1–0	6	3	1	Whitney (13 inn)
7/12/81H	Pro.	3–0	3	1	2	Ward
8/23/81A	Cle.	2–0	3	3	0	Nolan
5/3/82H	Chi.	5–0	6	1	1	Goldsmith
7/22/82A	Det.	3–0	2	4	2	Derby
8/24/82A	Pro.	4–0	5	3	0	Radbourne
8/2/83A	Cle.	3–0	7	2	2	Daily
5/25/83H	Phi.	4–0	3	5	0	Nagle
6/21/83H	Chi.	12–0	1	5	0	Corcoran
6/25/83H	Det.	2–0	4	3	1	Shaw
9/18/83A	Phi.	4–0	3	5	0	Purcell
5/26/84H	Chi.	4–0	8	4	0	Corcoran
6/7/84A	Det.	6–0	2	12	1	Meinke
6/12/84H	Cle.	3–0	3	3	0	McCormick
8/2/84A	Det.	2–0	1	5	0	Weidman
8/4/84A	Det.	18–0	0	8	0	Meinke
8/7/84A	Det.	9–0	3	0	0	Weidman
8/27/84A	Phi.	2–0	3	4	2	Ferguson
8/28/84A	Phi.	7–0	5	1	0	Vinton
9/9/84A	Pro.	2–0	4	4	1	Radbourne
9/11/84A	Bos.	1–0	5	11	0	Buffington
9/24/84H	N.Y.	6–0	4	6	1	Welch

The Great Shutout Pitchers

Date	Team	Score	Hits	S.O.	Walks	Loser
10/1/84H	Pro.	2–0	7	4	0	Conley
6/3/85H	Stl.	11–0	5	3	1	Palmer
6/12/85A	Stl.	2–0	3	4	0	Sweeney
6/16/85A	Stl.	5–0	4	7	2	Sweeney
6/7/86H	Cin.	3–0	7	3	0	Mullane
8/19/86A	Stl.	6–0	7	1	2	Caruthers
8/26/86A	Lou.	7–0	NA	NA	NA	Hecket

(game in question—still has to be determined if he is entitled to a shutout)

Date	Team	Score	Hits	S.O.	Walks	Loser
5/12/87H	Ind.	7–0	4	1	1	Boyle
6/28/87H	Wash.	8–0	5	9	1	O'Day
9/12/87H	Wash.	3–0	7	3	1	O'Day
5/21/88H	Wash.	5–0	2	8	2	Gilmore
6/20/88A	Chi.	5–0	4	5	1	Krock
7/13/88H	Bos.	6–0	1	2	0	Radbourne
7/20/88A	Ind.	4–0	10	2	1	Sherve
7/27/88H	Ind.	2–0	6	0	0	Sherve
8/23/88H	Ind.	7–0	6	1	1	Boyle
6/3/89H	Ind.	1–0	5	2	1	Boyle
6/28/89H	Phi.	3–0	6	1	0	Casey
7/1/89H	Phi.	6–0	3	2	0	Buffington
8/13/89H	Bos.	9–0	5	3	3	Daley
6/9/90H	Chi.	6–0	3	2	0	King
8/21/91A	Cin.	2–0	5	3	2	Mullane
9/4/91H	Brk.	6–0	8	2	1	Caruthers

Shutouts by Team

NL

Bos.	Brk.	Chi.	Cin.	Cle.	Det.	Ind.	N.Y.	Phi.	Pro.	Stl.	Syr.	Wash.	Wor.
6	1	4	3	5	6	5	1	6	5	3	2	3	4

AA

Cin.	Stl.	Lou.
1	1	1* (questionable game)

PL

Chi.
1

Shutouts by Position

1	2	3	4	5	6	7	8
4	7	0	7	7	9	12	12

Jim Galvin

	Home	Away
79	3	3
80	2	3
81	3	2
82	1	2
83	3	2
84	4	8
85	1	2
86	1	2
87	3	0
88	4	2
89	4	0
90	1	0
91	1	1
	31	27

Index

Aaron, Henry 67
Alexander, Grover Cleveland 17–26, 101, 112, 148
Altrock, Nick 124–125, 127, 129, 161
American Association 218, 222
Anderson, "Sparky" 113
Anson, "Cap" 39

Baker, Frank "Homerun" 34
Baltimore Orioles 41, 51, 172
Bench, Johnny 78
Berra, "Yogi" 77
Blyleven, Bert 98–108
Bostock, Lyman 90
Boston "Beaneaters" 40–41, 208–209
Boston Pilgrims 123
Boston Rustlers 47
Brown, Mordecai "Three Finger" 30, 126–127, 142, 158, 212
Bunning, Jim 182, 198

Carew, Rob 82, 90
Carlton, Steve 113, 115, 147–157
Chance, Frank 55, 126, 160, 163, 165–166
Chapman, Ray 123
Chesbro, Jack 44, 52, 123, 181
Chicago Cubs 31
Chicago White Sox 172

Clark, Fred 197–198, 211
Clemens, Roger 154, 173
Clemente, Roberto 77, 140, 148
Cleveland Spiders 39, 42
Cobb, Ty 162–163, 213
Cuellar, Mike 76

Dineen, Bill 140
Doke, Bill 142
Drysdale, Don 111–112, 125, 141

Ehmke, Howard 127
Einstein, Charles 130, 163, 197
Evers, Johnny 126, 212–213

Federal League 57–58, 132, 166
Feller, Bob 88–89, 170
Fingers, Rollie 99
Ford, Whitey 34, 68, 171
Fregosi, Jin 86, 90
French, Larry 68

Gabrielson, Len 142
Galvin, "Pud" 32, 216–225
Gibson, Bob 112, 135–136, 148, 150, 179, 192
Gill, Warren 212

Hahn, Frank "Noodles" 30
Harris, Bucky 11

Hemus, Solly 136–137
Hodges, Gil 77
Hornsby, Rogers 22–23
Hubbell, Carl 179
Hunter, Jim "Catfish" 78

Jackson, Reggie 116, 121
Jenkins, Fergy 181
Johnson, "Ban" 30, 43
Johnson, Randy 134
Johnson, Walter 5–16, 56, 74, 101, 128, 141, 144, 219
Jones, Fielder 124, 130
Jones, Randy 118, 151
Joss, Addie 126, 128–129

Keane, Johnny 137, 139
Killefer, Bill 20–21
Koslo, Dave 93
Koufax, Sandy 70, 88–89, 92, 110–111, 115, 140–142, 150–151, 153, 170, 173, 192, 202
Kuenn, Harvey 188

Landis, Kenesaw "Mountain" 11
Lazzeri, Tony 22
Leifeld, "Lefty" 161
Leonard, Hubert "Dutch" 149, 161
Los Angeles Dodgers 115
Lyons, Ted 99

Mack, Connie 51, 55, 165, 197–199, 201, 203
Maddux, Greg 154
Marichal, Juan 138, 187–195
Martinez, Pedro 154
Mathewson, Christy 18, 27–38, 56, 82, 128, 160, 167
Mauch, Gene 139
May, Ronald A. 27
Mays, Carl 123
Mays, Willie 65
McCarthy, Joe 21
McEleven, Pryer 33
McGinnity, Joe 29–30, 53, 127–128, 160, 210
McGraw, John 28–30, 44, 165
McLain, Denny 142–143, 148
Merkle, Fred 34, 213
Mumson, Thurman 88

New York Yankees 82, 183
Newcombe, Don 142
Nichols, Charles "Kid" 202–203
Niekro, Joe 116
Niekro, Phil 75, 119

O'Day, Hank 213
O'Mailey, John 222
Owen, Frank 124–125, 129

Palmer, Jim 117, 153, 170–176
Palmer, Peter 199–200
Perry, Gaylord 177–186
Philadelphia Athletics 55, 172
Philadelphia Phillies 152
Phillippe, Charles "Deacon" 44
Plank 31, 35, 46, 51–61
Player's League 222
Powers, Francis J. 130

Qualls, Jimmy 76

Radbourn, Charles "Old Hoss" 219
Reynolds, Allie 88
Rixey, Eppa 99
Roberts, Robin 111
Robinson, Frank 182
Robinson, Ray 197
Rose, Pete 78
Roseboro, John 111
Ruelbach, Ed 31, 129
Ruffing, "Red" 100
Ruth, George "Babe" 9–11, 12, 34
Ryan, Jack 163
Ryan, Nolan 70, 86–97, 99, 113, 117, 198

St. Louis Cardinals 172
St. Louis Terriers 58
Scott, Joe A. 198
Seaton, Tom 18
Seaver, Tom 74–85, 118, 153, 173
Shatzkin, Mike 119
Smith, Frank 124–125, 129, 130
Snod Grass, Fred 34
Southworth, Billy 63, 65
Spahn, Warren 62–73, 190
Speaker, Tris 34
Stallard, Tracy 71
Stengel, "Casey" 63
Sticklet, Elmer 124

Sutton, Don 75, 110–112

Temple Cup 41–42
Texas Rangers 119
Thomson, Bobby 67
Trucks, Virgil 88

Union Association 220

Valenzuela, Fernando 81
Vandermeer, Johnny 88

Waddell, Rube 43, 45, 52, 88, 196–207

Walk, Bob 19
Walsh, Ed 56, 119, 123–134, 210
Warhop, Jack 9
Washburn, Ray 179
White, Guy "Doc" 124–125, 128–129, 130
Willis, Vic 163, 208–215
Wood, Joe 7–8, 33–34, 55–56

Yastrzemski, Carl 148
Young, Cy 17, 35, 39–50, 52, 70, 89, 128, 130, 181–182, 201–203

www.ingramcontent.com/pod-product-compliance
Ingram Content Group UK Ltd.
Pitfield, Milton Keynes, MK11 3LW, UK
UKHW041945140426
5217IPUK00014B/672